INSECURITY POLITICS

Insecurity Politics

HOW UNSTABLE LIVES LEAD TO POPULIST SUPPORT

Lorenza Antonucci

PRINCETON UNIVERSITY PRESS
PRINCETON & OXFORD

Published by Princeton University Press
41 William Street, Princeton, New Jersey 08540
99 Banbury Road, Oxford OX2 6JX

press.princeton.edu

GPSR Authorized Representative: Easy Access System Europe -
Mustamäe tee 50, 10621 Tallinn, Estonia, gpsr.requests@easproject.com

ISBN 9780691262468
ISBN (pbk.) 9780691262475
ISBN (epub) 9780691287300
ISBN (PDF) 9780691262451

Library of Congress Control Number: 2025945348

British Library Cataloging-in-Publication Data is available

Editorial: Rebecca Brennan and Rebecca Binnie
Production Editorial: Theresa Liu
Jacket/Cover Design: Ben Higgins
Production: Danielle Amatucci
Publicity: William Pagdatoon and Kathryn Stevens
Copyeditor: Anita O'Brien

This book has been composed in Miller

10 9 8 7 6 5 4 3 2 1

To my mother for all her work
in making us less insecure

CONTENTS

List of Figures and Tables · ix

Introduction: The Widespread Insecurity Thesis 1

CHAPTER 1 Defining Insecurity in Life and Politics 14

CHAPTER 2 The Fear of Keeping Your Job and of Having a Stagnant Life 36

CHAPTER 3 The Transformed Welfare States and the Effects on Insecurity 61

CHAPTER 4 Demand and Supply in the New Politics of Insecurity 85

CHAPTER 5 From Insecure People to Populist Voters 113

CHAPTER 6 The Future of the Politics of Insecurity 137

Epilogue: The Social Basis of the Populism Momentum 152

Acknowledgments · *161*

Methodological Appendix · 165

Glossary of Key Terms · 177

Notes · 179

Index · 205

LIST OF FIGURES AND TABLES

Figures

1.1. Socioeconomic, Cultural, and Political Security Shifts Behind the New Politics of Insecurity 24
2.1. Agreement on the Dimensions of Work Conditions Among Case Studies in 2015 50
2.2. Evolution of Content Autonomy, 1995–2015 51
2.3. Evolution of Procedural Autonomy, 1995–2015 52
2.4. Evolution of Work Pressure, 1995–2015 53
2.5. Share of the Population Not Living Comfortably on Their Present Income per Security Regime 55
2.6. Average Share of Those Who Stated They Had Difficulties Making Ends Meet in the Previous Three Years and Had Not Recovered by the Fourth Year, Across Case Studies 56
2.7. Average Share of Those Who Stated They Had Difficulties Making Ends Meet in the Previous Three Years and Had Not Recovered by the Fourth Year, Across Security Regimes 57
3.1. Active and Compensatory Spending of Each Country in 2015 74
3.2. Unemployment Spending of Each Country in 2015 75
3.3. Changes to Generosity Scores of Unemployment Insurance, 1980–2018 76
4.1. Demand and Supply in the New Politics of Insecurity 88
4.2. Salience Analysis of Commodification and Security Agendas of Main Parties in Spain Based on Manifesto Data 100
4.3. Salience Analysis of Commodification and Security Agendas of Main Parties in Sweden Based on Manifesto Data 103
4.4. Salience Analysis of Commodification and Security Agendas of Main Parties in Germany Based on Manifesto Data 107

5.1. Predicted Probabilities by Education and Perceived Change in Financial Situation 117
5.2. Association Between Work Insecurity and Radical Populist Right Voting 121
5.3. Association Between Work Insecurity and Radical Left Voting 122
5.4. Probabilities of Voting for Populist Parties Based on Financial Insecurity, Precarity of Tenure, and Precarity at Work 127
5.5. Correlation Between the Evolution of Financial Insecurity and Voting for Mainstream Parties, Voting for Populist Parties, and Nonvoting 134
5.6. Correlation Between the Evolution of Financial Insecurity and Voting for Mainstream Parties, Voting for Populist Parties, and Nonvoting Among Those Who Voted for Populist Parties Before Covid-19 135

Tables

1.1. Work-Related Forms of Security 20
1.2. Financial Forms of Security 23
2.1. Security Regimes and the Forms of Protection 38
2.2. Work and Financial Security Shifts Within Each Security Regime 59
5.1. Measures of Tenure and Work Precarity 118
5.2. Measures of Financial and Work-Related Insecurity 125
5.3. Measures of Work-Related Insecurity: High Pressure and Job Dissatisfaction 130
5.4. Measures of Work and Financial Insecurity in the Longitudinal Panel 133
A.1. Measures of Content Autonomy, Procedural Autonomy, and Work Pressure 166
A.2. Populist Parties Mapping Across Case Studies Since 1990 168
A.3. Dimensions and Coding in the Manifesto Data 169
A.4. Selection of Parties in the Study, France and the Netherlands 172
A.5. Selection of Parties in the Study 174

INSECURITY POLITICS

Introduction

THE WIDESPREAD INSECURITY THESIS

IN 2019 THE popular Italian magazine *L'Espresso* investigated the "curious case" of Montesilvano, the seaside town with circa fifty thousand inhabitants where "everyone" had started supporting the right-wing populist party of the moment, Lega.[1] Interestingly, it was not the first time that Montesilvano had been described as the new center of populism. Just a few years earlier, the town was considered the bastion of another populist party, the Five Star Movement, which got over 36 percent of the votes in both the national elections in 2013 and the European elections the following year. Fast-forward to the national parliamentary elections in September 2022, and the winning party in Montesilvano was the latest right-wing populist party on the rise, the Brothers of Italy, which went on to lead the country's right-wing populist coalition.

Montesilvano is a microcosm of what has been happening in domestic politics in Italy, where, even by Italian standards, populist support has been extremely volatile over the last decade. If political scientists had wanted to investigate the party offer to try to understand if there were any special factors that explained Montesilvano's frequent electoral swings and shifts, they would not have found any, as the city presents a rather typical history of local politics. The Democratic Christian Party dominated for over forty years, until the early 1990s; since then, there has been a fragmented, unstable, and changeable political landscape, with a high diffusion of clientelism that is common in medium-sized cities in Southern Italy. Despite the political shifts, support for the populist party of the moment has been a constant in Montesilvano, almost as if the positioning of the party within the left and right divide was unimportant and what mattered was simply picking the newest diversion from the status quo. In addition to populism, there has been another constant in the city: a generalized social malaise that pervades its inhabitants—a feeling familiar to me, as I lived in Montesilvano for the first eighteen years of my life.

While Montesilvano is not in the poorest region of Italy, it embodies the decline of lower-middling areas. Montesilvano is in Abruzzo, culturally and historically in *Mezzogiorno* (Southern Italy), a part of Europe that is notoriously plagued by negative economic growth. Abruzzo has one of the highest rates of food insecurity in Italy, with a staggering 29.6 percent of people experiencing or being at risk of experiencing food poverty.[2]

The year 2016 is generally taken to signal the beginning of the contemporary populist wave or the Brexit/Trump momentum—or, perhaps more accurately, the year when the Anglo-Saxon media started paying attention to it. At that time, I worked in the Tees Valley in the UK, and I passed by Hartlepool almost every day to go to work. To me, the economic inertia of this deindustrialized town, the insecurity that characterizes the lives of people in the Tees Valley, and the preference in this area for antisystem politics, in the shape of Brexit, all felt incredibly similar to Montesilvano.[3] Hartlepool experienced a decline in its socioeconomic conditions during the 1980s and 1990s as an effect of the closure of the British steel industry and the general passage to a postindustrial economy. Even before Brexit, the Tees Valley had been at the center of journalistic and sociological interest due to the potential political implications of what might occur there. In the early 1990s the American investigative journalist Tony Horwitz wrote a long piece on joblessness and low-wage jobs in Hartlepool titled "British Society Is Mired in Class-Consciousness, Apathy and Under-Achievement. The Future Looks Bleak," which offered a rather gloomy vision of what local communities were experiencing as a result of deindustrialization.[4] The 2016 referendum led to a renewed interest in the enduring precarity of these areas. A staggering 70 percent of voters in Hartlepool supported leaving the European Union (EU), which prompted *The New Yorker* to dedicate another long report to the deprived "pro-Brexit coastal town."[5] This article, like much of the media coverage of the recent rise of populism around the globe,[6] strongly suggested a link between individual insecurity from the cost-of-living crisis and populist support. Despite these connections being widely acknowledged and discussed in public commentaries, social sciences lack a general theory that explains the political repercussions of widespread insecurity among the population. Intrigued by the fact that the same social malaise pervades the streets of Montesilvano and Hartlepool, I began to investigate the underlying social dynamics and the mundane experiences of insecurity that are found in these areas as in the rest of Europe.

In this book I advance two arguments: first, that socioeconomic insecurity has steadily increased in Europe, albeit presenting itself in different ways across countries and security regimes; and, second, that this increase has created the basis for support for populism. To understand the relationship between insecurity and populism, I propose a conceptually nuanced and empirically evidenced understanding of both. With the emergence of the post-Brexit populist momentum, research on populism stopped being a matter for political science alone and became (or returned to being) a subject for the entirety of the social sciences, with special issues and ad hoc analyses appearing in sociology, economics, human geography, and social policy, among others.[7] Sociological research has produced rich accounts of the cultural environment and cultural values that predominate in communities supporting populist right politics, particularly in the United States.[8] However, the tools and instruments used in research on populism have remained anchored in classic political science research, which tends to rely on an economic conceptualization of insecurity rather than utilizing a socioeconomic understanding of it.[9] This book attempts to reverse this trend. Conceptually, my work builds on the emerging field of insecurity research, which aims to capture the everyday experiences of people through objective and subjective indicators and therefore helps the investigation of populism by generating a bottom-up understanding of how the insecurity that people experience reverberates into their interaction with politics. In what follows, I will first define what socioeconomic insecurity is. I will then illustrate the implications of using an ideational notion of populism, before highlighting the mutual linkages between insecurity and populism.

A Socioeconomic Understanding of Insecurity

The conceptualization of insecurity I offer in this book is based on the way the term is used in the emerging field of insecurity and precarity studies, which has developed within and beyond sociology. Unlike analysis in the 1990s, which took a macro and institutional approach to risk, contemporary research on insecurity and precarity focuses on microlevel experiences that have both a material and a subjective component. I use the concepts of precarity and insecurity as adjacent terms, preferring insecurity because precarity is often used to refer strictly to precarious job contracts, while insecurity, in the way I define and operationalize it, is a broader notion, concerned with the ordinary effects of work on people's lives as well as their financial insecurity.

In this book, I investigate the relative loss of security in two areas that are central to people's livelihoods in Europe: work and finances. This focus builds on the existing research on insecurity conducted around the world, which has pointed out that microlevel insecurity is manifested in people's lives through work and via their financial experiences.[10] Work security is not just about having a job and, moreover, one that is secure: It also entails having secure work conditions with respect to work pressure, autonomy, work–life balance, and recognition. Similarly, financial security is not solely based on income levels or the ability to pay for food and the basics: It includes being able to pay bills, cover unexpected expenses, and live without financial anxiety. Individuals have always relied on three major providers to navigate insecurity: their family, the state, and the market. As I illustrate in the first part of the book, it is now harder to gain security through each of these.

The fact that precarity and insecurity are partially based on subjective evaluations does not mean that they have no scientific validity. Indicators of insecurity are empirical and more grounded in the everyday lives of individuals than the abstract and remote economic operationalizations that have been used to explain Brexit, such as trade shocks, macroeconomic indicators of growth, and unemployment rates, which can be imprecisely transposed to people's lives.[11] It is also true that, compared to income-based poverty and social exclusion, socioeconomic insecurity understands social disadvantage to be a more common and multidimensional phenomenon, and hence it is particularly suited to investigate the socioeconomic triggers of widespread social discontent.

My evaluation of the qualitative facets of Europeans' work and financial lives uses a socioeconomic understanding of insecurity. Such a conception moves beyond the focus on indicators that measure quantifiable aspects of people's lives, such as income or wealth. The issue of whether the insecurity of populist voters is only perceived or real lingers in the debate: Is insecurity objectively experienced, or are individuals feeling insecure because of their subjective feelings? This question underpins different methodological, but also moral, views of insecurity. A perspective that is purely economically based and is therefore measured through metrics that are defined objectively, such as income, wealth, and unemployment, is in opposition to an approach that leaves it to respondents to express qualitative opinions about their lives, which is generally considered subjective. Do we only trust purely numeric and economic measures (e.g., income, job contract type), or do we also include measures of quality of life that allow people to express their own opinions? Using the latter approach enables us to capture elements of people's work and economic lives that inevitably require a personal evaluation on the part of respondents.

Understanding Populist Support as a Process

From the beginning of this century, there has been a steady interest in populism both in the public debate and in academia. Since 2016, however, the interest has boomed. There have been twice as many mentions of populism in the news, and the number of academic articles with "populism" or "populist" in the title or abstract has also doubled.[12] Populism continues to be studied not just because it is an overlooked or unexplored field of research per se—indeed, it is now a rather crowded field—but because it permits academics to uncover and discuss the various underlying and overlooked causes of an ongoing social dissatisfaction that manifests as populism, which academics failed to predict. Therefore, since 2016, research on populism has become the way to investigate the geography of discontent and address the grievances of the working class. In other words, this research has carried a certain moral urgency in highlighting the social problems that can result in political discontent.

The term "populism" is in itself controversial. Depending on which side of the debate one is on, populism can be a negative term, almost an insult, or a euphemistic expression employed to underplay the rise of ethnonationalism.[13] Populism is helpful due to its capacity to capture not just its right-wing expression, but all directions of antiestablishment sentiments. In this all-encompassing conceptualization, populism denotes the centrality of the people to politics and the belief that politics is characterized by an opposition between the people and the economic, intellectual, political, and media elites.

Instead of focusing purely on voting patterns or parties' agendas—which results in a rather static understanding of populism—I aim to delineate the process behind its rise. When examining the concept of a populist outlook or viewpoint in addition to the notion of populist voting, populism appears to be more dynamic and less black-and-white. What is helpful about understanding populism as a set of beliefs rather than a fixed behavior ("if you vote X, you must be populist") is that it allows us to move past the idea of populism as a rigid everlasting phenomenon and enables us to investigate the process that made populist voting more prevalent in this historical moment. Do we believe that the current political status quo does not serve its purpose? Do we think that populism is the product of winner-takes-all politics and entrenched inequalities? Seen through these lenses, people-centrism and anti-elitism are more commonplace than they might appear, and we could all, potentially, partially or totally adopt a populist viewpoint.

Furthermore, a sociological examination of populism looks at other expressions of antiestablishment politics, such as nonvoting and shifting between nonvoting and voting for a populist party. In this historical dimension, the popularity of populism becomes circumstantial and a key element in understanding the crisis of the European project and the decline in established party politics across the continent. Despite the noise that it generates in every national and EU election, populist voting is not the full or sole form of social unrest in Europe given the considerable rates of nonvoting and the political mobilization of those who are not entitled to vote, such as migrants.[14]

The Missing Links Between Insecurity and Populism

Having introduced my definition of insecurity and the understanding of populism used in this book, I will now clarify the links between the concepts. At first, explanations of the post-2016 populist momentum revolved around what scholars labeled the "it's the culture, stupid!" (or the cultural backlash) argument. For example, the very influential work by Pippa Norris and Ronald Inglehart found that populism emerged from the cultural clash of those who hold traditional and conservative views regarding migration and societal diversity, and that, through populist right support, express an opposition to progressive ideas in respect to migration, multicultural diversity, gender roles, and LGBTI+ rights.[15] Furthermore, earlier socioeconomic explanations of populism put forward by several scholars theorized that the post-Brexit populist vote represented a protest by a neglected working class affected by material hardships, unemployment, and a decline in their material conditions.[16] Empirical analyses showed inconclusive evidence for the theory of the economic left-behind, indicating that populist voting did not seem to be associated with extreme socioeconomic disadvantage, such as being unemployed or being a recipient of welfare benefits.[17] Similarly, when it has been investigated through objective economic measures, such as income, wealth, and employment status, precarity has not been effective in explaining the rise of the right-wing populist vote.[18] In the words of Sheri Berman, "despite the plausibility that individual economic setbacks and/or insecurity would lead voters to support populists, the evidence linking individual economic grievances to populist voting is not particularly strong."[19]

This led part of the scholarship to conclude that the grievances voiced by individuals voting for populist parties were mostly post–material cultural concerns (e.g., on gender equality, multiculturalism, and LGBTI+ rights), rather than based on material issues or socioeconomic changes in individuals' conditions.[20] It also led to the emergence of another strand of literature. As it became apparent that populist voting was not explained by indicators used to measure the disadvantage of left-behind groups, the work that I and my colleagues authored in this period suggested that the rise in populism was representative of a decline in the conditions of the intermediate segments of the population (i.e., the squeezed middle) and also indicated that socioeconomic disadvantage was spreading to the point that it was being experienced by multiple social groups.[21] The focus on the political behavior of the squeezed middle was accompanied by a change in how disadvantage was investigated, from a static type experienced by left-behind groups to a more commonplace and dynamic experience of insecurity that also affects the declining intermediate classes.[22]

Research on populism has not completely neglected insecurity. For instance, the political theorist Albena Azmanova defined the current political momentum as "precarity capitalism"—a term she coined to stress how the current political climate is characterized by the "universalization of insecurity, which is now afflicting the majority of the population, almost irrespective of employment type and income level."[23] In the empirical research on populism, however, insecurity has been investigated as an economic process, rather than being studied in the way I have defined it, namely, as a socioeconomic phenomenon experienced by individuals. As mentioned earlier, scholars who have investigated populism in relation to *economic* insecurity have found that a number of macroeconomic processes are associated with populist voting, such as trade shocks, public cuts at the local level, and economic crises. Influenced by economic framings, economists and political scientists have perceived the emergence of new social cleavages between the winners and losers of globalization and have interpreted populist voting as a reaction by the losers, who represent the populists' primary constituency.[24]

The studies focusing on economic processes have found important trends, but the explanatory process linking macroeconomic phenomena (i.e., loss of GDP, trade shocks, and globalization) to populism is macro, abstract, and remote and misses a connecting element that relates to individuals. The Brexit voters from Hartlepool mentioned earlier would not have been attracted to the populist sentiments of Brexit because they felt they had lost from globalization or due to the macroeconomic effects of trade shocks. Presumably, they would have voted for it because something in their individual conditions had changed *as a result* of macroeconomic changes in globalization and trade. Furthermore, the direction that their discontent had taken was deeply connected to their cultural framings, as well as the political options that were presented to them. Instead of considering just macroeconomic conditions, I use an integrated understanding of how economic, cultural, and political shifts occur in people's lives. Insecurity is deeply connected to the political sphere because the European social model that emerged after the Second World War was never about economic growth per se. Rather, it has always been about the balance between a moderate level of growth and a relatively good quality of life, comprising good working conditions and financial stability, for the majority of Europeans.[25] Endorsed by established parties, this implicit European social pact—which lacks the economic ambition of the American Dream but guarantees a certain level of security for large portions of the population—has come under threat. Populist parties have offered new political scripts that restore and underscore the importance of the main security providers (the family, the state, and the market) in sustaining socioeconomic stability. In addition, they have proposed new political solutions to address insecurity: The radical populist right have argued in favor of closing borders, while the radical populist left have campaigned for the redistribution of wealth by taking resources from the elites.

The Consequences of Using Insecurity to Explain Populism

I argue that using an approach centered on insecurity has three major implications for the way we investigate populism. First, it provides a more nuanced notion of what social disadvantage means in relation to political preferences. Second, rather than maintaining a distinction between cultural and economic explanations and using either one or the other, it integrates them, thereby positioning opposition to migration among the forms of status threat emerging from insecurity. Finally, it highlights insecurity's potential to divide people and to bring them together.

INSECURITY AND INEQUALITY: POPULISM BEYOND THE WORKING-CLASS VOTE

Investigations into the recent rise of populism have been highly influenced by the political sociologist Seymour Martin Lipset and his analysis of the rise of authoritarianism, which, he argued, was politically driven by the culturally authoritarian, yet economically liberal, working class.[26] However, the recent turn to populism has features different from those that Lipset analyzed, and the empirical research conducted to understand the recent populist rise did not find class voting to be a clear explanation for populist support; instead, it found a more complex class profile comprising traditional left-out segments and a portion of the middle class, whose economic and social position has been declining.[27] This generated an interest in examining not just class cleavages but also shared experienced and common social factors across classes that could become aggregators of political support.

Insecurity is helpful in analyzing the social basis of populist support because it has the capacity to capture common conditions and wider processes of inequalities, rather than focusing on crystallized class cleavages.[28] Not everyone who is affected by generalized conditions of work or financial insecurity will be equally affected by them, and the impact of insecurity is unequally shaped by the resources that people can access to navigate insecurity. As both the traditional working class and emergent service workers experience elements of precariousness, this can drive them toward a shared sense of being part of the people, a mass of individuals coming together around similar insecure conditions and in opposition to those who contribute—in their understanding—to make them insecure, be those migrants or the economic elites.

INTEGRATING CULTURAL AND MATERIAL EXPLANATIONS

The tendency to separate cultural and economic explanations of political processes is well-known in sociology. For instance, the sociologist Michèle Lamont once stated: "Political scientists ask the question: 'Is it culture or the economy?' To me it is about both."[29] The dualization Lamont is referring to—which has strong roots in Lipsetian political sociology—resurfaced during the most recent analyses of the populist momentum, particularly in the influential cultural backlash theory mentioned earlier.

Although its application has been challenged, Norris and Inglehart's theory remains extremely influential among political scientists and economists, especially in the way it investigates culture in isolation from the material aspects of people's lives, and it continues to be replicated in numerous studies on populism.[30]

From the cost-of-living crisis to growing work insecurity, material concerns are highly visible in Europe and elsewhere. In his last monograph, even the late Ronald Inglehart, the main theorist to support the idea that politics has become postmaterialist (i.e., no longer concerned with material issues), dedicated an entire chapter to the role economic insecurity has played in the rise of right-wing populism. While denying that insecurity would be "the proximate cause of the Populist Authoritarian vote," Inglehart—reproducing the common Lipsetian separation between the economic and cultural spheres—admitted that *economic* insecurity "plays a crucial role earlier in the causal process, helping explain why the Populist Authoritarian vote is much stronger today than it was 30 years ago."[31] As I explained earlier, insecurity is not purely an economic variable that precedes a series of cultural variables that are detached from people's material realities, but rather a concept that integrates cultural and economic aspects of their lives. The sharp division between a selected number of cultural attitudes and investigations that focus solely on economic insecurity is at odds with current cultural sociology, which has introduced a number of influential reference frameworks (such as recognition, symbolic boundaries, and social status) that are built on the interactions between the socioeconomic structure around people and the resonating cultural frames.

An example of this distinctive way of treating the cultural and the economic is how the literature on populism uses attitudes toward migrants as purely cultural variables,[32] in opposition to how cultural sociologists themselves discuss migration in relation to the rise of neoliberalism, material concerns, and wider divisions between insiders and outsiders.[33] Although associations have been found between opposition to migration and populist right support, attitudes toward migration have not explained if and how populist support increased in Europe at a specific point in history. Furthermore, the proliferation of antimigration attitudes does not help to explain another aspect of populist support: namely, the parallel rise in Europe of left-wing populism, whose enemy is the economic elites, rather than migration. To use technical terminology, the cultural backlash theory considers migration attitudes not as a product of the outside world (exogenous variables) but as endogenous variables that are separated from the socioeconomic conditions experienced by individuals, making the explanatory process behind populism circumscribed and based on a restricted understanding of how antimigration attitudes are formed. Instead, as I will illustrate in chapters 1 and 4, culturally based evaluations of race, ethnicity, or deservingness intersect with a generalized climate of socioeconomic insecurity, determining whether oppositional frames are directed against the economic elites or against someone with a different skin color, accent, or economic position.

INSECURITY AS A UNIFIER OF CONDITIONS AND A DIVIDER OF POLITICAL SOLUTIONS

A paradoxical aspect in the new politics of insecurity is that, in principle, rising insecurity leads to a harmonization in the condition of individuals that is, nonetheless, often expressed in divisive terms through the use of out-group framings. As I will show in chapter 4, populist parties' agendas are not simply oppositional. These parties also plan to restore security through the two actors that have been absorbing the rise in market-based insecurity: the state and the family. Hence, a typical right-wing populist agenda endorses a strong role for the state in combating the threat of citizenship status via migration, but also in taking action against undeserving citizens, because both threaten access to limited economic resources. Right-wing populists also typically support traditional family structures because of the role these play in upholding conservative values and because they wish to reestablish the family as a crucial provider of security in highly insecure times. Therefore, support for the family and opposition to migration are not disconnected from the socioeconomic realities of people's lives.

Cultural frames are important in understanding the direction of political discontent. People express their insecurity in an oppositional way because opposition between "us" and "the others" is embedded in the current political script. Policies, mainstream political discourse, and even songs encourage individuals to compete to earn a life free from insecurity. The opposition between "us"—the people—and "the others," which is constructed at the individual level, is also present at a country level. For instance, while the widespread insecurity experienced by Europeans is making the continent more homogeneous than it used to be in respect to living conditions, deservingness and merit are often evoked to establish out-group dynamics between the productive countries of the North and the "lazy" countries of the South.[34]

Chapter Outline

The first part of the book aims to illustrate the rise of socioeconomic insecurity in Europe, discussing how it is connected to economic, political, and cultural shifts. Chapter 1 establishes socioeconomic insecurity as a central concept in political sociology and describes the components of the new politics of insecurity. The chapter presents the sociological definition of insecurity used in the book, clarifies its links with the emerging sociology of insecurity, and discusses how this notion helps us to expand our understanding of socioeconomic disadvantage. The remainder of the chapter discusses how the new politics of insecurity emerges from the integrated effects of socioeconomic, cultural, and political security shifts.

In chapter 2 I illustrate how insecurity has increased across security regimes. I present a systematic review of the qualitative evidence of the rise in insecurity in the selected case studies and then show how insecurity affects the lives of individuals in Europe, using analyses of European datasets. The chapter identifies and discusses two shifts that have served to make insecurity a widespread and ordinary experience in Europe: the increase in work-related insecurity since the 1990s, and the exacerbation of financial insecurity since the 2010 crisis. The chapter concludes by questioning the compensatory role that welfare states play given the wide diffusion of work and financial insecurity across regimes.

Chapter 3 analyzes how political economic shifts have resulted in a microlevel rise in insecurity. First, the chapter presents the secular economic shifts that have occurred in Europe, such as changes in macroeconomic trends and the effects of the 2010 economic crisis. Second, it examines the current evidence on how the changes to national and European welfare-state interventions—centered on individual incentives and reducing the use of passive income support—have indirectly led to work and financial insecurity.

The second part of the book examines in more depth the conceptual and empirical links between insecurity and populism. Chapter 4 illustrates the microlevel mechanisms that pull insecure individuals toward populism and away from supporting established parties, presenting an integrated conceptual framework that considers the mediation of cultural frames. Through closer examination of the case studies, the chapter looks at how insecurity has entered welfare-state politics. It analyzes how mainstream parties have stopped incorporating socioeconomic security in their discourse and agendas, and how populist parties have exploited this gap to propose new political offers to address insecurity.

Chapter 5 presents the findings from multiple cross-national studies of work and financial insecurity that I have led, which have tested new indicators of insecurity either through ad hoc online surveys or by matching existing probability-sampling datasets. After showing how the notion of social disadvantage expanded to the squeezed middle, the chapter presents the empirical associations between populism, in the shape of an outlook and voting behavior, and insecurity.

In chapter 6 I discuss the responses to the rise in insecurity during Covid-19, arguing that this was a missed opportunity to change how policies address it. I then argue that although insecurity is not able to aggregate political support into a single class of voters (the precariat), it still influences politics in several ways. The final section offers a prescriptive list of ways that parties could address insecurity by intervening in the family–market–state nexus and hence influence how individuals can use family, state, and market sources to navigate insecurity. The epilogue summarizes the main arguments of the book and discusses the implications of the findings for research and political debates.

Empirically, this book employs a mix of quantitative and qualitative analyses, which I have conducted with the support of my research teams since 2016. I look at nine European countries, offering a qualitative analysis of their security regimes (chapter 2) and examining their political responses to insecurity (chapter 4).[35] These case studies contain a variety of populist sentiments in the shape of support for radical populist right (RPR) and radical populist left (RPL) parties; the justification for the case study selection and the details about the empirical analyses are provided in the methodological appendix. I present quantitative analyses of European datasets on an even larger number of European countries to find generalizable patterns concerning work and financial insecurity (chapter 2) and to investigate the association between insecurity and populism (chapter 5).

CHAPTER ONE

Defining Insecurity in Life and Politics

INSECURITY IS EVERYWHERE.[1] In 2023 Astra Taylor penned one of the most popular guest opinion pieces in *The New York Times*, asking: "Why Does Everyone Feel So Insecure All the Time?"[2] She referred not just to psychological sentiments of individual insecurity, but to how the economic conditions around individuals—the expensive housing market and shrinking social policies—contribute to these feelings. Insecurity can be hard to grasp. It is often defined in negative terms, as a loss of security, or purely as a feeling, and is hence disregarded in favor of more material, objective, and therefore tangible notions of economic disadvantage.

Drawing on the influential field of insecurity studies, I highlight the political implications of the concept and how it is positioned across cultural and economic research within and beyond sociology. Part of the interdisciplinary field of socioeconomic studies, the burgeoning research on this topic investigates conceptually and empirically its forms, qualities, and distribution.[3] This literature investigates insecurity not merely as a subjective feeling but as a condition emerging from how the changes in people's material lives intersect with cultural scripts of what security is in a certain society. For example, in the European context, as in a number of Western countries, it refers to work conditions and financial security. The fact that the middle classes express increasing insecurity is not a reflection of the purely subjective nature of the measures that assess this phenomenon, but rather a sign that insecurity is a quite common experience that, due to the rise of inequalities, affects the declining middle class, as well as poorer segments of the population.

The first part of this chapter illustrates and justifies how socioeconomic insecurity is used in this book, which builds on the emerging field of research on insecurity in socioeconomic studies; in particular, it highlights how and why the current focus on microlevel insecurity differs from the previous emphasis on new social risks. The second part of the chapter presents a multidimensional framework to understand the integration between the economic, cultural, and political elements of insecurity. Using a socioeconomic understanding, as discussed in the introduction, is important for the investigation of the socioeconomic triggers of populism in the second part of the book because it captures the subjective state felt by voters, which is missing in objective operationalizations of economic insecurity.

What Is (Socioeconomic) Insecurity?

Socioeconomic insecurity has long been a central concept in social sciences, although the way it has been discussed has changed over time. Having been described as a key effect of neoliberalism by Pierre Bourdieu in a speech delivered in 1997, insecurity continued to be mentioned in the work of several social scientists, from Judith Butler's investigation of how experiences of lived insecurity reverberate into the cultural sphere, to Michael Graetz and Ian Shapiro's exploration of its role in US politics.[4] For many years part of the sociological literature has conceptualized socioeconomic uncertainty as a form of social risk. In these studies, social risk was viewed as an external and macro factor, affecting and disrupting previously stable structures, such as families, class relations, and the ability of the state to regulate.[5] Insecurity first entered late modernists' illustration of uncertainty as an existential and individualized psychosocial feeling, as exemplified by Zygmunt Bauman's words:

> Insecurity affects us all, immersed as we all are in a fluid and unpredictable world of deregulation, flexibility, competitiveness and endemic uncertainty, but each one of us suffers anxiety on our own, as a private problem, an outcome of personal failings and a challenge to our private savoir-faire and agility. We are called, as Ulrich Beck has acidly observed, to seek biographical solutions to systemic contradictions; we look for individual salvation from shared troubles.[6]

While the most recent body of research has examined the processes of individualization in navigating socioeconomic instability, it has also been fundamentally concerned with clarifying the untapped interaction between structures and individuals' experiences of insecurity.[7] In particular, this recent research has investigated how individuals experience and react to uncertainty at the micro level, looking at how insecurities are reproduced endogenously within our societies in concrete terms, such as in work and in navigating financial uncertainty, and clarifying the interaction with the structures around them, as well as how inequality is reproduced through experiences of uncertainty.[8]

Initially, this most recent strand of research focusing on microlevel insecurity focused primarily on employment precarity and understood insecurity as a derivative state emerging from precarious work.[9] For instance, Guy Standing's work on precarity was first and foremost an analysis of work-related insecurity, although it mentioned the spillover effect that this has on people's finances.[10] Similarly, research on precarity conducted in the United States linked the state of precariousness to work conditions and experiences of labor-market uncertainty.[11] In parallel, another strand of research has revolved around how policy reforms have resulted in individuals experiencing higher levels of financial insecurity.[12]

The emerging field of insecurity research tends to pay attention to both work and financial insecurity, which have been identified as the two pillars of contemporary experiences of socioeconomic instability.[13] While precarity refers to a generalized sense of insecurity that results from the changes in work practices, sociologists have used this concept to examine the detrimental financial effects of labor market insecurity on workers.[14] To be clear, the notion of insecurity used in this field, and the one that I adopt, differs from a purely economic notion of insecurity, because rather than being about the risk of *future* economic occurrences, or about economic losses, it concerns current experiences. That is not to say that insecurity does not have a temporal dynamic linking the past, present, and future socioeconomic circumstances of individuals; clearly, it does.[15] However, the exploration of insecurity I use focuses on the *present* everyday realities of instability that individuals face in both their work and their financial lives, which often reflect changes from a previous state of financial and work security.

Another element that characterizes contemporary research in the field and that I adopt in this book is the view that insecurity is, as Bourdieu stated, "affecting an increasing proportion of the population, even the middle classes."[16] Loïc Wacquant, whose research generally focuses on extreme forms of precarity, took a similar perspective, theorizing a generalized insecurity since the Fordist era, which he defined as a state that "mixes the fear of the future, the dread of social decline and degradation, the anguish of not being able to transmit one's status to one's offspring in a competition for credentials and positions that is ever more intense and uncertain."[17] Yet, scholars who investigate socioeconomic insecurity do not suggest that insecurity is equally distributed among or experienced by socioeconomic classes. Quite the opposite—while the sociology of risk has been criticized for its treatment of social class and its conceptualization of risk as a factor that transcends enduring inequalities,[18] the sociology of insecurity has investigated uncertainty at the micro level precisely to uncover the contemporary processes that reproduce inequalities.[19] For example, in my own research, I have investigated socioeconomic dependence on state resources, family contributions, and the labor market (what I call the "welfare mixes") to clarify how individuals (specifically, young people and platform workers) navigate insecurity, finding that being in precarious work does not necessarily translate into experiences of precarity and financial insecurity, and that the latter are shaped by the unequal distribution of welfare mixes across social classes.[20] The most recent research exploring insecurity and class also indicates that precarity emerges as "the consequence of an unequal distribution of protection within society."[21] It is also a condition that affects several socioeconomic classes.[22]

A central element in the contemporary research on socioeconomic insecurity is the use and embeddedness of subjective measures, namely, questions that ask participants to evaluate various aspects of their lives. Work and financial security have both an intrinsic socioeconomic meaning in people's lives, in terms of supporting them in a material way, and an extrinsic value, in terms of sustaining the status and recognition that they have in society and hence upholding their sense of stability.[23] This aspect characterizes the work of many sociologists, who have discussed how social insecurity destabilizes status hierarchies of nationals and colonial immigrants in Western Europe and redefines gender relations in the insecure labor market.[24]

Before moving on to justify the specific operationalization of work and financial insecurity used in this book, I shall add a couple of clarifications on why I refer to insecurity instead of calling this process precarity, as some scholars based in Europe do. As mentioned in the introduction, while I rely on research on precarity and use both this term and insecurity as adjacent concepts, I utilize the notion of socioeconomic insecurity as a more effective concept and one better equipped to be employed in a comparative setting to describe the phenomenon that precarity scholars allude to. Having been translated from French (*précarité*) and Italian (*precarietà*), the term precarity has been extensively used by the Italian radical autonomist literature, in which it was initially applied to report extreme experiences of work poverty among those affected by globalization.[25] Over time, precarity has evolved to refer to a generalized condition of insecurity experienced beyond work and employment.[26] However, a discrepancy remains between the way the term is used in contemporary social sciences (in Europe) to define everyday and mundane forms of socioeconomic insecurity, and how extreme "precarity" sounds in everyday English. For this reason, I prefer the more commonly used concept of socioeconomic insecurity.

Outside sociology, insecurity can refer to matters of personal safety. Such use of the term, and its reduction from a broad concept encompassing socioeconomic experiences to a matter of physical safety and protection from external attacks, is in itself a process for social sciences to consider.[27] Using Wacquant's words, material socioeconomic insecurity has been "captured" by "the new martial discourse of politicians and the media on delinquency . . . , fixating it onto the narrow issue of physical or criminal insecurity."[28] Hence, using insecurity in the socioeconomic sense is also a way of reclaiming the term, by ensuring that it is used to consider people's work and financial experiences.

WORK INSECURITY

The classic economic operationalization of insecurity in relation to work conceptualizes it as the risk of losing one's job or as the insecurity that comes from having a contract with uncertain tenure, which is defined as job insecurity. This affects so-called labor market outsiders: individuals—such as young people, women, and migrants—who are excluded from the labor market and who consequently face barriers in accessing the welfare state. The assumptions that underpin this conceptualization are that security comes mostly from having a job and that insecurity represents a future and potential risk. Political science research has been highly influenced by the restricted conceptualization of economic insecurity: Scholars have investigated the political preferences of labor market outsiders and individuals who work in sectors with a higher diffusion of atypical contracts.[29] Insecurity that is related to the tenure and length of work is on the rise in Europe, especially for young workers, but it still affects only a small proportion of the total workforce, and "there has been no clear secular trend for job durations to become shorter or subjective job insecurity to become more prevalent."[30] Therefore, while measures of insecurity based on the tenure of job are important, they exclude the majority of the working and nonworking population.

Scholars who conduct research on work, meanwhile, have emphasized the presence of a more hidden form of job insecurity that relates to the changing conditions of work.[31] In Europe, employment rates remain relatively high, but a large portion of the workforce struggles with the presence of higher workloads, increasing work pressure, and declining autonomy.[32] In the sociological literature on work security and job quality, the loss of the features of work involves both its intrinsic features (pay, material aspects) and its extrinsic features (work–life balance, work pressure, intensification, skills, recognition, etc.). Table 1.1 presents the multidimensional definition of work-related security I use in this book, which covers various areas that the work literature has revealed to be under threat and builds on the existing studies on work conditions. Many of the forms of labor market insecurity identified in the table do overlap with the forms of job quality identified by the sociology-of-work literature, which aimed at retaining a focus on the quality of work instead of simply monitoring the quantity of work.[33] Indeed, after the 1990s, public policy specialists and scholars developed measures of job quality to monitor the quality of work in Europe as a reaction to the emphasis on employment creation and work activation that had emerged in EU policymaking and could have resulted in a trade-off between the quality and quantity of jobs created.[34] In particular, with regard to table 1.1, job security refers to the classic operationalization of insecurity as instability in the tenure of work;[35] employment security is a reflection of the individual effects of employment labor protection;[36] work–life balance has featured in influential studies on work-based insecurity;[37] work pressure and work intensity are core elements of the hidden forms of job insecurity identified in the sociology-of-work literature;[38] autonomy is an operationalization of the security of the worker vis-à-vis the instability of work generated by employers/managers;[39] career security is included in classic analyses of at-work security in Europe;[40] income security has been described as a central component of work-related security;[41] and qualitative research has highlighted the role of work-based recognition in fostering workplace security.[42]

According to Guy Standing, the obstacles in obtaining these forms of work security, which have constituted the bonding factor of European societies since the post–World War II growth, have resulted in an increase in citizens' experiences of precarity.[43] One could consider these ways of conceptualizing insecurity as arbitrary, too broad, or purely elements of

Table 1.1. Work-Related Forms of Security

Form of work security	Description
Job security	Having a long-term contract and/or not fearing losing one's job in the following six months
Employment security	Employment protection (regulation against arbitrary dismissal, hiring and firing regulations, etc.) and the possibility of finding similar jobs in the labor market
Work–life balance	Having time to engage in nonwork activities during the working week; not having to work during unsociable hours
Sustainable work routines	Not having to work at high intensity, lack of work pressure, and absence of stressful patterns of work
Autonomy	Autonomy in making decisions at work and autonomy in deciding on how to conduct one's work (e.g., vis-à-vis management or the central organization)
Career security	Opportunities to gain skills and use them at work; possibilities to progress in the workplace
Income security	Work providing an adequate and stable income, minimum/living wages, taxation to supplement low income
Work-based recognition	Feeling that one's role and work are valued and recognized in the workplace

the varying quality of work, which does not reflect a threat to socioeconomic security. This criticism is not new: In the 1990s, scholars debated the need to overcome economic-centered definitions of insecurity. Two sociologists of work lamented in 1999 that "insecurity sceptics are often economists and tend to favor fairly narrow and 'objective' definitions of insecurity in terms of changes in job tenure, the use of temporary labor and employment legislation regulating the dismissal of employees."[44] Their perspective—like mine—is that simply having a job with a permanent tenure does not make someone secure in their work life. Ultimately, opinions of what to include in and exclude from the notion of insecurity will vary among academics, and the interpretation of these measures is likely to be the subject of disagreement. It is relevant to note, though, that work–life balance, future prospects, job content, relationships with management, and work pressure are not only core elements of empirical measures used to investigate job quality in Europe but also distinctive elements of how Europeans, in particular those in Western Europe, evaluate the quality of work in comparison to workers elsewhere.[45] Facing more obstacles in fulfilling core components of what generates job satisfaction in a certain social context would result in a loss of security according to the way I have defined and described insecurity. Those who investigate work conditions through restrictive definitions of what makes a job secure neglect the fact that the majority of citizens in Europe, according to comparative studies on job quality and European values, still expect their jobs to provide more than just contractual security.[46] As a consequence, these scholars might miss crucial components of socioeconomic concerns that can potentially have political repercussions.

It should also be noted that the operationalization of security in relation to work can change across time and space (e.g., a sustained time of collective decline in job quality could potentially reduce the influence of job satisfaction on people's security), though the existence of studies that investigate insecurity in respect to work conditions in the Global South pushes scholars to deepen our understanding of the sources of security that all humans need across the globe.[47] Crucially, there is no other way to find out how people evaluate their experiences of work besides asking individuals, which makes these measures more complex than the purely behavioral measures used by economists, but also substantially more interesting in respect to their political implications.[48] Furthermore, despite being largely underused in political science research, subjective measures of insecurity are extremely accurate in predicting political preferences—as much as, if not more than, objective measures.[49]

FINANCIAL INSECURITY

Work-related insecurity is central in capturing people's discontent, but it is not the only form of insecurity, and it would be reductive to rely on it for several reasons. For one, this notion privileges a market-centered vision of security, and it neglects the experiences of those who have more difficulties in accessing formalized labor markets to obtain security, such as young people, home care providers, and disabled individuals. Financial insecurity is a more democratic way to investigate what brings security to individuals through the financial sphere. As mentioned, studies conducted in the Western context (namely, the United States, Europe, and Australia) have found work and financial insecurity to be two central pillars of current experiences of socioeconomic insecurity, and studies from the Global South point at the same finding.[50] Work and financial security are both independent and partially connected. They are independent as they capture different dimensions of what makes people secure: two major areas of individuals' lives that connect them to the market, the state, and their family. At the same time, a "precarity trap" can emerge from the combined effect of work and financial insecurity, as work-related precarity has a knock-on effect on individuals' financial security, and financial and work insecurity interact to reinforce each other.[51]

Socioeconomic insecurity is concerned with present financial struggles. Economic insecurity, on the other hand, refers to the inability to buffer *future* shocks. For example, Jacob Hacker's investigation in the United States included a measurement of past exposure and potential future exposure to economic shocks of relevance to US citizens (past or future expected experiences of losing a job in the household, health, loss of value of the house, etc.).[52] While it is important to dissect the connections between present and future insecurity, I found it more pragmatic to investigate first and foremost what individuals felt about their present financial conditions.

Many aspects of the current investigations of financial insecurity were already present in the work of the British sociologist Peter Townsend, who had the ambition of capturing a culturally based notion of deprivation by identifying the items that were deemed necessary for the majority of the population in a certain country, and by investigating how many people were not able to afford these items, despite wanting them.[53] As deprivation is a much more restrictive notion than insecurity, my analysis focused only on items that could potentially affect a broader sample of individuals than just the extreme poor, such as the capacity to repair broken goods or face unexpected expenses. Townsend wanted to understand what made the most vulnerable part of the population deprived, whereas my interest is in what makes the majority of the population financially secure. Hence, drawing from the literature on financial security and deprivation, table 1.2 provides a comprehensive list of the main indicators of financial security. These include the more extreme forms of financial insecurity from the items of deprivation developed by Townsend; items of deprivation that can apply potentially to a broader segment of the population, as they relate to everyday financial commitments;[54] indicators of the capacity to meet potential unexpected expenses, to make savings, and to increase debt, which are part of the literature on financial inclusion;[55] and, finally, a psychosocial and widely used indicator of financial anxiety that measures distress in managing everyday expenses.[56] Readers will note that these items do not aim to investigate outcomes in people's lives as well-being measures do but refer

Table 1.2. Financial Forms of Security

Form of financial security	Description
Lack of deprivation in relation to basic needs	Being able to afford essential needs: heating to keep home adequately warm; meat or equivalent to eat at least once a week; all recommended dental work; a holiday away from home for one week a year, not staying with relatives
Capacity to make ends meet/ face financial commitments	Enough money to pay rent, mortgage, utility bills, or loan repayments; having enough money to cover the necessary expenses for the household
Capacity to face unexpected expenses	Enough money to replace or repair broken electrical goods such as a refrigerator or washing machine; enough savings and/ or external support to manage a loss of income in the short term
Savings	Having savings for unexpected financial expenses; having the ability to save
Ability to reduce debt/ avoidance of debt	Ability to pay off debt; no need to access credit
Lack of financial anxiety	Not having anxiety or distress in meeting day-to-day expenses

specifically to the experiences that people live, and in particular to how difficult or easy it is to fulfill financial commitments.

Mapping the Current Socioeconomic, Cultural, and Political Security Shifts

The new politics of insecurity emerges at the intersection of parallel socioeconomic, cultural, and political shifts. After the golden age of welfare state expansion (1945–1975), European societies underwent complex socioeconomic transformations, such as the passage from a planned economy to an economic structure that emphasizes individual competition. This macroeconomic shift, as I will discuss, led to a reconfiguration of welfare such that individuals began to struggle to sustain their security through each of the welfare sources available within their welfare mixes (the state, the market, and the family).

The direction that socioeconomic discontent takes is mediated by the cultural societal frames, which are in turn influenced by the structure of the

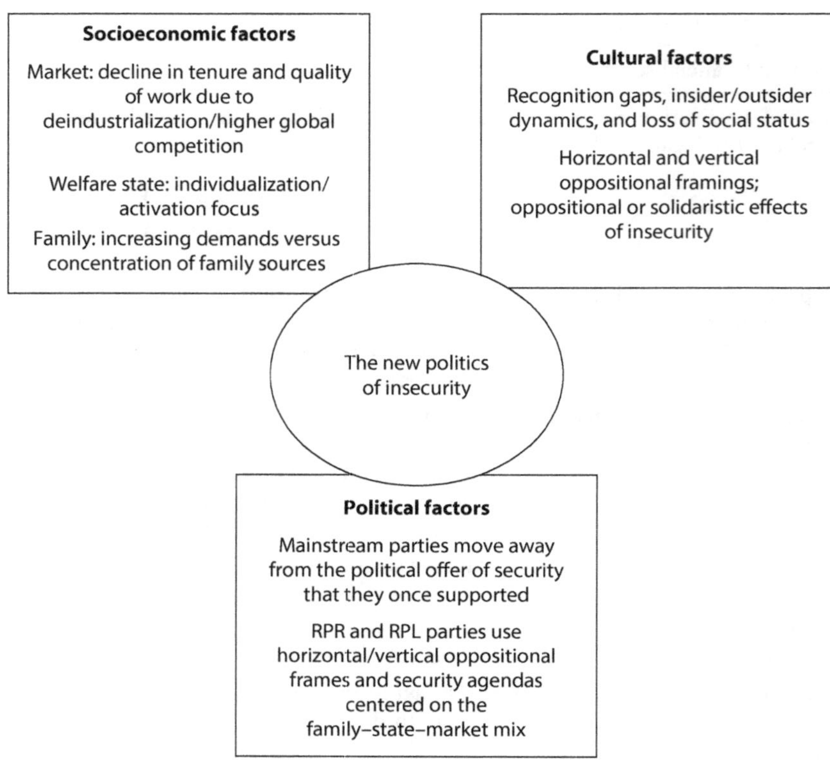

FIGURE 1.1. Socioeconomic, cultural, and political security shifts behind the new politics of insecurity.

economy: Contrary to what postmaterialist theory postulates, the connections between the economic and cultural spheres are mutual. The analysis of cultural scripts informs us about the direction that discontent takes in insecure times. Socioeconomic discontent can take the shape of ethnonationalism and in-/out-group dynamics or can become a bonding source or a feeling of shared insecurity in people's opposition against the elites.

Moving to the political sphere, European societies have been interested in a shift in terms of the public recognition of who ensures socioeconomic security. Established and mainstream parties moved away from providing a response to the insecurity of individuals, which was part of the construction of the role of the state in Europe. At the same time, new actors (such as RPR and RPL parties) entered the political sphere or repositioned themselves within it to provide different political solutions to address insecurity through oppositional frames. The three security shifts are summarized in figure 1.1.

THE SOCIOECONOMIC DRIVERS OF INSECURITY

One of the major sources of insecurity in contemporary debates is the fear that machines and technological automation will result in a loss of jobs—an idea that has entered academic investigations. When scholars investigate how automation affects security, the issue is often framed as a potential future risk of how the use of artificial intelligence (AI) and automation can result in a loss of human jobs, and hence the question participants are asked is whether technology could potentially lead to them losing their job at some point.[57] While technology might affect the security of workers, it is far more pressing to investigate the past and current shifts—those that have already occurred and that risk being overlooked by the focus on potential future effects of automation.

In respect to present disturbances to work security, labor market risks began to be transferred from employers to employees as far back as the 1990s, through companies making wider use of jobs with a fixed tenure and more frequently linking remuneration and employment to performance.[58] The insecurity revolution has been a subtle one in Europe, because it has not taken the shape of a full surrender to the role of the market, and the state has been involved in this silent revolution. Across the continent, the institutional shift that has occurred has had a more nuanced manifestation: Individuals are assisted by institutions, with states changing their function from seeking to avoid market-based sources of insecurity to helping individuals by serving as a buffer against insecurity. Welfare states have reacted to external economic changes by developing a new approach: the Schumpeterian workfare model of state intervention. (Note the use of "workfare," meaning work-related welfare interventions, rather than simply welfare.) In opposition to the previous Keynesian welfare state (KWS), with the Schumpeterian workfare state (SWS), the state abandons the ambition of shaping demand through internal policies, because this would not be feasible within the system of international market capitalism, and instead pursues the ambition of influencing the supply of work, through active labor market policies and social investment. States have not left everything to the market but have taken on additional responsibilities on behalf of companies to ensure that they attract or retain multinational organizations that operate in the knowledge economy, so that those firms do not move to countries with cheaper labor costs. In a piece that reads like a manifesto from any mainstream political party agenda of the 1990s to 2000s, Bob Jessop described the welfare transformation in the following way:

> States have a key role here in promoting innovative capacities, technical competence, and technology transfer so that as many firms and sectors as possible benefit from the new technological opportunities created by R&D activities undertaken in specific parts of the economy. [And finally] the crucial point is that state action is required to guide the development of new core technologies and widen their application to promote competitiveness.[59]

For Jessop, this change in welfare functions represents a form of policy neoliberalism, though he also concedes that the concept of neoliberalism might be too vague in the way it is usually defined to capture how the changes to the state-market nexus might affect societies.[60] In specific terms, Europe has not been subjected by welfare state retrenchment, as the transformed welfare state has, paradoxically, become even more pervasive in the lives of individuals than the passive welfare state of the so-called Golden Age. To start with, almost everywhere in Europe, state spending as a percentage of GDP is now higher than it was in that Golden Age of the welfare state.[61] The state also takes a more active role in the reproduction of the labor force, generating high-skilled individuals by putting more young people in higher education, upskilling workers, and providing training to get unemployed individuals back into the labor market. The responsibility for upskilling and providing education lies with the state, although it partially transfers this to individuals, for instance by increasing the cost of higher education for young people and their families.[62] Where companies operating in Europe have looked to cut corners, states have compensated by making workers more productive and by "reactivating" them through training and upskilling. In other words, states have not been retrenching but have been actively working to make the individual more entrepreneurial by investing in them.

Indeed, studies on the evolution of European social policy indicate the continuing role of the state in terms of spending even during periods that were characterized by a political commitment to austerity. During the 1980s, Paul Pierson showed how the new politics of the welfare state had protected the main welfare-state functions (pensions and health).[63] Even at the peak of the European crisis in 2010, retrenchment was not the only policy being pursued, as social investment spending was still dominant.[64] In fact, social investment policies took an even more prominent role in Europe after the 2010 economic crisis.[65] So, if welfare state retrenchment does not provide an accurate description for the subtle shifts that have taken place in welfare politics, what exactly has changed that might have caused an individual increase in insecurity?

To tackle this question, I need to address the perspective of the most strenuous defenders of social investment as an absorber of populist demands. Iversen and Soskice, in their latest work, *Democracy and Prosperity*, laid out a persuasive argument to demonstrate how the proactive role of the state has acted as a form of protection against economic and technological risks, allowing European economies to stay competitive and enabling most individuals to remain employed and protected through labor market access.[66] Their thesis was that such a system creates a minority of losers who support populism, but that, due to their limited quantitative impact, these people cannot affect the overall support for this structure of welfare capitalism.

Even if one agrees with the authors that the shift to a social investment state model has succeeded in sustaining employment, productivity, and growth, which is itself debated (the effects of active labor market policies on employment seem to be mixed and mechanisms-dependent[67]), this might still have created unintended consequences in other components of people's lives. I identify, in particular, two effects that the transformed welfare state has had on socioeconomic security: the indirect effects of out-of-work and in-work policies, and the decreasing compensatory effects of welfare states—both of which have been proven to be linked with populist support.

The development of out-of-work policies implied a move away from passive forms of income protection, and for part of scholarship it negatively affected the capacity of welfare states to address extreme forms of insecurity and poverty.[68] Furthermore, when one examines in detail the type of social investment welfare-state interventions that are promoted in Europe, it becomes clear that the most diffused form of social investment is not upskilling but rather the provision of incentive reinforcement and activation, which cannot be considered a type of intervention that reinforces security because it pushes individuals to accept any job that they can find.[69] In fact, the presence of incentive reinforcement affects not only those looking for work, but also employed individuals, as it reduces workers' ability to say no to suboptimal types of work in favor of being unemployed.

The shift to a social investment state also had effects on financial insecurity. At a fundamental level, it resulted in a reduction of cash-based transfers from states to individuals and their families, as spending is directed toward funding social investment services and policies to assess and monitor how individuals are using them. Indeed, while there are differences across countries and welfare regimes, retrenchment and adaptation became the dominant trajectories of welfare-state reforms, in part due to cutbacks of unemployment and family allowances, but also because active labor market programs were not counterbalanced by a higher level of spending on family policies.[70] Hence, in Europe welfare states have progressively transferred to individuals and their families part of the cost of being activated to join or rejoin the labor market, in a process that Jacob Hacker has defined in the United States as the privatization of social risk.[71]

Despite the atomized vision of the competitive individual at the basis of the new workfare model, Europeans are increasingly dependent on their families to cope with insecurity while being told that they need to be self-reliant to navigate the insecure paths of life, in a way similar to what Allison Pugh describes for American tumbleweed society.[72] A good illustration of this shift in Europe is the expansion of higher education and how it has consisted of a progressive process of privatization of social responsibilities from the states to young people and their families, resulting in an increase in financial insecurity not only for traditional working-class students in Europe but also for young people from declining middle-class segments.[73] The increasing demands on families are occurring at a time when family resources are unequally distributed as a result of the rise of wealth and income inequalities.[74] This means that fewer families are able to use family sources as a mechanism to compensate for financial insecurity, even if the expectation that we would help our relatives if something were to happen is even greater than it was a few decades ago.

Compensation theory postulates that the welfare state has an ability to lessen the impact of financial insecurity on livelihoods, reduce the extent of grievances, and limit the appeal of populism. At the same time, a number of empirical investigations have suggested that the reduction of passive interventions for individuals experiencing financial insecurity can help to explain the rise of populist support in Europe.[75] As I will examine in more depth in chapters 2 and 3, the symbolic and material loss of security in European welfare states reverberates into populist support through the reduction of the compensatory role of the welfare state.

INSECURITY AND CULTURE

Using the enlarged vision of culture established in the introduction (i.e., one that goes beyond attitudes toward migrants, gender, and LGBTI+), we can discuss in more depth the connections between insecurity and dominant cultural frames. Work and financial security, as mentioned earlier, have not only an intrinsic meaning in supporting voters' lives in a material way, but also an extrinsic value in representing the cultural conditions that determine one's worth in European society. People experiencing precarity use dominant cultural narratives to make sense of their condition of insecurity individually, as well as to make sense of how their past experiences influence their present.[76]

Furthermore, as resources do not simply have the function of maintaining material positions but are also a way to uphold or sustain one's status, the experience of social insecurity due to a lack of resources that bring safety can have the sociological meaning of reducing the perception of one's social status compared to others.[77] As Tali Mendelberg stressed, "Political systems allocate not only valued material resources but also collective social value," and hence a political system that is not able to sustain people's socioeconomic security would be perceived as devaluing people.[78] The experience of insecurity is connected to the adoption of a cultural outlook that can be considered populist through the mediation of dominant cultural scripts investigated by sociologists. For example, as Bart Bonikowski pointed out, the challenging economic climate contributes to the heightened salience of majority-group identities.[79] Similarly, Lamont found that economic transformations have profound cultural repercussions that challenge workers' social status and recognition.[80]

As mentioned in the introduction, at its core populism is a discursive frame centered on the will and value of the people (people-centrism) and the separation between the people and the others (anti-elitism), with a third belief that derives from the other two (people-centrism/anti-elitism), which attaches to populism the tendency to view good and bad as dualized (Manichaean outlook).[81] As the rise of financial and work insecurity is perceived to be a condition that the people share, insecurity begins to define the social category of the people and how valued they are by the political system. The concept of the people is also formed in opposition to the other, either those who are in proximity to us (horizontal opposition) or those who are above us (vertical opposition). Horizontal oppositional frames exclude others from the notion of the people through existing cultural hierarchies of worth and value based on race, ethnicity, nativism, or productivity, while vertical oppositional frames express the distinction between the people and those who have a higher position in the social hierarchy, such as the economic or cultural elites. According to this framework, more insecure voters are going to be drawn to populist views because these offer a narrative in which "the people," who are affected by shared experiences of insecurity due to worsening work and financial conditions, are recognized and given value, in contrast with the secure elites, who are perceived to be responsible for this situation. The construction of "the people" is influenced by the dominating cultural frames in a society: Who is part of the solidaristic construction of the people and who is excluded from it clarifies the in-group/out-group dynamics and the horizontal oppositional frames that are present based on existing cultural distinctions.

As Mabel Berezin explained in her analysis of the rise of Euroscepticism, antimigrant sentiments are neither the only manifestations nor the direct explanatory factors of the rise of antiestablishment orientations but rather are embedded in a reconfiguration of feelings of disadvantage and out-group dynamics that result from insecurity. In this context, "xenophobia is a contingent and not necessary response to the social problems that immigrants pose."[82] Hence, using an enlarged framework that considers both horizontal and vertical oppositional frames allows us to include other forms of antiestablishment sentiments that have become popular in Europe and that include an opposition to other categories of people who are not deserving of solidarity because they are reliant on welfare or considered undeserving. The opposition between "us" (the "people") and "the other" can also take a different form and rely on solidaristic horizontal frames. Culture enters the new politics of insecurity not only in relation to voters but also with regard to the populist views that parties and leaders are espousing, the discourses they are promoting, and the views of society they are framing—and hence to their political offers of security, as I will discuss in the next section.

THE POLITICAL OFFER OF SECURITY

A third shift that has taken place concerns the changing offer of socioeconomic security through politics. The new politics of insecurity—namely, "the ways in which political actors frame and reframe perceived threats while offering potential responses to these threats"[83]—is mostly applied to the politics of domestic rather than socioeconomic insecurity, even if socioeconomic "security" was as important as decommodification or stratification in establishing the welfare capitalism consensus in Europe after World War II.

The use and articulation of socioeconomic security within the political sphere have changed in Europe over the last decades. The consensus that emerged after World War II among Social Democrats and Christian

Democrats was built on the politics of welfare, as the welfare state was the machine that helped the majority of individuals to obtain socioeconomic security, which in turn enabled parties to secure political support. This was very evident in Nordic countries, as the social democratic consensus in Sweden was built on the notion of *trygghet*, a term that refers both to material concerns and to a deeper feeling of "comfort, well-being, and belonging" that is obtained through collective public intervention, while *otrygghet* was understood to derive from "competition between unprotected individuals in the marketplace or from insufficient public responsibility and collective solidarity."[84] Beyond the Nordic model, Christian Democratic groups of the center right, particularly those in the continental countries, have a well-established history of social capitalism based on ensuring the security of Europeans.[85] Even in the liberal model of the UK, there was a long history of a left-wing and liberal consensus behind the development of the welfare state that concerned sustaining citizens' security.[86] One of the pivotal features of welfare capitalism before the turn to precarity capitalism was the "policy consensus between the two centrist political families on curbing the free market via state-managed redistributive policies," not simply as an ideological tool to keep the role of the market under control, but also as a pragmatic way to maintain socially acceptable levels of security among the majority of the population with the implicit understanding that welfare state interventions were not meant to support certain social groups.[87]

The so-called Golden Age of European welfare states has been characterized by entrenched social divisions based on gender, race, and ethnicity that excluded several segments of the population from accessing socioeconomic security, while at the same time by the political intention of framing the welfare state as a provider of security for most of the population, in particular for white middle-class voters.[88] The existence of a welfare-state consensus on security for most in Europe becomes even more evident when analyzing the shift in the political discourse that started in the 1980s and became more common during and after the 1990s. The 1990s and the post-2008 crisis years fundamentally challenged the social capitalist basis of centrist groups in Europe.[89] A new consensus between the center left and the center right emerged during the 1990s and 2000s in particular, replacing the focus on providing security for most, and these two factions converged even more in their views of what it was possible to do.[90] For Azmanova, this new consensus concerned "the need to free the market from political intervention."[91] More subtly, as underlined in the section on economic security shifts, the consensus has been on the need to modernize welfare state intervention to sustain the goal of making the workforce competitive in a new global economy. Social Democratic and Christian Democratic parties have not abandoned the welfare state but have repackaged its function as an instrument to sustain economic competitiveness.

The indirect and partly unintended effect of the established parties adopting a political discourse that proposes a different balance between growth and security was the abandonment of socioeconomic security as a concept used to gather political support. From the 1990s onward, the Social Democrats, in particular, in order to achieve or maintain coalition potential, adopted policies and discourses that accepted and favored the shift toward flexible labor markets, diluting their defense of welfare-state provisions, trade unionism, social equality and justice, and redistribution of wealth.[92] While it might be true that, in terms of political veto powers and overall spending, welfare states remained immovable objects, visible changes took place in how the two main political groups were justifying or presenting the welfare state to their electorates: as an insecurity buffer or as a competition-enhancing machine.[93]

Examining the change to political discourse that occurred after the 1970s in Europe, Vivien Schmidt noted the change from "security-driven" values of solidarity to those that put an emphasis on individual responsibility and competition. In the UK, while the Conservative government under Thatcher did not succeed in cutting social welfare expenditure or other welfare-state interventions (pensions and healthcare), her longstanding legacy was the promotion of productivist values that undermined the support for the welfare state as a provider of security.[94] This made it easier for the Labour government under Tony Blair to reform social security and workfare in favor of opportunity and individual responsibility over passive dependence, while at the same time intellectually surrendering to the spread of social insecurity in society—defined in New Labour terminology as "new social risks."[95]

This shift was not limited to liberal countries. In the Netherlands, a continental country, the public was presented with no alternative other than to support reforms to a welfare state that focused more on job creation than on passive dependency, because both coalitions (that between Christian Democrats and Social Democrats, and the left-liberal coalition) were in support of this new vision of welfare.[96] In Italy, a Southern European country, the discourse also changed in the direction of reforming the labor market to make it more competitive, partly as an effect of the external constraint of the EU. Despite the fact that competition between unprotected individuals was framed as a negative form of insecurity in Sweden in the previous era, Social Democratic groups and Christian Democratic parties in the country had, by the late 1990s, agreed on a new framing of welfare-state intervention that prepared workers to better compete with one another in the labor market.[97] Hence, the changed positions of established parties indirectly contributed to the societal acceptance of insecurity.

Conversely, as I will examine in chapter 4, populist parties have offered concrete political solutions not just to migration concerns but to the issue of insecurity. For now, it is sufficient to note how populist parties combine oppositional frames with discourses and scripts that fill the security gap. One of the most distinctive features of the political offer of RPR parties has been the reliance on horizontal oppositional frames, which position the people in opposition to migrants and other "undeserving" citizens and serve as both a cultural and an economic political response. The symbolic boundaries created by RPR parties are a solution not only to the domestic security threats posed by migrants (i.e., an authoritarian solution), but also to the socioeconomic insecurity felt by citizens vis-à-vis their socioeconomic lives, as, alongside highlighting those who are excluded from it, they also reinforce who is entitled to socioeconomic security from welfare interventions (in-group/out-group dynamics). It might be reductive to define the agendas of RPR parties as leftist and welfarist, as their idea of welfare state interventions excludes outsiders, such as migrants and poor, undeserving citizens.[98] It is also relevant that, as noted earlier, RPR parties make extreme a degree of horizontal exclusion that was already present in European welfare states even during their leftist and welfarist years.[99] Most important, in addition to using oppositional frames, the distinctive function of RPR is that, in a new democratic settlement where mainstream parties have lost touch with citizens by prioritizing market responses over voters' demands, RPR parties at least formulate political agendas that offer an explicit political response to voters' microlevel insecurity.[100] For example, alongside their focus on state-based notions of exclusionary welfare, RPR parties are known for placing the family at the center of their political offer, which reflects not only their cultural agenda but also an understanding that the family can help individuals to navigate insecurity in material terms.[101] As I will discuss in chapter 4, several RPR parties in Europe also propose a new partnership between the state and the market as a potential fixer of people's insecurity.

In the case of RPL parties, in addition to a vertical opposition to the economic elites, they propose expansive and inclusive agendas to restore security based on radical forms of redistribution from the economic elites to the people.[102] Chantal Mouffe illustrated how in left-wing populism insecurity is mobilized as a bonding factor to construct a collective notion of "us" based on shared negative experiences.[103] This point is also evidenced by how Íñigo Errejón, the former secretary for policy and strategy and campaigner for the RPL party Podemos in Spain, used the concept in relation to the construction of a community: "Reactionary populism has been able to recuperate the powerful idea of 'community'—that we must build a spirit of community at a time when there is more insecurity, more anxiety and fear, more uncertainty about tomorrow."[104]

It is important to note, however, that the collective notion of "the people" does not necessarily include everyone who experiences insecurity, as cultural frames intervene to influence who is perceived as an insider and who is excluded from the solidaristic understanding of community—for example, migrants' insecurity might not be recognized in the same way as that of the nativist population due to their outsider position. In chapter 4 I will look in more detail at how radical populist right and radical populist left parties build their support by using vertical or horizontal oppositional frames that exist in a generalized climate of insecurity, and how these resonate with individuals based on their material experiences of insecurity and the insider/outsider cultural frames.

Summary

Examining macroeconomic changes—or operationalizing insecurity in a restricted way, for instance as the risk of unemployment or as having a precarious contract—offers a limited understanding of the sociological transformation that has occurred in Europe. The socioeconomic security shift influenced the balance between three sources of welfare that individuals use to buffer insecurity: the market, the state, and the family. Like other parts of the world, Europe has been affected by secular economic changes, such as deindustrialization, economic crises, and the technological shift to a service economy, which have resulted in more market-based sources of insecurity for individuals. Economic restructuring shook the relative stability in workers' tenure and the way people conduct their work (i.e., work intensification and work pressure). Furthermore, the changed role of the workfare state, from influencing the demand to shaping the supply, affected welfare states' capacity to function as security buffers. Families have been required to intervene to materially sustain individuals and help them to navigate insecurity, but due to the concentration of family wealth and income, a significant proportion of families are less able to function as security buffers.

The rise of socioeconomic insecurity is channeled either through oppositional frames targeted against migrants or those who are perceived as not belonging to the solidaristic notion of the people, or through more inclusive frames. The dominance of the first type of horizontal oppositional frames is influenced by the lack of recognition for large segments of workers and the existence of insider/outsider dynamics, both of which are a consequence of the generalized state of socioeconomic insecurity. However, the existence of anti-establishment discourses based on radical redistribution shows that discontent can be framed through more solidaristic lenses and via the use of vertical oppositional frames targeted against the elites.

Finally, the new politics of insecurity emerges as a consequence of the shift in how political parties address socioeconomic stability, which has consisted of mainstream parties progressively moving away from offering political responses to people's socioeconomic insecurity and from using socioeconomic security in their political discourses. In response, RPR and RPL parties have stepped in, providing political agendas that contain oppositional frames to the perceived sources of insecurity while also proposing policy solutions to address the problem. Before delving into the institutional origins of the shift to a politics of insecurity, I will examine in more depth the forms that insecurity takes across welfare regimes.

CHAPTER TWO

The Fear of Keeping Your Job and of Having a Stagnant Life

WHEN THE BIG populist wave hit Europe in 2016, many commentators were taken by surprise: Europeans live secure lives by Western standards, sheltered by relatively generous welfare states. The idea that the turn to populism could not be explained by a decline in their material lives suffers from a lack of understanding of the recent developments within European societies. Furthermore, insecurity emerges not simply from a reduction in people's standard of living but from a loss of what makes lives secure in a certain cultural context, which in Europe entails stable work conditions and relatively safe financial lives for the majority of citizens. What I provocatively suggest in the title is that the real fear of Europeans is not that they will lose their job—as most measures of insecurity used to explain populism assume—but that they will keep having a job with mediocre conditions and a life that is stagnant in financial terms.

In a piece for *The New York Times* in 2005, Alan Krueger, trying to explain the steep rise in job dissatisfaction in Europe in comparison to the mild drop experienced in the United States between the mid-1970s and early 1990s, speculated that this difference was due to a decline in job discretion and in the social elements of work among Europeans.[1] Financially, too, while Europe has never been a place for becoming a millionaire, the implicit promise that most people in society will not struggle to pay their bills at the end of the month has progressively dwindled. According to the second European Barometer on Poverty and Precariousness, in 2023—after the 2008 crisis, Covid-19, and the cost-of-living crisis—almost a third of Europeans stated that they were in a precarious financial and material situation, while the majority of Europeans were just getting by but stated that they needed to be careful.[2] According to the same study, the majority of Europeans have had to compromise on their choices regarding food and expenses due to difficult financial conditions in the last few years, which has involved skipping meals, turning the heating off, borrowing money, or not treating a health problem. This study indicated that experiencing financial insecurity is becoming, in one way or another, increasingly commonplace.

Two essential components of the European security model were a stable and secure job, with a high level of work satisfaction, and security in the ability to manage financial commitments. This chapter discusses what has shifted in both respects. First, I examine the evidence on the prevalence of work and financial insecurity across five security regimes, referring in particular to the case studies analyzed in the book. While the effect of security shifts has been magnified in the periphery of Europe, there has been a generalized rise in insecurity across the continent, which covers countries that were previously considered secure, such as the UK and France. I discuss two shifts that have made work and financial insecurity highly diffused in Europe by presenting new analysis, respectively, on the increase in work-related insecurity since the early 2000s, using the European Working Conditions Survey (EWCS) dataset, and on the most recent increase in financial insecurity, using the European Social Survey (ESS) and the EU statistics on income and living conditions (EU-SILC) dataset (see the methodological appendix for more details on the analysis of microdata). As stated in the previous chapter, the promise of high-quality work and secure financial lives in Europe has been a shared value among the large center-right and center-left parties that have dominated the political scene in Europe since the Second World War. The decline in the features of work and in the capacity of individuals to meet their financial commitments therefore carries profound political implications.

The Forms of Insecurity Across Security Regimes

Regime analysis is often used to investigate the variations in institutional settings across countries. I refer here to "security regimes" rather than simply welfare-state regimes, as each model of welfare that was investigated had specific strategies to achieve work and financial security, as defined chapter 1. While welfare regime analyses focus on what institutions provide, their assumptions, and their dominant features, I will use a real-worlds-of-welfare approach that examines the impact of welfare-state arrangements on societies, particularly on the work and financial security

Table 2.1. Security Regimes and the Forms of Protection

Security regime	Strategies for work and financial security	Sources of work and financial insecurity	Case studies
Southern	Job security and work quality for insiders; passive mechanisms	Informal market, labor market exclusions	Italy, Spain
Eastern	Protection of extreme poverty and some forms of work-based security for insiders	Work and income insecurity from the post-Soviet transition	Hungary, Poland
Liberal	Protection from extreme poverty, the market as a source of security	Failures from the market generate insecurity	United Kingdom
Continental	Job security and work quality for insiders, family protection	Labor risks for labor market outsiders	The Netherlands, Germany, France
Nordic	Diffused job security and work quality, active and passive support	Extreme poverty, youth poverty	Sweden

of individuals and their families.[3] I analyze the evolution of insecurity within a selection of case studies that will be used to qualify the features of each security regime: the United Kingdom (the liberal security regime); Italy and Spain (the Southern European security regime); the Netherlands, Germany, and France (the continental security regime); Sweden (the Nordic security regime); and Hungary and Poland (the Eastern European security regime).[4] I conducted a systematic review of the evidence available in this set of case studies (more details about the review are included in the methodological appendix) to get an insight into the descriptive changes to work and finances that have occurred within each security regime, summarized in table 2.1.

The core–periphery division that has characterized the European project since its inception was reinforced after the European crisis, and the changes to work insecurity have had a particular impact in the periphery of Europe.[5] The decline in security is, however, a pan-European phenomenon for several reasons. First, the rise in inflation after 2022 contributed to an unexpected convergence in the likelihood of Europeans to experience insecurity, which we can suspect resulted in a harmonization of insecurity across Europe.[6] Second, the move toward insecurity is a *relative* move—that is, it can take different forms within different security regimes, depending on the point of departure. In other words, if individuals in the

Nordic security regime expect highly diffused job security and work quality, the reinforcement of an insider/outsider dimension, by which labor protection is maintained for insiders, results in an overall loss of security within that regime. Third, the way insecurity increased in certain countries suggests that no security regime is truly "security proof." For instance, insecurity sharply increased in France, even if the country belongs to a relatively secure regime (the continental security regime).

These various movements generate a tipping point in the distribution of insecurity, whereby a considerable number of individuals across security regimes experience insecurity at work and financially. The importance of looking at qualitative manifestations of insecurity within the various case studies and not relying solely on quantitative generalizable data cannot be overstated: A few scholars have contested the notion of a widespread insecurity using economic data that examine only the tenure of work, without considering the multifaceted features of insecurity illustrated in the previous chapter.[7] Multidimensional measures of work and financial insecurity might offer a partial view if they are not interpreted within the qualitative and descriptive changes to work and financial security that have occurred within each regime and case. My review encompasses the narratives of insecurity that have emerged within each security regime in order to capture the relative loss of security. This is a crucial step in the interpretation of the comparative data on the political effects of insecurity that follows.

THE LIBERAL SECURITY REGIME

As hinted at in chapter 1, the beginning of the insecurity shifts in the UK can be found first in the Conservative agenda of the 1980s and later in the government of New Labour in the 1990s/2000s, not just, or even primarily, because of the policy changes that they were able to implement, but due to the progressive establishment of a political script that normalizes rising and constant insecurity, intellectually legitimized by the notion of new social risks.[8] The normalization of insecurity was reflected in how the British workplace changed during this time, with a steady rise of job intensification even before the economic crisis.[9]

The Great Recession in 2010 brought about a temporary rise of unemployment and underemployment in the UK.[10] The record low unemployment rates that followed, however, were the result of the radical transformation of the UK labor market, as unemployed people were reinserted into the workplace mostly through the creation of precarious work.

Indeed, the growth in employment postcrisis has been largely attributed to self-employment, precarious contracts, and agency work, with zero-hours contracts becoming extremely diffused working arrangements.[11] Given the presence of a dual labor market structure that distinguishes between low-skilled/low-wage jobs and high-skilled/high-wage jobs, a large share of low-skilled workers in the UK tends to be segregated in jobs that are highly precarious, with atypical contracts, low pay, or high uncertainty and instability, expanding the experience of so-called in-work poverty.[12] Alongside the increase of insecurity among the so-called labor market outsiders, a more pervasive, yet hidden, face of insecurity that became highly prevalent in the UK is the loss of the core qualities of work among the majority of labor market insiders, characterized by a progressive rise in work intensity, a decline in autonomy at work, and the general threat of experiencing diminishing working conditions.[13] Furthermore, the Covid-19 pandemic resulted, as it did elsewhere, in an even more evident normalization of work-related insecurity within society, given that many working in relatively safe sectors experienced redundancies and spells of unemployment.[14]

As a legacy of poverty studies, research into financial insecurity in the UK has usually focused on low-income households and their use of welfare and other strategies to cope with highly volatile income. Until a few years ago, being middle class in the UK meant being financially secure and able to support one's family without too many issues. This has changed quite profoundly, particularly since the 2010s, when economic policies had the double effect of concentrating wealth and income within a smaller portion of the population while transferring the costs of living from the state to British families, particularly in the areas of housing, higher education, and health.[15] As a result of this shift, the "shattered nation" described by Danny Dorling is not just an island with rising levels of hunger and precarity among the poorest (hardly new for an economic model that developed alongside the Poor Laws), but also a country where "the vast majority of middle-class people are now in the getting-poorer group, no longer part of the truly well-off."[16] The families of the British intermediate class, who are being squeezed, face financial insecurity even if they do not belong to the traditionally unskilled working class, as they often hold skilled jobs, own their own houses, and have assets.[17]

Due to the combined pressure on both the poorest and the intermediate segments of the population, the UK, together with Mediterranean countries, presents the highest diffusion of temporary poverty and financial strain among the case studies.[18] Since Covid-19, some of these tendencies have been exacerbated, as even families from intermediate classes have found themselves in the position of having to use food banks.[19]

THE SOUTHERN EUROPEAN SECURITY REGIME

In many respects, insecurity is not a new characteristic of the Southern European security regime but one of its defining features, as exemplified by the cases of Spain and Italy. One of the key reasons for this is that a not insignificant portion of workers join the labor market not through regulated work contracts but via undeclared work, which exposes them to even higher work-based insecurity.[20] Historically, the Spanish and Italian labor markets have been characterized by a dualization of insecurity, with labor market insiders being relatively sheltered through state-regulated labor market protection (e.g., employment protection legislation) and labor market outsiders being more exposed to irregular contracts, job insecurity, and substandard quality of work.

From the early 2000s, and with a sharp acceleration following the Great Recession, which hit Southern Europe very hard, two changes occurred simultaneously within the Southern European cluster: a rise in the insecurity of labor market outsiders and a decline in work conditions for insiders. In the Spanish case, outsiders were also subjected to more job insecurity as a result of reforms designed to make the Spanish labor market more flexible, which resulted in job dismissals becoming the main strategy that was used to cope with negative economic shocks in Spain.[21] While it is true that unemployment decreased after the crisis, this seems to have occurred at the expense of labor market outsiders, with young people, migrants, and women with low education being particularly affected by work-related precarity.[22] Furthermore, the changes to the Spanish labor market did not only affect labor market outsiders, as subjective job insecurity increased in Southern European countries, while Spanish workers in particular experienced an increase in strict control by management.[23]

In Italy, too, the recession resulted in an exacerbation of job insecurity for labor market outsiders, which affected in particular two groups that struggle to enter the Italian labor market: young people with low levels of education in the South, and women.[24] Since the Monti government in 2011, the 2008 recession was used as an opportunity to implement reforms to make the labor market more flexible. Adopted to revitalize the Italian economy by facilitating the entry of newcomers to the labor market, the Jobs Act implemented in 2015 during the center-left Renzi government has had the negative effect of creating temporary jobs over permanent ones, thereby increasing overall job insecurity in the Italian labor market.[25] Work-related security in Italy decreased not only among labor market outsiders but also among "mid-siders"—that is, workers who do not belong to the traditional category of outsiders identified by the literature and yet do not obtain the labor market protection of labor market insiders.[26]

Italy and Spain also feature among the countries with the highest rates of financial insecurity in Europe, particularly in the shape of poverty and financial strain, and the preexisting trends were exacerbated after the crisis.[27] The economic crisis, and the subsequent austerity reforms implemented in Italy during the 2011–2012 technical government to reduce spending, diminished state-based forms of cash transfers for several segments of the population.[28] The declining fortunes of those below the median in Southern Europe, and in particular in Italy, became more evident after the economic crisis, when the middle class experienced a phase of impoverishment.[29]

THE CONTINENTAL SECURITY REGIME

The continental regime is generally considered to be one of the regimes that is most shielded from the rise in insecurity, due in part to its relative economic stability. However, the relative lack of reforms within this cluster meant that its citizens were not necessarily protected from the emergence of new forms of insecurity, due, for example, to the decline in the quality of work for insiders, which challenges the idea of an automatic security of labor market insiders within this regime.

Changes to work security have corroded the foundations of the continental security regime as exemplified by the case of France, where work security historically holds a fundamental role in sustaining the collective values of French society. For the past thirty years, the obsession with reducing the cost of labor in France has led to a number of reforms that have reduced the workforce, intensified the work for those who have stayed, and reduced their job quality.[30] The 2010 crisis resulted in an inevitable decline in growth and a temporary rise in unemployment and constituted a window of opportunity to make the French labor market more competitive via work flexibility. The attempt to curtail differences between insiders and outsiders resulted primarily in a lessening of employment protections for insiders.[31] The trend of reducing rigidity continued in the reforms in 2013 and 2016, and during Emmanuel Macron's terms. The changes in the French labor market were twofold. First, the increased flexibility in the labor market led to the adoption of fixed-term contracts, which became popular for jobs that were not seasonal, particularly those that were held by new entrants to the labor market and young workers.[32] After the crisis, these contracts constituted about 15 percent of salaried jobs, and the median duration was about eight days, with employees facing constant switches from employment to unemployment. The second type of labor market change in France, and arguably the one that affected work security most profoundly, was the decline in job quality for labor market insiders. Between 2005 and 2010, France experienced the biggest drop in job quality among the countries considered in this study and had a comparatively high level of tenure insecurity.[33] As a result, possibly, of the financial effects of work-based insecurity experienced by French workers, France also presented, after the 2010 crisis, levels of financial strain that resemble those found in Southern Europe and the UK.[34]

Germany is often cited as an example of how populist ideas can spread in a country with relatively low levels of objective insecurity. While it is true that Germany has lower levels of insecurity than its European counterparts, there are also multiple signs of how insecurity is quietly creeping in and making Germany fertile ground for insecurity-led political discontent. The Hartz reforms were introduced in 2003–2005 to structurally change a German labor market characterized by high unemployment rates, labor costs, and regulation, by introducing flexible working arrangements and discouraging unemployment via cuts to benefits. The reforms seemed to encourage shorter unemployment spells but also resulted in a decline in wages among low-skilled workers.[35] They also resulted in some unintended consequences in respect to the qualitative level of work available, as the tightening of benefits resulted in people with financial insecurity accepting low-quality jobs, thereby increasing overall work-based insecurity.[36]

In economic terms, the Great Recession did not affect the German labor market to the same extent that it did in other countries, and given the market's dualized nature, it was mostly labor market outsiders who experienced job insecurity.[37] Due to flexible working contracts produced by collective bargaining, employers primarily resorted to cutting working hours rather than laying staff off during the crisis, which allowed production to resume in sufficient capacity once demand returned after the crisis.[38] As Europe's most secure member state, Germany helps in showing what has been happening across the continent, which is to say that conditions have been deteriorating: A comparison of wages between 2007 and 2010 shows that wages of workers in Germany were severely affected during the crisis, while work–life balance also declined.[39]

Financial insecurity is comparatively lower in Germany than in other countries, but recent studies indicate that there are visible effects of the cost-of-living crisis also on working-age households with low incomes in Germany, which experienced losses of 8–10 percent of their disposable income.[40] Furthermore, studies looking at specific aspects of insecurity have shown that there are emerging issues such as poverty and food insecurity that affect specific groups. Poverty among individuals at the periphery of the labor market (women and low-educated workers) has increased in the past few decades.[41] There are also important regional differences within Germany, with the east of the country—an area that notoriously breeds populist support—presenting higher levels of poverty and insecurity.[42] Looking at the country as a whole, Pfeiffer and her colleagues, who found that 7 percent of the population intermittently live in food insecurity and 46.6 percent are not able to afford a drink or meal with others at least once a month, went as far as to state that there is a "delegation, denial and stigmatization of hunger and nutritional poverty in Germany."[43]

The Netherlands is usually classified as belonging to the continental regime. However, given that it displays features of other regimes, it represents a hybrid case that incorporates aspects of the continental, liberal, and Nordic security regimes. In general, the Dutch labor market is characterized by a high flexibility of contracts and a normalization of high job insecurity.[44] This includes a comparatively high level of contracts with nonregular tenure, though these tend to be taken up voluntarily, which should result in workers reporting lower subjective tenure insecurity.[45] The Netherlands had one of the lowest levels of job-quality loss in Europe, although issues with work–life balance have become much more common after the European recession in 2008.[46] Similarly to Germany, the Netherlands shows comparatively lower levels of financial insecurity, although qualitative studies indicate the presence of persistent poverty among specific social groups, such as single mothers and migrants, and a high presence of food insecurity among older people and marginalized groups.[47] Financial and work insecurity are still present in the Netherlands in a more qualitative and subtle way, as a consequence of the changing compensatory role of the welfare state: Due to the institutional normalization of temporary work, and to the individualized and productivist orientation of the transformed Dutch welfare state, welfare recipients report experiencing an increase in job insecurity and financial insecurity.[48]

THE NORDIC SECURITY REGIME

The Nordic security regime is considered to offer higher levels of security than other models, but looking at the case of Sweden, I found a relative increase in work and financial insecurity, which can explain the relative loss of security that is also found in this country. The main change in the Swedish labor market has been the alteration in welfare-state regulations, which has made the Swedish labor market similar to a continental labor market in that it presents a sharper insider/outsider division in respect to employment protection and plays host to a larger proportion of outsider and precarious workers.[49] Sweden also has high proportions of involuntary part-time and temporary employment, with part-time employment accounting for 25 percent of contracts in 2013, about 30 percent of which were involuntary.[50] Temporary employment, and therefore job insecurity, is to a large extent the domain of young workers who are either in education or early entrants to the labor market, but it is also adopted in significant numbers by cohorts above the age of sixty-five.[51] While Swedish welfare-state interventions have focused on labor market outsiders, another important change has occurred in the country in relation to insecurity: a decline in at-work insecurity for labor market insiders as an effect of the declines in job security, working conditions, and career security (i.e., the security related to skills and career development).[52]

Regarding financial insecurity, Sweden, along with Denmark, is the country with the lowest levels of long-term multiple economic insecurity in Europe. Relative poverty is present in Sweden, with one-fifth of the population having an income below what most Swedes think is necessary to make ends meet, while more extreme forms of financial insecurity tend to affect outsider groups in particular, such as migrants and young people.[53] Temporary extreme financial insecurity is actually quite high in Sweden and Denmark, as market-related risks are present in these two countries; however, due to the presence of state-based buffers, insecurity becomes a more transitional experience.[54] The transitional experiences of insecurity, however, might well serve to create a climate that is more receptive to new political provisions of security: Recent research reports that, much like in the Netherlands, the stigmatized dependence on the state and the high control of the transformed Swedish social assistance system increased financial insecurity among welfare recipients.[55]

THE EASTERN EUROPEAN SECURITY REGIME

The higher levels of job insecurity and at-work insecurity in Eastern Europe, in comparison to Western Europe, are the result of the levels of poverty in Eastern Europe during the Soviet period, the economic shocks that Eastern European countries experienced after the move to Western capitalism, and the transition to welfare capitalism in these regions.[56] Within Eastern Europe there are different submodels: the neoliberal welfare state, with minimalist welfare-state interventions and high levels of poverty (e.g., Romania); the dual regime, with relatively high spending, low corporate taxes, and high personal taxes, and with fragmented welfare states that are relatively developed but host a large portion of outsiders that do not access social protection (such as Hungary and Poland); and the social corporativist regime, which has maintained higher levels of social spending and shows lower levels of poverty (e.g., the Czech Republic).[57] My analysis will focus on two cases that have a dual regime and form part of the Visegrad Group of countries: Hungary and Poland.

In the 1980s Hungary had a Scandinavian level of income inequality, but by the early 2000s it had become one of the most unequal countries of the EU in respect to income.[58] The loss of 1.2 million jobs out of 5 million, coupled with the privatization of public services and a highly means-tested welfare state, resulted in rising work and financial insecurity, with a growing number of Hungarians experiencing low wages and long-term unemployment.[59]

Unlike the other security regimes I have looked at, the Eastern European regime does not have a welfare capitalist past with a strong welfare state as a central provider of security, and welfare capitalist reforms by all political parties have often distanced themselves from the Soviet past by supporting light state interventions over a more prominent market role. This has also been the case in Hungary. Supported by a blind faith in the market as security provider, the RPR-led Fidesz government, under Viktor Orbán, has adopted a number of reforms that have increased job insecurity: The Labor Code reform of 2012 brought more flexibility to the Hungarian labor market and enabled foreign multinational companies to invest in the country and create jobs, while the abandonment of collective agreements increased job insecurity and labor market vulnerability, particularly in northern and eastern regions.[60] The social security reforms also had a regressive effect on inequality and income distribution, as they favored higher incomes, increased the burden on those on low incomes, and resulted in a rise in financial insecurity for low and lower-middle income groups and the exacerbation of poverty among historically socially excluded groups (e.g., Roma).[61]

In Poland, the posttransition phase was characterized by a high level of deregulation of labor markets, doubling rates of temporary employment between 2002 and 2015, and a rise in job insecurity; during this period, Poland was able to increase employment rates almost exclusively through the creation of temporary and precarious work.[62] It is not just labor market outsiders, of whom there are a large number, who endure work insecurity in Poland, but also labor market insiders, as the multidimensional indicator of job quality indicates that the country has the worst job-quality performance in Europe.[63] While a slight improvement in job quality has been reported among those in permanent contracts, workers in temporary contracts experience high rates of work pressure and a lack of autonomy, as measured through work scheduling quality and job strain.[64]

Compared to its Hungarian counterpart, the government led by the RPR party Law and Justice (PiS) adopted a more welfare chauvinist approach in areas that it deemed would help to sustain political support by doubling family and child expenditures between 2015 and 2019 and increasing expenditures on health and retirement.[65] The Family 500+ program in particular consisted of the most significant cash transfer since pre-Soviet times, which helped to reduce poverty and inequality.[66] The reforms PiS has made to address the profound and entrenched levels of job insecurity and insecurity at work in Poland have been less expansive, although the PiS-led government put a three-year limit on fixed-term contracts and extended the unemployment allowance to more workers with temporary contracts.[67] A study on perceived socioeconomic insecurity among those at work, in terms of perceived employment insecurity and income insecurity, showed that the interventions adopted had a partial effect, as between 2007 and 2017 Poland remained among the most deprived countries in Europe, but the perceived insecurity among the population decreased.[68] However, the pandemic contributed to a deterioration in the financial situation also in Poland.[69]

How At-Work Insecurity Became a Majoritarian Concern in Europe

As mentioned in the previous chapter, the main feature of insecurity that is discussed in scholarly publications and popular narratives is the diffusion of precarious jobs and the use of short-term contracts or jobs with a fixed tenure (i.e., job insecurity). Since the Great Recession in 2008, there has been an increase in the proportion of temporary employment contracts among the total jobs created in each country. The Netherlands, Poland, Portugal, and Spain have the highest rates of temporary contracts—between 21 and 27 percent of the working-age population, which is much higher than the OECD average of 11.5 percent—while temporary employment contracts have sharply increased in France and Italy as well.[70] However, the gloomiest and darkest predictions regarding the diffusion of job insecurity that would result from the crisis—that is, that the majority of jobs in Europe would become precarious jobs with fixed-term contracts and precarious tenure—have been refuted.[71] Indeed, other than in Spain and Greece, the employment rates across Europe before the onset of the Covid-19 pandemic were higher than they had been before the 2008 crisis. Furthermore, while the number of short-term and precarious positions has increased, they remain a relatively small segment of the total number of jobs in the labor market, a fact that has been used in sociology to challenge the idea of a diffused precarity.[72] If there is a diffused insecurity in Europe, in what way is this work-related insecurity manifesting itself?

As argued in the previous chapter, the percentage of short-term and precarious jobs is not the main indicator to monitor the evolution of insecurity. The diffused insecurity relates to the quality and composition of the job market and the fact that working conditions in European labor markets are now vastly different from what they were a few decades ago. Work insecurity, as discussed in chapter 1, refers to a loss of the features of work: a declining level of pay, a poor work–life balance, more pressure and control from management, and less autonomy for employees to conduct their work in the way they would like. As I have started to show with the analysis of the case studies, changes have occurred in European labor markets that are not just a result of the rise in short-term irregular jobs but are above all connected to the altered relationship between employers and their employees, even if employees have permanent contracts and are therefore considered labor market insiders.

Despite the rising wages and falling hours in the 1990s, this was the decade when job dissatisfaction started to steadily but quietly increase in Europe.[73] Comparative studies that investigated work autonomy, job intensification, work pressure, and job satisfaction found a pattern of decline in work conditions between the 1990s and 2000s, indicating that, rather than the diffusion of precarious contracts per se, it was the quality of work that had really declined, in particular in the form of job intensification.[74] While the European labor market recovered after the 2008 crisis, even this improvement—as discussed in relation to the case studies, and as European-wide analyses have confirmed—has occurred at the expense of good jobs, with more bad jobs being available around Europe.[75]

Existing studies, and the analyses of the case studies presented earlier, have indicated the presence of a decline in job quality, but I want to investigate in more depth how diffused, or even majoritarian, the lack of satisfaction at work has become in Europe, using the multidimensional measures of work security presented in chapter 1. I empirically test this using the variables in the major dataset on work conditions in Europe, the European Working Conditions Survey, a cross-national dataset on job quality in Europe, which is run by Eurofound and has been conducted at regular intervals. My main goal here is not to analyze trends across waves per se (the latest available round of the EWCS is from 2015, as the pandemic affected the collection of data in 2020) but to appreciate the extent to which individuals tended to report work-related insecurity in 2015, and hence even after the Eurocrisis.

The usual measure employed to evaluate insecurity—the fear of losing one's job within the next six months—reached its highest level, 34 percent, in 2010, during the crisis and had only partially recovered by 2015 (see fig. 2.1). Around Europe, the rates varied between about 20 percent and 40 percent, with the EU average being 29 percent. The wide diffusion of job insecurity in Europe is, however, much more evident by looking beyond the fear of tenure and examining the conditions of work. On average, across both the EU and the case studies, 59 percent of individuals believed it would be hard to find a similar job to the one they had at the time, even after the postcrisis recovery. This measure is a good proxy to understand, alongside other items, how trapped individuals feel in their jobs. Another dimension that conveys sentiments of insecurity among European workers is whether they believe they are paid fairly. In 2015 some 48 percent of workers on average across the EU and 49 percent on average across the twelve countries considered in the analysis did not believe that they were paid fairly. A slight majority of the working population (56 percent in EU countries and 57 percent in the twelve countries considered) also reported that they had bad career prospects. In other words, more than half the workers in Europe expressed a generalized dissatisfaction with their work lives. This means, of course, that there was another half of the population who felt relatively secure at work, but having about half the population reporting multiple forms of work-related dissatisfaction is an important element to consider when exploring the social basis of populist support.

FIGURE 2.1. Agreement on the dimensions of work conditions among case studies in 2015, using EWCS data.

In 2015 specific questions were asked to understand the effects of company restructuring in Europe. Restructuring could indicate a worsening of work conditions, with the same work being shared among fewer workers. According to the data available in the EWCS, 22 percent of workers both in the case studies I consider and across the EU agreed that the number of staff in their companies had declined, while 31 percent of workers agreed that their duties had increased. Hence, almost a third of workers reported an increase in work intensity as a result of workplace restructuring.

To understand when the decline in work security occurred, I extended the analysis of work autonomy and work pressure introduced by Lopes et al. by considering the postcrisis period, which was not included in the original study.[76] Similar to the original study, my analysis examines two measures of autonomy of workers: procedural autonomy, which refers to the degree of control that workers perceive they have over when and how they carry out their tasks; and content autonomy, which refers to the learning opportunities available in their job and whether workers assess the quality of their work. It also included a measure of work pressure, which is constructed by combining measures on work intensity (working at very high speed and to tight deadlines) and questions related to potentially stressful patterns of work, such as reliance on work done by colleagues, defined performance targets, and time constraints. My analysis

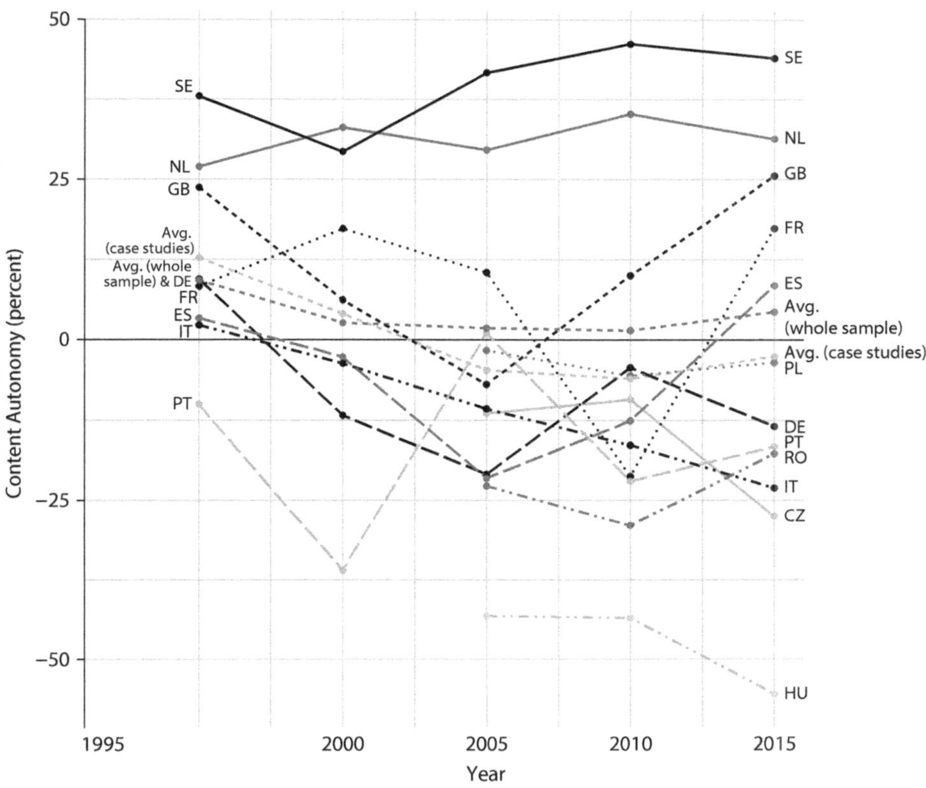

FIGURE 2.2. Evolution of content autonomy, 1995–2015, using EWCS data.

revealed that both procedural autonomy and content autonomy have been declining, on average, since 1995 across the countries considered; in both cases, there was a slight increase after the crisis (between 2010 and 2015), but the level in the latest available round (2015) was lower than the starting point (1995) (figs. 2.2 and 2.3).

An even more interesting result comes from looking at work pressure, which includes an operationalization of work intensity and stressful patterns of work. Figure 2.4 shows a steep increase in work pressure both on average and in individual countries from 1995, with a steep rise between 2000 and 2005. This seems to indicate that the reforms of the labor market that took place in the 1990s and early 2000s had a negative effect in terms of increasing work pressure.

To sum up, the analysis of the items related to income security, employment security, and career security showed that about half the working population experience work-related insecurity. It also

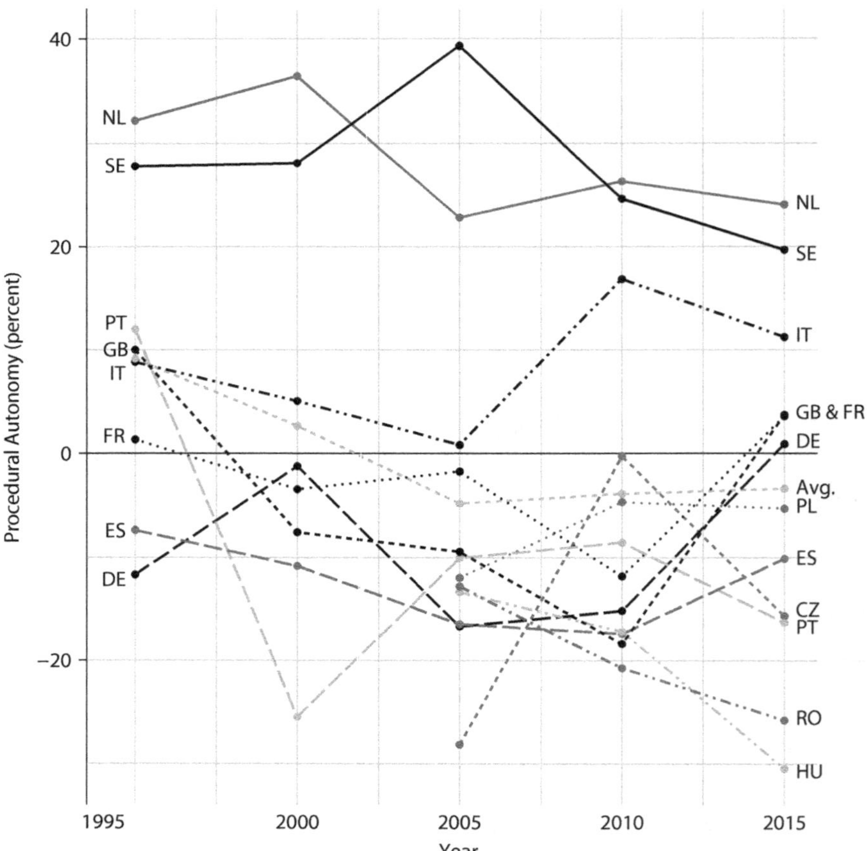

FIGURE 2.3. Evolution of procedural autonomy, 1995–2015, using EWCS data.

highlighted that more negative feelings are expressed for the indicators that capture insecurity in work conditions than for those linked to job insecurity. In addition, the analysis of the trends of work-related insecurity revealed that content and procedural autonomy have declined and not recovered while work pressure has steadily increased, and that these trends occurred not after the crisis but after 1995 and 2000—that is, during the period of labor market reforms. The picture that emerges so far is that of a work environment in which the majority express issues over the main features of their work. These trends do not appear to be simply economically led, as their timing indicates that they are also the effects of a transition to the new Schumpeterian workfare model implemented in the 1990s and 2000s.

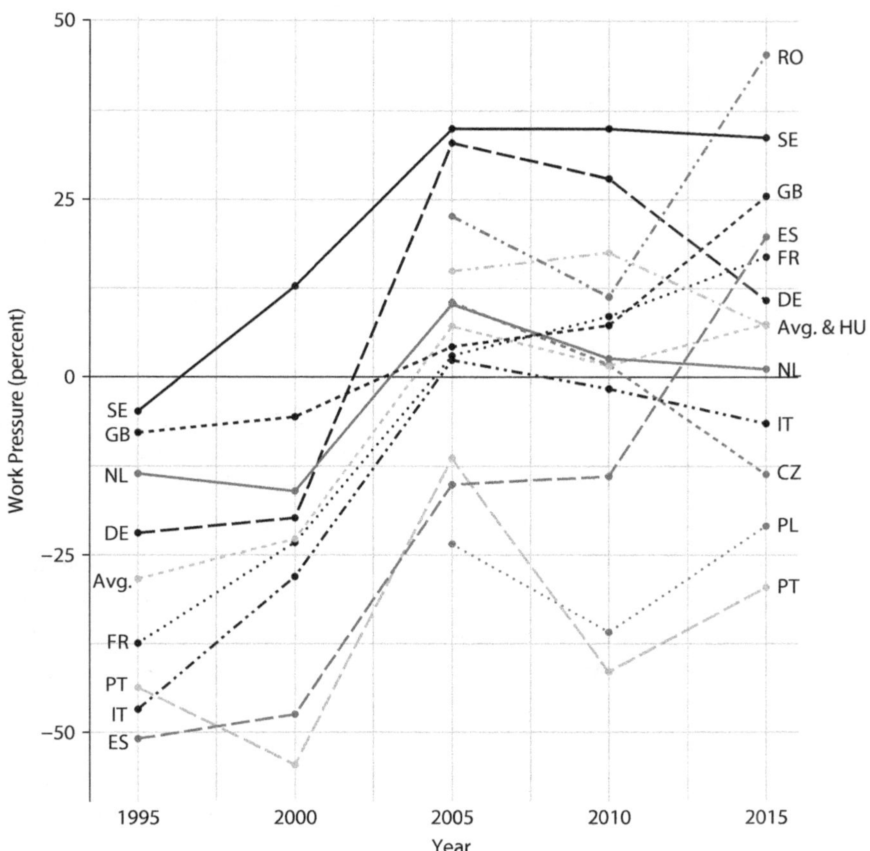

FIGURE 2.4. Evolution of work pressure, 1995–2015, using EWCS data.

How Financial Insecurity Spread Across Classes and Regimes

The descriptive analysis of the case studies that I presented indicated that the diffusion of financial insecurity varies across security regimes, but that financial insecurity might have become a more prevalent phenomenon in Europe. We have two hints that this might be the case: the way financial insecurity has become part of the experiences of the middle classes, and the role of the economic recession in exacerbating financial insecurity even within more secure regimes.

On the first point, I referred before to the concept of the "squeezed middle" to describe how financial insecurity spread to new social groups in the liberal and Southern security regimes, where such a change is more evident. Europe in general has experienced a "great squeeze"—that is, a significant reduction in the resources available to families and individuals—which has affected not only lower-income groups but a larger percentage of the population that includes intermediate income groups. Generally used to refer to individuals or families with lower-middle incomes (10–50 percent of the median), although sometimes extended to include upper-middle incomes (50–70 percent of the median), the notion of the "squeezed middle" describes the social position of "ordinary" families who have intermediate or even upper-intermediate levels of education and stable jobs and yet struggle to maintain their lifestyles.[77] The start of the reduction in aggregate household income of middle-income households in most European countries due to declining wages, rents, and pensions has been identified to have occurred between 1991 and 2010—therefore, well before the period immediately preceding the 2008 crisis.[78] The negative evolution of middle-class fortunes in Europe can be explained partly by the redistribution of economic resources at the global level: Due to economic globalization, the losses for (lower-)middle-income groups in Europe have been particularly severe and even higher than the losses for low-income groups globally in relative terms.[79]

The 2008 recession in Europe affected the social basis of financial security, leading to an increase in insecurity both within countries and across security regimes. The decline in work conditions and the pressures on wages felt by workers and reported in the previous section contributed to an erosion of middle-income and wealth returns for the middle classes in Europe.[80] Income distribution is becoming more polarized in many European countries, leading to sharper income-based cleavages within society, while—beyond income—middle-income groups are more likely to experience more economic stress (liquidity, ability to make ends meet, debt, etc.) and higher moderate deprivation (e.g., measured as the ability to go on holiday or keep the home relatively warm).[81] Looking at financial insecurity, defined as the difficulty experienced by a household in managing financial resources in order to meet its needs (through temporary exposure to poverty and financial strain, and an inability to meet financial obligations), Ranci and his colleagues found that financial insecurity since the Great Recession extends across income groups and occupational classes, including the middle classes, and that insecurity is more normalized across Europe and present even in more secure welfare regimes.[82]

Based on this emerging evidence, I wanted to explore in more depth how prevalent financial insecurity is and how it is distributed across

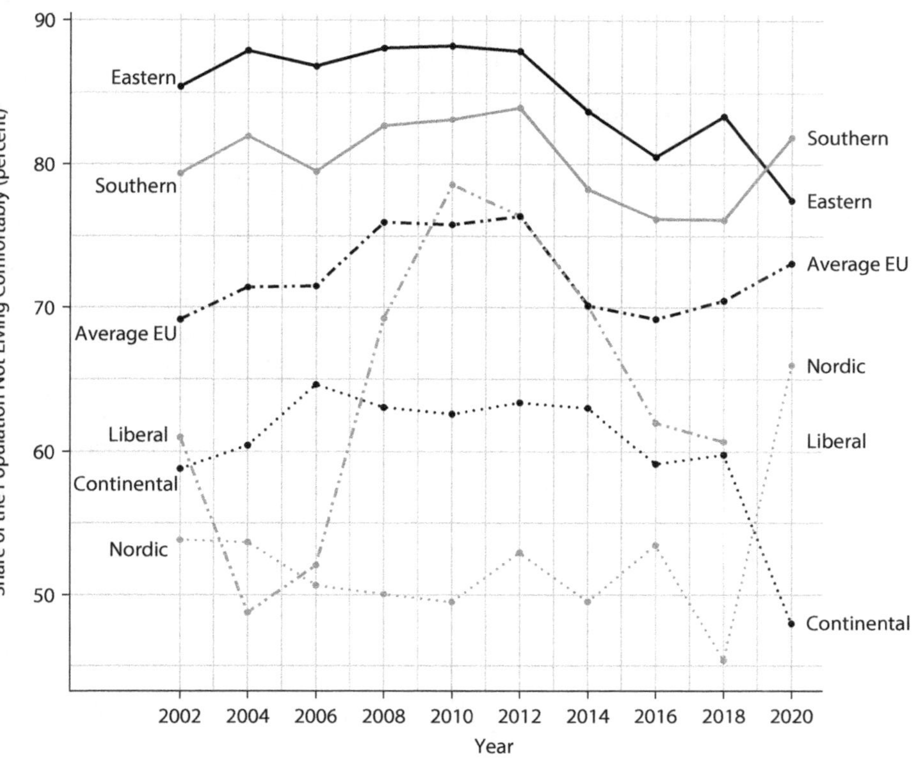

FIGURE 2.5. Share of the population who are not living comfortably (that is, who are "coping," "finding it difficult," or "finding it very difficult") on their present income per security regime, ESS 2002–2020.

security regimes. Using data from the ESS waves between 2002 and 2020, I looked at the only item investigating financial insecurity, namely, the one that asked whether the respondent was "living comfortably," "coping," "finding it difficult," or "finding it very difficult" on their household income. Figure 2.5 presents the share of those who did not state that they were living comfortably, divided per security regime.[83] In both Eastern and Southern Europe, that share constituted a significant majority, while there was a substantial increase in the liberal cluster. The average, both in the case studies I consider and across the EU, was over 70 percent, making the lack of financial security a prevalent feature among the population. While the Nordic and continental countries showed much lower rates, the data reported a recent increase in the Nordic cluster even before the last cost-of-living crisis that happened after Covid.

Wanting to understand more about the pervasiveness of extreme financial insecurity—in other words, how prevalent it is in people's

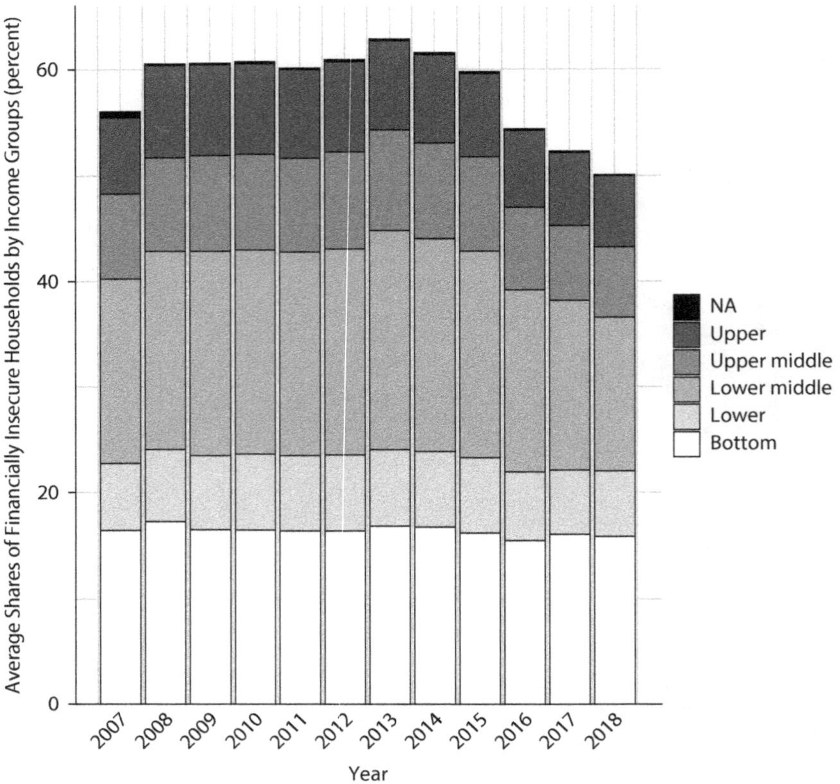

FIGURE 2.6. Average share of those who stated they had difficulties making ends meet in the previous three years and had not recovered by the fourth year, across case studies, EU-SILC (2007–2018).

recent experiences and across different socioeconomic groups—I tried to use the existing indicators in the EU-SILC in a more expansive way. This part of the analysis focused on the longitudinal portion of the EU-SILC dataset to find out the percentage of individuals who stated that they had difficulties making ends meet over the previous four years. Figure 2.6 shows the percentage of individuals who stated that they had difficulties in making ends meet during the previous three years and that they had not recovered in the fourth year, with a breakdown per class based on income groups.[84] To be clear, this measure is not simply a measure of financial insecurity but one of extreme financial insecurity—far more restricted in its diffusion among the population than the measures of financial insecurity I used earlier and will use in chapter 5. Despite the extreme formulation of this indicator, more than half of households stated that they had difficulties making ends meet over the four-year

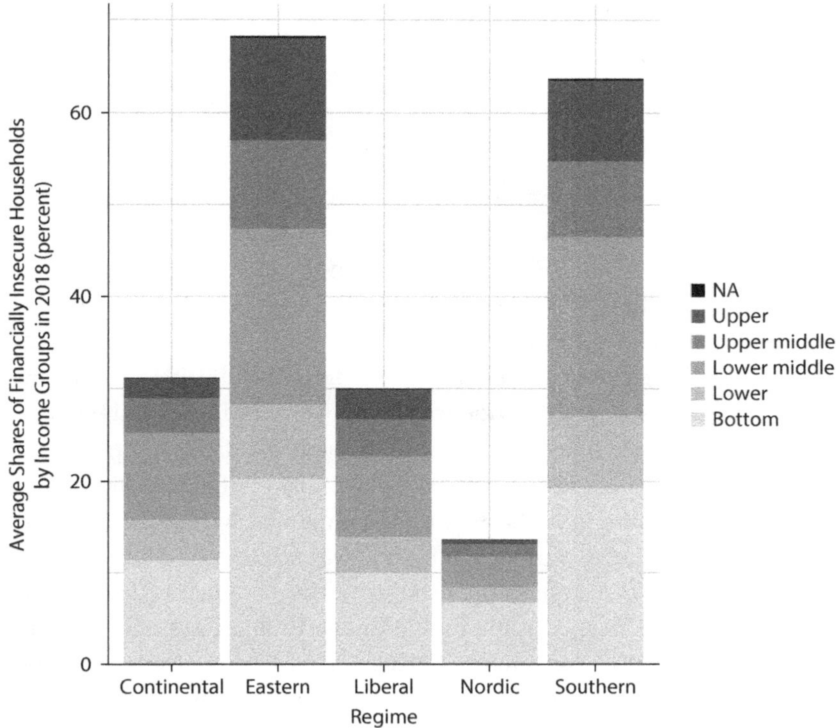

FIGURE 2.7. Average share of those who stated they had difficulties making ends meet in the previous three years and had not recovered by the fourth year, across security regimes, EU-SILC (2014–2018).

span, indicating that this occurrence might not happen every year but may be more common in the short-term experience of individuals than we think. Most important, the class composition indicates that there is a very high diffusion of difficulty in making ends meet among lower-middle-income groups, which is comparable to, if not higher than, the bottom group.

I found lower levels of financial insecurity in the Nordic security regime, average levels in the liberal regime and (quite surprisingly) also in the continental regime, and, predictably, extremely high levels in Eastern and Southern Europe, as per figure 2.7, which indicates the breakdown according to each security regime and referring to the final available year (2018). It is also relevant to note that particularly in Eastern and Southern Europe, but also in the continental and liberal models, the lower-middle-income groups are greatly affected by this form of financial insecurity—as much as, if not more than, the lower- and bottom-income groups. In fact, it is only in the Nordic security regime that financial insecurity affects the bottom more than the lower middle class.

Summary

It is common to reduce the issue of insecurity in Europe to marginalized groups or to a problem that concerns only the periphery of Europe, such as Southern and Eastern Europe. I have demonstrated that this is not the case and that patterns of insecurity related to work and finance emerge, to different degrees, across security regimes. Both the literature and the analyses presented here have highlighted differentiated shifts within security regimes and suggested a wider diffusion of insecurity beyond the poor, as summarized by table 2.2. Starting with the most affected regimes, the Southern European security regime saw a diffusion of job insecurity and a significant decline in work quality, accompanied by a rise in in-work poverty and insecurity. The liberal regime was affected by a sharp rise in the precarious forms of access to the labor market, a reduction in the quality of work for insiders, a rise in in-work poverty, and the emergence of a squeezed middle. The continental model, while being relatively protected from the rise in job insecurity that was happening elsewhere, experienced a decline in the quality of work, which was particularly visible in France. In terms of financial insecurity, the continental model is more protected than other regimes but is not immune from the decline in the middle class and the rise in work poverty. The Nordic cluster, while quite resilient in the provision of security, was also affected by a decline in work quality and a rise in job insecurity for labor market outsiders; financial insecurity in these countries has affected mostly socially excluded groups and individuals at the bottom of the income distribution. Eastern Europe is a bit of an outlier as far as the trend of rising insecurity goes, as in this regime the high levels of job insecurity and financial insecurity can be ascribed to the transition to the market-based economy, the impact of which has persisted, overshadowing more recent insecurity shifts that have occurred in Europe.

What are the implications of the changes illustrated for how institutions compensate individuals to protect them from market-based risks? A popular idea among political economists is the "compensatory hypothesis"—that is, that exposure to globalization leads to an expansion of welfare-state interventions in order to compensate individuals, and especially globalization losers, for the risks of economic international exposure. This hypothesis assumes that macroeconomic preferences are

Table 2.2. Work and Financial Security Shifts Within Each Security Regime

Security regime	Work security shifts	Financial security shifts
Southern	Job insecurity; decline in work quality	Rise in in-work poverty; increase in extreme insecurity; decline in financial security for the middle class
Eastern	Increase in job insecurity after the crisis; persistence of insecurity in work conditions	Increase in financial insecurity, especially for socially excluded groups
Liberal	Rise in the proportion of labor market outsiders; rise in job insecurity; decline in the quality of work	Spread of in-work poverty; declining financial security for the intermediate class
Continental	Decline in the quality of work; more job insecurity/work insecurity for welfare claimants	Decline in the lower-middle-income group; persistent poverty/work poverty; rise in financial insecurity among claimants
Nordic	Decline in work quality; rise in job insecurity	Impoverishment of he income groups at the bottom/socially excluded

at the center of state policies and that individuals' preferences on welfare are related to these macroeconomic considerations.[85] The starting point of this argument is that economic compensation is automatically a form of socioeconomic compensation—in other words, that what protects individuals economically is also what protects them from a socioeconomic perspective. This is not necessarily the case: Welfare-state expansion can take place to sustain systems' market-based competitiveness while also diverting from the initial "security-oriented" goals of welfare-state interventions. The first type of insecurity, work-related insecurity, concerns not only the spending function of the welfare state (e.g., employment policies, out-of-work options), but also its indirect role in occupational welfare and in the creation of quality jobs. The second type of insecurity, financial insecurity, is directly related to the compensatory function of the welfare state, particularly in its cash-based form, such as via unemployment benefits.

Based on the analysis of the case studies, we can suspect that both economic and institutional drivers might be involved in individuals' declining ability to buffer their insecurity, which I have demonstrated in this chapter. Even when mechanisms are in place that compensate individuals in economic terms (e.g., by creating jobs or by upskilling individuals), they might fail to compensate them in respect to their work and financial insecurity—for instance, by not creating quality jobs, or by reducing the income-based resources they receive in favor of an emphasis on reinserting individuals in the labor market. The next chapter will focus on clarifying the economic shifts and the institutional drivers of the changes I have described.

CHAPTER THREE

The Transformed Welfare States and the Effects on Insecurity

UNLIKE THE OPENLY politically divisive 1980s, the 1990s were an era of subtle and yet profound changes in European societies. In 1996 a prominent economist at MIT, Rudi Dornbusch, penned an influential piece called "Euro Fantasies" that critiqued the new European Monetary Union as an organization that would institutionalize high unemployment, low growth, and an unaffordable welfare state. "Competitive labor markets is the answer, but that is a dirty word in social-welfare Europe," he lamented.[1]

The pressure on the European project mounted, and Rudi Dornbusch's words did not go unheard. Just a few months later, in 1997, the German Social Democratic government recruited a professor from the Max Planck Institute for the Study of Societies as the main adviser to the "Alliance for Jobs," the complex tripartite negotiations to make the German labor market more competitive. This German economic sociologist argued that unions should have a "responsible" role in the process and should accept "competitive corporatism" in order to create more jobs.[2] His main argument, outlined in the pieces he authored at that time, was that the social standards that the German welfare state had had during the industrial period were not suitable for the emerging service sector.[3] The intellectual shift endorsed by the professor determined the beginning of a new pact in the German and European labor market: The state had to support individuals in becoming competitive but would be less likely to offer direct protections to individuals.[4]

Twenty years later, in 2017, the same professor, Wolfgang Streeck, penned a powerful critique of how the reforms to make the labor markets more competitive through flexibility and cost-cutting had become "the *pensée unique* of both the center left and the center right," arguing that the dominant political script fueled populist support.[5] Why did one of the major intellectuals involved in the transformation of the European welfare state end up adopting such a critical view of the political effects of these reforms? And how did the attempt to modernize European welfare states result in fuel for populist support?

In chapter 1, I introduced the paradoxical status of welfare-state interventions in Europe: Despite continuous support for social investment spending and a lack of dramatic cuts to welfare-state spending, even during the crisis, the normalization of insecurity has been progressively embedded within welfare-state interventions.[6] I argue that the ineffectiveness of the welfare state in addressing insecurity, as illustrated in chapter 2, stems from the new goals of the transformed welfare state, which puts more emphasis on funding institutional mechanisms to reactivate individuals in the market. The altered institutional language, values, goals, and targets of the state function in relation to the social sphere have had profound effects on individuals' sense of socioeconomic security, which can be described as a process of "desecuritization" of the welfare state function in Europe. In this sense, we ought to move beyond an assessment of the economic changes to appreciate the trickle-down effects of institutions on people's lives and delve deeper into how individuals and their families have been presented with a different balance of market and state resources to address insecurity. This chapter discusses the *institutional* premises, assumptions, and outcomes of the new welfare model. While several important analyses have been published regarding the implications of welfare transformations for institutions and for the collective management of risks and responsibilities, we are missing a deeper understanding of the implications of welfare state transformations on microlevel security.[7]

The Reconfiguration of the Market–State Nexus

The economic sources of insecurity in Europe cannot fully explain why individuals across European countries are experiencing different impacts in terms of work and financial stability, but they help us to understand the features of the transformed welfare state, which is based on a different balance between what the economy, institutions, and society aim to do to navigate insecurity.

Europe has experienced an acceleration in its exposure to the globalized world economy that has had profound effects on its levels of insecurity. Globalization and the economic exchanges between world economies are not recent occurrences according to world-systems theory, as we have seen a progressively integrated world economy since the sixteenth century. The higher level of security achieved in Europe after World War II that I described in the previous chapters has been in part achieved through racialized and colonial systems of relations that have kept European insiders secure through resource extraction, migration, and colonial relations with other countries.[8] The role that Europe has played in this world economy, in part through colonization, has gradually changed, however: The creation of capital gains in the integrated world economy has shifted from Europe to, first, the United States and then a multipolar world-economy structure in which Europe, the United States, and parts of Asia all represent core centers of capital accumulation.[9] As the capitals of the world economy have moved and the world economy has developed through a multipolar structure, the central position of Europe as a core economy has been diluted, making it more exposed to losses from economic globalization.

The rise of China, India, and other emerging countries has increased the global supply of work, characterized by poor work conditions and low wages. This has indirectly weakened the bargaining position of workers in Europe.[10] Globalization has helped to lift new segments of the global middle class out of poverty,[11] but the presence of supply chains in China has also generated downward pressure on wages in Europe. Furthermore, the global movement of capital and the rising proportion of foreign shareholders in European firms have resulted in a normalization of restructuring and contracting out that often results in individual experiences of stress and work pressure for employees.

Rigid European labor markets have become more flexible than the public discourse on European labor market rigidity would concede. Companies' emphasis on reducing labor market costs has resulted in a more flexible hire-and-fire culture, which is visible in the rises in functional changes to the division of labor, flexible hiring through agencies, and the diffusion of atypical or nonstandard forms of labor. As I have discussed in the previous chapters, however, insecurity is not just manifested with respect to work tenure but is experienced by workers in more mainstream and mundane ways. Indeed, the recommodification of firms has also had microlevel effects on blue-collar workers, making the division of labor much more fluid and less oriented toward lifetime employment—an element that just a few decades ago was considered to be a pillar of the rigid but secure European work model. As companies are less likely to invest in long-term creation of professions, individuals are now more dependent on the short-term changes in the labor market, and their positions are uncertain. The impact of restructuring on European working lives—a departure from the tradition of the secure continental workplace—is epitomized by the case of the privatization of a publicly funded company, France Télécom, which was so unsettling for the workforce that it led to sixty-nine suicides and a generalized discontent among workers.[12]

The impact of economic globalization is also visible in the normalization of financial insecurity, as in a climate of global competition, wages tend to fluctuate more, and wealth is kept unequally distributed. Indeed, the historical evolution of global inequality shows that between 1988 and 2008, the losers of economic globalization were the lower middle classes of the rich world, including Western Europe.[13] This group of individuals—who are certainly much richer than the poorest sections of the world in absolute terms—has been affected by the biggest relative decline in income as an effect of increased global competition and the pressure on wages.

States have not been passive observers of these economic changes and have taken part in the reconfiguration of the market–state nexus and in the transition to a Schumpeterian workfare state (SWS).[14] While in the previous model the circulation of money occurred primarily within the national economy and was controlled by the national state, in the new SWS there is a cross-border flow of financial capital. States recognize their national economic vulnerability to volatile currency movements and accept that economic intervention must take the form of influencing the supply side instead of shaping the demand, as the demand is now determined by global markets.

A first sign of the embeddedness of market logics within state interventions is visible in the rise of what scholars have called "corporate welfare."[15] Popularized during the British electoral debate in 2015, corporate welfare is a term coined by the founding father of British social policy, Richard Titmuss, to indicate that welfare states contribute to the functioning of the market by directly or indirectly funding enterprises and corporations via public taxation. In addition to the amount of spending involved in corporate welfare, which has been open to debate, what is politically relevant is that a large part of this spending does not result in any form of conditionality or influence on businesses and therefore represents a renunciation by the state of its tools to influence the corporate world.[16] The rise of corporate welfare indicates that the state, due to the pressures of intensified globalization, has "(often voluntarily) relinquish[ed] its various tools of constructive economic intervention over recent decades [and] has become increasingly dependent on corporations to fulfil the primary goal of providing for prosperity and social stability."[17] Changes to how social policy is financed and delivered due to the financialization of the welfare state have also affected people's financial security in a number of areas. For example, the financialization of the housing market has increased the exposure to financial risks by people through housing insecurity, particularly through sudden changes to housing costs, mortgages, or rents that are consequential to fluctuations of the stock market.[18] Similarly, the privatization of pensions in Europe has subjected new categories of middle-class pensioners to potential future financial insecurity, as their pensions are attached to stock fluctuations.[19]

The transition to a new type of welfare state has also had profound effects in terms of defining the boundaries of what the state decides to intervene on, and which policies are prioritized in this new economic environment. In the previous Keynesian welfare state model, the state regulated wages, productivity, and work so that consumer demand would better align with the production sector in order to avoid crises of underconsumption/demand. The contemporary SWS does not retain this ambition, as the alignment between supply and demand is disturbed by the fact that the demand is global and export-oriented, and wages are seen simply as a cost of production, not as a way to sustain demand. In this context, the transformed welfare state has a different priority: keeping labor costs under control through short-termism, a hire-and-fire culture, and higher labor market flexibility to sustain competitiveness.[20] In the new competitive globalized economy, the state's main function is to invest on the supply side—to make workers educated, upskilled, trained, and ready to enter or reenter the labor market. In other words, to have the function of a social investment state. What are the impacts of the transformed welfare state on the security of individuals?

The Transformed Welfare State and the Loss of Security

Different terms have been developed in the literature to define the changed role of the welfare state from the 1990s onward, which I have also described as the shift toward a Schumpeterian workfare state: the enabling welfare state, the postindustrial welfare-state transition, the postcapitalist welfare state, and the social investment welfare state.[21]

The implications of the shift toward social investment remain a source of much debate in the literature. For some scholars, social investment has been able to maintain social stability in Europe and reach groups that are not usually covered by traditional welfare-state interventions.[22] For others, social investment is the embodiment of the adoption of neoliberalism by the state, because the inclusion of market-based logics—and not spending per se—is already a concession to neoliberalism.[23] Another group of scholars argued that social investment would potentially have a positive social effect if it were applied in its entirety, but that the adoption of selective social investment has privileged its neoliberal components.[24] Despite the different evaluations of the social investment agenda, there seems to be an agreement that the welfare state has been transformed in Europe, social investment spending has increased, and more social investment policies have been adopted across Europe. In this section I show that the transformed welfare state is, at its core, a desecuritized welfare state—namely, one that has implicitly accepted that individuals will be subjected to a higher level of insecurity.

Different variations of social investment have been implemented, and it is perhaps not surprising that scholars from liberal countries like the UK, where social investment has been implemented with a more optimistic view of the role of the market, tend to be more skeptical about social investment than scholars examining Nordic European social policy, where social investment has been interpreted with more emphasis on the social democratic rationale.[25] Whether social investment represents a neoliberal shift or not is not, at the end of the day, the key element when it comes to evaluating the implications of welfare state reforms for European societies. It is far more relevant to discuss how the inherent assumptions of the transformed welfare state affect the security of individuals in symbolic and material terms. Therefore, I shall first analyze the assumptions and goals of social investment to understand the implications for the security of society and individuals, and then discuss the effects of the transformed welfare state on work security and financial security.

ASSUMPTIONS OF THE SOCIAL INVESTMENT STATE AND HOW THEY RELATE TO SECURITY

As a first step in my analysis, I will take the theory of social investment and unpick its inherent assumptions and goals in relation to socioeconomic security. In a recent edited volume examining the politics of social investment, the authors argued that "social investment policies aim to prepare, mobilize, and equip individuals in a way that increases their chances of supporting themselves in the knowledge economy (notably through employment) and reduces their future risks of income loss and poverty."[26]

From this definition, we can tease out several significant premises that social investment builds on. The ultimate goal of the social investment state is to equip *individuals* and support them in a bumpy economy. The emphasis on individuals (and not societies) is relevant here, as the focus on succeeding in the knowledge economy is intrinsically on individualized effort. The first theorizations of social investment identified a continuity between social investment and neoliberalism, in that "the social investment perspective's macroeconomic analysis retains the focus on the supply-side that neoliberalism instituted,"[27] but they also stressed that compared to a purely neoliberal regime, the state participates in taking some of the responsibility for human capital creation to compensate for market failures and tackle poverty. Even if social investment differs from neoliberalism, the transformed welfare state still shakes the social and collective principle of sustaining socioeconomic security: As society, under this system, is organized according to market principles, and as the state has given up the ambition of containing the market in the social sphere, it would be up to individuals and their families to invest in their human capital creation and make their members competitive against others.

Market logics have a key role in the theorization of social investment, as "in terms of economic returns to individuals, the social investment perspective expects to enhance labor market opportunities and earnings potential."[28] The aims of the transformed welfare state are to "prepare, mobilize, and equip" individuals so that they have more chance to compete in the knowledge economy by finding work, and to address "future risks of income loss and poverty."[29] Here, there is an understanding of risk that is heavily influenced by the definition of economic risk as future risk or as poverty (see chapter 1), again confirming that the symbolic boundaries of our understanding of social policy interventions are limited to the *economic* interpretation of disadvantage. The economic terminology of social investment also permeates the slightly different framing by one of the main policy entrepreneurs in EU policymaking, Anton Hemerijck, for whom social investment's essential aims are increasing or maintaining human capital stock, easing work transitions, and having social safety-net buffers, either to reduce poverty or to improve job matching.[30] By admission of its proponents, this framing of social investment relates to "concepts of human capital investments and productivity," but also to human capability.[31] Its limitation in relation to the socioeconomic sphere is its large concessions to the market over an uncommodified notion of welfare.[32]

A corollary of the focus on the market and on addressing capabilities is that, in both the original theorization and its most recent one, the social investment state mostly intervenes to address one type of social failure generated by the market—poverty—thereby leaving other social concerns, such as socioeconomic security, out of the welfare state's sphere of influence. Using the state to stabilize individuals' security is simply, and very explicitly, *not* one of the aims of the social investment state. This is quite openly disclosed in *Never Enough* by Neil Gilbert, whose main argument and claim of "progressive conservativism" is that the welfare state has already reduced poverty and sustained our societies' affluence and that we should not expect a welfare state that can fulfill more than this.[33] By limiting the symbolic boundaries of state intervention to a less ambitious array of interventions than addressing human needs or decommodifying people's lives, and through a revised logic on how to intervene, the transformed welfare state has several knock-on effects on insecurity.[34]

The main assumption is that the level of security or insecurity in a country will be more dependent on the level of employment security in that country, because by focusing on those at risk of being out of work, the welfare state is implicitly attaching security to work. The corollary of this assumption is that individuals in environments with higher employment protection legislation and more powerful unions will have more secure work lives, as suggested by my analysis of security regimes in chapter 2. Furthermore, the security of individuals will be more dependent on the economic cycles present in the labor market: Periods of high unemployment will be more affected by losses of security, as has been confirmed by the analyses of job quality and financial security after the 2008 crisis. This brings us back to the origins of the welfare state as a provider of socioeconomic security that protects against the fluctuations of the market, an argument made by Karl Polanyi. For Polanyi, market instability could reverberate into human insecurity, and Western welfare-state interventions offered a means by which to temper those effects. As citizens living in Europe are learning the hard way, through a cost-of-living crisis that has been taking place since 2020, leaving security in the hands of the market is a risky business, as the market is able to maintain stability only if wages and prices are aligned, which does not occur automatically. For Polanyi, attaching livelihoods to the market "implied for the worker extreme instability of earnings, utter absence of professional standards, abject readiness to be shoved and pushed about indiscriminately."[35]

According to Polanyi's analysis, the work and financial security that Europe has historically enjoyed have been attached to mechanisms of decommodification—in other words, partial independence from the market—because of the market's inherent cyclicity and instability. The adoption of a productivist social investment approach, with its explicit reliance on the labor market as a source of welfare, necessitates an acceptance of greater instability in the lives of individuals.

In addition to the market, the state itself has become a collective machine to reproduce and normalize insecurity, as the type of welfare-state intervention that is currently being delivered is qualitatively different from the decommodified state intervention in Polanyi's time and aims to individualize the management of security. This is clearly indicated by the qualitative studies on welfare recipients cited in chapter 2, which have shown how the new institutional logics of the transformed welfare state have served to generate higher levels of job insecurity and financial insecurity for welfare recipients—even, and especially, in countries with relatively generous and secure regimes, such as Sweden and the Netherlands. This has occurred through several mechanisms. The high level of control and negative frame of dependence perpetuated by the new welfare interventions generate shame among welfare users, as well as higher financial insecurity, while the transformed welfare state also has the function of pedagogically instilling an individualized form of optimism, a higher level of responsibilization, and a vision of security that is projected toward the future while neglecting the experiences of insecurity in the present.[36] We can suspect that the effects of the different political scripts and mechanisms of welfare interventions go well beyond the experience of welfare users: Potential welfare users and people in work will likely want to avoid the shameful experience of having to depend on a stigmatized, controlled, and highly conditional form of state support and hence will choose not to take up what should serve as a core source of security in navigating insecure labor markets.

The third negative effect of the transformed welfare state on security is that by focusing on reducing future risks of income loss and poverty, the welfare state lacks the ambition to redistribute or provide security to lower-middle- and middle-income groups. Indeed, as discussed in the previous chapter, financial insecurity is not equally distributed among different income groups, and the decline in previously safe middle-income groups makes insecurity a more mainstream experience than it used to be. The classic critique of social investment's capacity to effectively protect those at risk refers to how the social investment agenda facilitates the Matthew effect, namely, the accumulation of disadvantage among the poorest sections of the society. In short, this critique argues that social investment does not even succeed that well in protecting the poor because it is intrinsically biased in favor of high- and middle-income earners, and it is much harder for those at the bottom to be competitive in society or have the initial tools to access policies that enable social investment.[37] The main policy goal of the social investment state is to target the groups at the bottom and those who have fewer opportunities to support themselves through the knowledge economy—in other words, those more at risk of poverty. The assumption here is that high- and middle-income groups will be automatically protected by access to education and via the use of market sources. The weakness of social investment relates to this precise assumption, because while it might be true that social investment interventions can boost an individual's chances of finding a job, the inference that their socioeconomic security is guaranteed by having a job is entirely questionable.

As I will discuss, the drawbacks of social investment are far broader than the Matthew effect and have to do with the fact that there is a large segment of individuals who are negatively affected by the focus on poverty as the only societal issue to be addressed by social policies, the most visible example being working-poor individuals. This is not simply a manifestation of the paradox of redistribution—that is, the principle that it is important to keep the middle class involved in the welfare state for political support, the validity of which has been debated.[38] It is also the effect of a miscalculation by the transformed welfare state, which assumes that those in employment will be financially secure. I will break down the argument by examining the impact of the transformed welfare state on work security, first, and then financial security.

THE TRANSFORMED WELFARE STATE AND THE SECURITY OF WORK

Among the negative evaluations of social investment, it has been suggested that the presence of active labor market policies (ALMPs) could generate negative spillover effects on insiders. The focus on activating individuals and putting unemployed workers back to work indirectly affects the labor market, as it diverts the focus to the number of people who are employed and away from the quality of work generated. For this reason, scholars have theorized the presence of a trade-off between the quantity and quality of work, viewing the declining job quality as an effect of the focus on the quantity of work in institutional policies.[39] According to this theory, ALMPs affect not only those who are out of work but also those seeking work or in work, as, given the incentives to be in work, their "out of work" options, in the presence of ALMPs, become less attractive, and workers will accept or stay in jobs with, for instance, higher intensification and work pressure.

When one considers in detail the types of social investment interventions promoted in Europe, upskilling remains marginal, and the most utilized form of social investment—even in the early 2020s—is one that provides incentive reinforcement and activation.[40] These policies could have a different effect on job quality: Incentive reinforcement to be in work is likely to have negative effects on job quality, as it diminishes the capacity for workers to refuse "bad jobs," because they get the incentives only if they do not refuse jobs.

What is the evidence on what social investment policies do? If we limit ourselves to looking at labor market and social protection policies, ALMPs have had a positive effect in creating employment opportunities and increasing labor market security.[41] ALMPs, in particular those focusing on upskilling, can in principle have positive effects on elements of job quality such as autonomy, although these policies remain underused among the social investment range of instruments.[42] I investigated the impact of welfare reforms on work security for insiders and outsiders in a recently coauthored paper using multilevel analysis.[43] At a superficial level, the findings of the study are reassuring for social investment proponents, as both content autonomy (which refers to the learning opportunities available to workers at work) and procedural autonomy are mostly positively influenced by a climate in which, through ALMPs, training and upskilling opportunities are available for those who are out of work. Passive labor market policies (PLMPs), such as unemployment benefits, also have a positive effect on job insecurity and most elements of job quality, confirming what was found in previous studies.[44]

However, this study also found a few caveats that indicate the presence of a trade-off between the quantity and the quality of jobs following the transition to the new welfare-state settlement. First, the positive effects of ALMPs and PLMPs on job dissatisfaction and career prospects were present up to the 2010 wave. Furthermore, there was an important exception to the trend described, which relates to work pressure, an indicator that captures the growing intensification of work since the mid-1990s. If the generosity of benefits has a positive effect on work pressure by reducing it, the same cannot be said for ALMPs, whose presence increases work pressure for those in the workplace. This can be explained by the fact that, by placing an emphasis on the quantity of work, a labor market with consistent supply-side interventions tends to create fewer incentives to say no to jobs with lower work conditions, thus pushing people to accept jobs with higher work pressure.

Moreover, the positive effects of ALMPs and PLMPs on job quality were more modest once the study examined the breakdown in relation to skills between 2010 and 2021. Here, the analysis revealed that while labor market policies reduced job insecurity for all skill groups, they only improved job quality among low/manual levels of skills. Manual/lower-skilled workers are often depicted as the losers of the knowledge-based transition in European welfare states,[45] but the analysis showed that the welfare state has a positive spillover effect on job quality mostly among this category of workers, leaving service workers (who represent the majority of the workforce in Europe at the moment) either unaffected by welfare-state interventions or negatively affected in some areas, like work pressure.

The findings illustrated here are the logical effect of the aims of transformed welfare states. Indeed, transformed welfare states aim to enable those more at risk and target incentives to be in/out of work via ALMPs and PLMPs that are mostly aimed at lower-skilled workers, but they do not generate positive spillover effects on the quality of work for all workers, as was the case in the Keynesian welfare model. Furthermore, ALMPs in the transformed welfare state have a more marked effect on job insecurity than on job quality. This is the direct effect of having a transformed welfare state that aims to reduce the risks of employment, not the insecurity in the quality of employment per se.

This study only investigated the direct effect of labor market policies on individuals. As discussed, there is a more profound effect that relates to how the welfare state limits its interventions on the supply side without intervening in the demand side of the labor market. In the transformed welfare-state model, individuals compete against one another in a work environment made more precarious due to the economic changes described on the previous pages. Furthermore, in a context in which states have abandoned the ambition of shaping the demand for work and in which corporate welfare is provided to firms without conditions being placed on the type of work they create, the implicit message sent by states to firms is that the quality and the security of the jobs they create are not a societal priority.

THE TRANSFORMED WELFARE STATE AND FINANCIAL SECURITY

The other important effect of the transformed welfare state on insecurity concerns the lower capacity of welfare states to provide financial security as a consequence of their changed roles, which have shifted from a cash transfer and redistributive function during the KWS to a reactivating machine during the SWS. Part of the literature has stressed the negative effects of developing ALMPs instead of investing in passive policies. In particular, Bea Cantillon linked the development of social investment spending to the decrease in the generosity of traditional passive income support schemes.[46] Alongside early studies that tended to be more skeptical about the shift from passive to social investment spending,[47] others found that in Europe a trade-off occurred between spending to support individuals and spending to activate people. For instance, Marchal and colleagues found that the low levels of minimum income schemes before the crisis were a direct consequence of the boosting of activation and social investment over passive policies during this period.[48]

Early critiques of social investment underlined the negative effects that this trade-off has, particularly for poor people. In a debate that has involved prosocial investment scholars and social policy scholars who are rather skeptical about this strategy, social investment has been criticized for its ineffectiveness in addressing poverty and protecting vulnerable groups.[49] Indeed, despite the rise in income and growth levels, poverty has stagnated or even increased in recent years.[50] According to this critical perspective, the lack of consideration of social class and the broader mechanisms of stratification that result from the economic focus of social interventions render social investment unfit to address poverty.

While this is a valid critique of social investment, I would argue that the drawbacks of social investment go well beyond its ability to tackle poverty, with the most concerning impact being the progressive decline in the compensatory effects of the welfare state for all citizens. Examining the evolution of active and passive interventions across Europe, one can see that welfare states have experienced a dual movement, whereby retrenchment of spending on compensatory policies has been accompanied by an expansion of spending on employment-oriented policies such as ALMPs.[51] Retrenchment and adaptation have been dominant trajectories of welfare-state reforms due to cutbacks in unemployment and family allowances, making the new social investment state less compensatory for

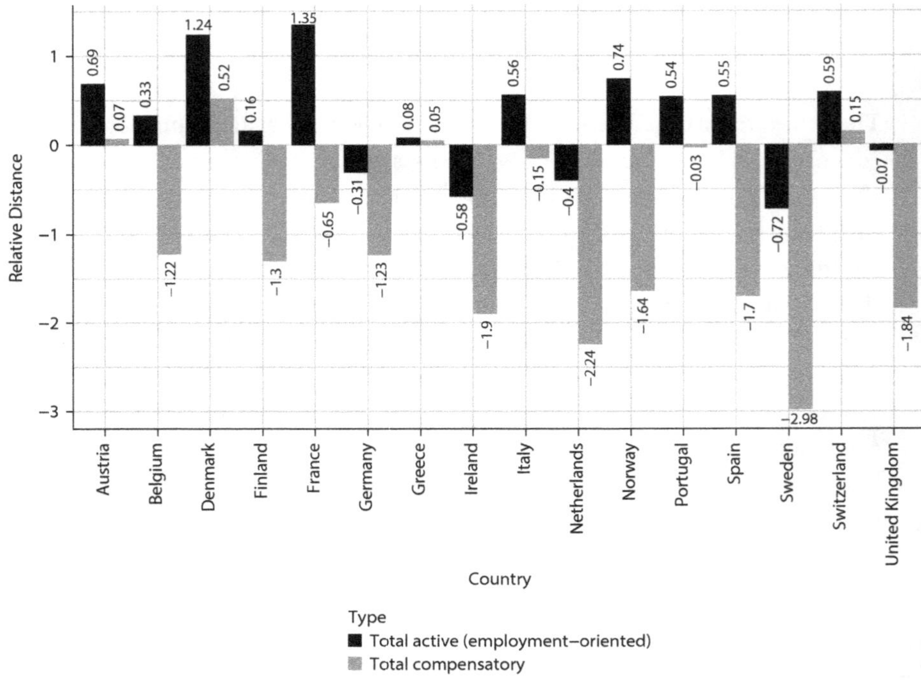

FIGURE 3.1. Active and compensatory spending of each country in 2015, considering their spending records. Image elaborated by the author using data reported in Emanuele Ferragina, "Welfare State Change as a Double Movement: Four Decades of Retrenchment and Expansion in Compensatory and Employment-Oriented Policies Across 21 High-Income Countries," 2022, 715. Ferragina uses a three-step approach to calculate this indicator, estimating the difference between the maximum and minimum values of spending ever made by a country and comparing it to the level reached in 2015.

individuals and households. Figure 3.1 shows the extent of the dual shift, with active spending increasing and compensatory spending decreasing in most countries, while figure 3.2 also indicates the decline in unemployment spending in most countries.

Not only was the *amount* of spending reduced, but, looking at the most comprehensive historical analysis of the evolution in welfare-state generosity through the Comparative Welfare Entitlements Dataset (CWED), the *level of generosity* of social insurance policies for individuals decreased in most countries between 1980 and 2018, as shown in figure 3.3, which indicates a general decline in generosity in unemployment insurance, with a few exceptions.[52] The reduced generosity can be explained not only by the evolution of spending, but also by the fact that unemployment benefits have been reoriented toward forms of activation

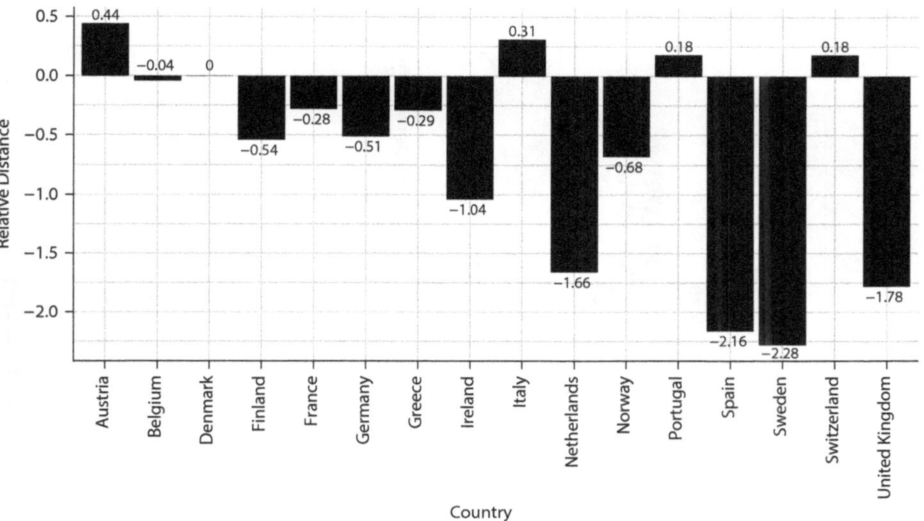

FIGURE 3.2. Unemployment spending of each country in 2015, considering their spending records. Image elaborated by the author using data reported in Emanuele Ferragina, "Welfare State Change as a Double Movement: Four Decades of Retrenchment and Expansion in Compensatory and Employment-Oriented Policies Across 21 High-Income Countries," 2022, 715. Ferragina uses a three-step approach to calculate this indicator, estimating the difference between the maximum and minimum values of spending ever made by a country and comparing it to the level reached in 2015.

and targeting, hence lowering the compensatory effects of so-called passive policies.[53]

The declining compensatory effects of the welfare state since the 1980s accelerated as a result of the 2008 financial crisis and the subsequent welfare-state responses, which, as mentioned earlier, entailed an increase in social investment interventions—the main exception to retrenchment in European welfare states.[54] If one were to examine welfare-state spending from the outside, it would be easy to perceive European welfare states as still relatively large and therefore able to have the same compensatory effects. For example, the reported rise of consumer debt in Europe could have been interpreted to be an effect of welfare-state changes if the decline in the generosity of the welfare state had been accounted for; instead, the analysis of the rise of consumer debt in Western Europe tends to exclude that the reduction of welfare state generosity could be a contributory factor, depicting Europe as a place where individuals are still financially protected by the state.[55] In reality, in a type of welfare-state arrangement targeted at the poorest, it is understandable that financial insecurity is on the rise and that the lower and lower-middle classes would

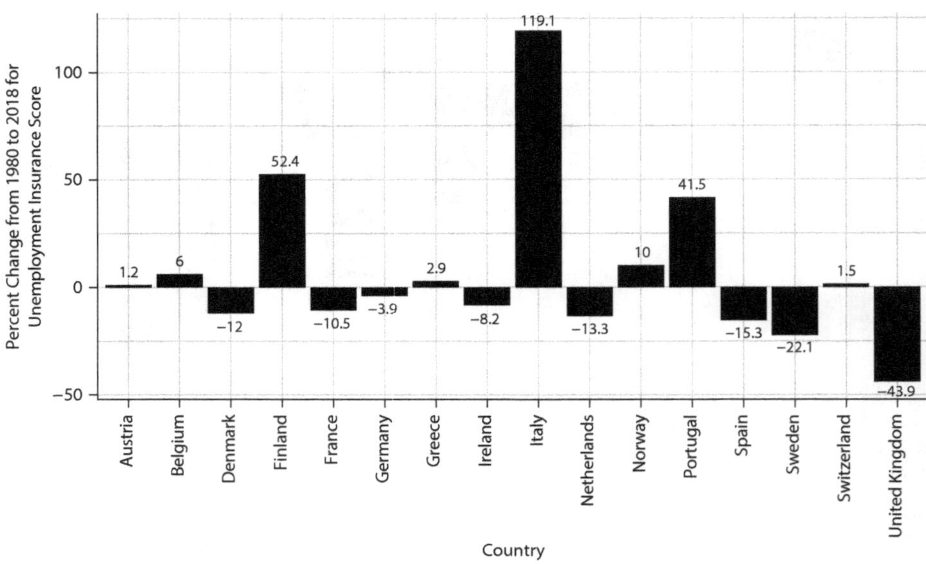

FIGURE 3.3. Changes to generosity scores of unemployment insurance, 1980–2018. Image created by the author using data reported in Lyle A. Scruggs and Gabriela Ramalho Tafoya, "Fifty Years of Welfare State Generosity," *Social Policy & Administration* 56, no. 5 (2022): 798.

find individualized solutions to address their insecurity, such as increasingly resorting to the use of credit cards and consumer debt. People from low- and middle-income households in Europe are indeed increasingly relying on what is defined as customer debt, even in countries that have been considered to be resistant to debt, such as France, Germany, Spain, and Italy.[56]

The effects of cutbacks on financial security have been marked in Southern European and liberal countries, and they have affected younger people more than older people: While countries with bigger welfare states have been more able to stabilize and avoid financial shocks for individuals, there has been an intensification of pressure in these countries to increase the targeting of cash transfers, which was the case even during the economic crisis.[57] In fact, the only divergence from the trend of higher targeting is represented by the response to the financial shocks of the Covid-19 pandemic, when several welfare states, having reached a point of no return in the level of targeting of their instruments, exceptionally and temporarily reintroduced higher levels of cash transfers (see chapter 6).

EU Policies and Discourses and Their Effects on Insecurity

Up to this point, I have discussed the effects of national policymaking on work and financial security. In this section, I will examine the effects of EU policymaking, given that the institutional sources of insecurity in Europe have increasingly been transferring from the national to the supranational level and that this transfer accelerated following the Eurocrisis in 2010 and, more recently, the Covid-19 pandemic. Rather than referring simply to national welfare-state reforms, it would be more correct to define the welfare-state transformation as a transition to a Schumpeterian workfare state and supra-state, as the institutional provision of welfare in Europe is the product of a supernational state (the EU) as well as individual member states. EU discourses, framings, and institutional choices have had numerous effects on national security regimes, which can be divided into three phases:

1. Phase 1, 2010–2014: austerity as a shock to security. Characterized by an explicit rhetoric of limiting spending in order to relaunch the European economy, this phase resulted in shocks to socioeconomic security in several countries on the periphery of Europe, as well as legitimation of the austerity policies in liberal countries (e.g., the UK and Ireland). In this phase, the EU acquired enhanced powers to intervene in the policies of national welfare states through new governance mechanisms.
2. Phase 2, 2015–2020: the contested socialization process after austerity. This phase was characterized by a change in discourse, from one of austerity to a new political script that welcomes the involvement of EU social actors. However, both the procedure and the content of the recommendations made by the EU to its member states were oriented toward policies that can activate and reinsert individuals into the labor market, rather than policies that could address socioeconomic insecurity.
3. Phase 3, 2020–present: the recent change to EU policymaking, such as Next Generation EU. I will examine this phase more closely in chapter 6, using recent evidence to show that the rise of insecurity that took place in phase 1 was not surpassed during the pandemic phase.

PHASE 1: AUSTERITY AS A SHOCK TO SECURITY, 2010–2014

More than ten years on from the Great Recession in 2010, there seems to be a consensus on how profound the socioeconomic effects of the austerity response have been on a large section of EU countries and social groups living in Europe.[58] EU institutions explicitly reassessed the expectation that states would provide a social safety net to individuals over the crisis, and the EU began to produce and reproduce insecurity in three main ways.

First, during the 2010 phase the EU acquired more powers to make national policies more competitive through structural reforms. This happened through new governance frameworks and procedures, such as the European Semester, which was intended to be a mechanism to communicate policy recommendations to member states, monitor their implementation, and assess the response by member states. As the EU increased its powers in realms that had previously been left to member states, the balance between social policy and market policy changed within EU policymaking. Parts of the commission, such as the economic section, DG ECFIN, gained more importance within this process than the parts that dealt with social affairs, such as DG EMPL and its related social partners. Writing about the EU's response to the Eurocrisis, A. Crespy and G. Menz noted that "social policy is becoming increasingly . . . subsumed to economic objectives focused on competitiveness, narrowly defined as low labor costs . . . and stringent fiscal discipline."[59] The European Semester contributed to a subjugation of other policies, including social policies, to macroeconomic criteria, and in particular to budgetary discipline to correct macroeconomic imbalances.[60]

Second, the EU used new narratives during the period of austerity that normalized the presence of work-related insecurity in Europe, particularly in Southern Europe. An important policy framing in this period revolved around cost-cutting to restore competitiveness, which was endorsed by Germany and other dominant countries in EU policymaking (core countries) against countries of Southern Europe, and neglected the economic benefit that core countries gained by exporting to the deficit-spending South.[61] This new discourse entailed a shift in the public discourse as the emphasis was placed on restoring competitiveness via export-driven growth, even though this resulted in an inevitable transfer of costs from capital to labor via the precarization of the workforce, and in an implicit acceptance of the normalization of social insecurity among the population.[62]

Third, the new agenda had effects on individuals, which tend to be overlooked in policy and institutional analyses. A core strategy of the EU response to the crisis was what economists call internal devaluation—namely, an economic and social policy strategy that aims to restore the international competitiveness of a country by reducing its labor costs through wages or indirect costs that employers face. During this phase of explicit austerity, unions also had less power as central mechanisms that are able to mediate negotiations between employers and workers.[63] The countries most affected by this were those that were directly involved in the Memorandums of Understanding (MoUs)—in other words, countries on the economic periphery of Europe, including Greece, Ireland, and Portugal. Comparative analyses have shown that EU interventions were particularly intrusive and attempted to move countries like Portugal and Greece to a new phase of modernization of the labor market. However, this also translated into pressing demands to cut public expenditure in order to improve competitiveness at a time when more individuals needed to access support mechanisms due to high unemployment. In addition to the MoUs, the European Semester was particularly effective in reforming social policies in countries in the South and at the periphery.[64] In the cases of Greece and Portugal, the generosity of the system was reduced even for Greek labor market insiders, while in Portugal an attempt was made to extend coverage of the system by lowering the length of the required contributory career. Social investment policies were central to this shift. The MoUs required a temporary expansion of the short-term programs for the long-term unemployed and young people not in employment or training, alongside the provision of a youth voucher scheme to private-sector employers to promote the training and reskilling of young unemployed people. Regarding employment legislation, measures were to be taken with the aim of reducing the costs of and other restrictions associated with the dismissal of workers on regular contracts, passing from flexicurity to "flexilience"—that is, flexibility for resilience. Finally, the MoUs in both countries sought to change collective wage bargaining structures in favor of a decentralized system, based on the principle that wage agreements should reflect the productivity developments and ultimately the competitiveness of individual firms.[65]

Comparative analyses of the distributive effects of austerity packages have indicated that the regressive effects of austerity—and therefore their potential to increase financial insecurity for those at low and middle levels of income—were present beyond the South/periphery. Sotiria Theodoropoulou and Andrew Watt analyzed the composition of austerity measures in terms of the proportions of expenditure cuts and tax rises that were employed, finding that such measures were mostly funded through expenditure cuts and regressive measures, such as taxes on consumption, that had a negative distributional effect on the low and lower-middle levels of the income distribution.[66] Apart from France and Luxembourg, which adopted some progressive measures for taxing high-income earners, the bulk of the spending reductions that occurred during this period in Europe can be categorized as regressive because they were implemented either through cuts in social protection and public services or by indirect tax rises via consumption.

The shift toward austerity concerned not only the countries of the periphery. In addition to advocating reforms on the periphery, countries that had a more proactive role in shifting the discourses of austerity from the national to the EU level pushed for internal policy changes that promoted austerity. The UK was a frontrunner in this respect, outdoing the EU in its emphasis on austerity and adopting measures with socially regressive effects before Brexit, while austerity also became a dominant policy orientation in Germany during this time.[67] For these core countries, reforming the orientation of their welfare states resulted in profound changes (see chapter 2) and established them as symbolic promoters of insecurity-driven policies in Europe.

PHASE 2: THE CONTESTED SOCIALIZATION OF EUROPEAN SOCIAL POLICY AFTER AUSTERITY, 2015–2020

According to some scholars, by 2015, which marked the beginning of the Juncker Commission, the European Semester was starting to change some of its defining features, becoming more social or socialized.[68] These researchers used the term "socialization" not as an indicator of an expansion of social policies at the level of member states; rather, they suggested that there was more attention on the social sphere within the new European Semester framework and a greater involvement of social partners in the process. Not all observers have been convinced of such a shift, however. According to Amandine Crespy and Vivien Schmidt, although there was a change in the discourse and in the formal involvement of social partners, the framing of structural reforms continued to exemplify the European Semester's focus on labor market reforms, with almost a third of recommendations concerning labor market reforms, and with the interpretation of social investment placing a firm emphasis on flexibility over security.[69]

An important question mark has remained over whether this higher involvement of and increase in attention on social aspects translated into a substantial shift from the previous phase and whether it compensated for the insecurity shock that occurred between 2010 and 2015. Attempting to find an answer to this question, I coauthored a study that investigated the social implications of the European Commission's recommendations.[70] Unlike most of the literature in this area, which has focused on policymaking and institutional exchanges, the analysis attempted to create a framework to capture the qualitative outcomes of the types of policies promoted through the country-specific recommendations (CSRs) communicated from the EU to member states, and to evaluate their potential impact in 2019—at the end of phase 2 and right before the Covid-19 crisis.

In this investigation, the recommendations the EU made to member states were categorized into four types: (1) social retrenchment—those that envisaged the retreat of the state as the key provider of social solidarity in terms of both benefits and social rights, such as social benefit curtailment, cost-containment strategies, labor-market deregulation, and pension privatization; (2) social investment—those that aimed to prepare, support, and equip individuals to increase their chances of participating in the labor market, through either activation or upskilling; (3) social inclusion—those that were intended to include socially excluded and targeted groups in education, access to healthcare, etc.; and (4) redistribution—those that implied a redistribution of resources toward middle- and lower-middle-income groups and that could be perceived to address the presence of financial insecurity.

The analysis of the CSRs between 2015 and 2020 showed that 67 percent of the recommendations in the area of labor market policies presented a specific focus on activation and employability, circa 10 percent focused on inclusion of disadvantaged groups in the labor market, while only 20 percent explicitly sought to tackle inequalities in the labor market. Those that referred to addressing inequality mainly mentioned the need to reduce the fragmentation of the labor market, promote and extend adequate social protection for nonstandard workers, and provide higher minimum wages. CSRs therefore made no reference to issues of labor market security, such as job insecurity, work–life balance, work intensification, autonomy, or pressures—all areas that, as analyzed in previous chapters, pertain to the rise of work-related insecurity.

Concerning the area of social protection, the vast majority of recommendations from the commission (75 percent) focused on developing highly targeted instruments to counter poverty and social exclusion in line with the social inclusion framework—for example, guaranteeing adequacy of unemployment benefit, healthcare, and minimum income, particularly in Eastern European countries. The recommendations that proposed a redistribution of resources represented 25 percent of the CSRs and tended to adopt a very narrow interpretation that focused on the bottom distribution of income and targeted marginalized groups. While having policies that target marginalized groups is not negative per se, this narrow definition of social interventions implies that most members of the population are or can be excluded from accessing any form of social protection. This has resulted in an absence of interventions for the majority of individuals even though financial insecurity became a more generalized issue among Europeans during the Eurocrisis, contributing to the erosion of the European middle class.[71]

The framing and content of CSRs shows that social investment was dominant during this phase of EU policymaking, with the Juncker Commission making explicit references to it. Several prominent social policy scholars acted as policy entrepreneurs of social investment agendas, as they were directly involved in European policymaking and in implementing European social investment policies, particularly at the EU level.[72] On the whole, these scholars viewed social investment as a new paradigm that could modernize antiquated European welfare states and ensure that they remain able to positively influence individuals' lives in the competitive global economy, particularly because of social investment's focus on groups that are usually excluded from national policies, such as young people. They also perceived social investment as a palatable policy agenda given its emphasis on economic incentives, at a time when austerity was a popular option in Europe during the Eurocrisis.[73]

Were those scholars satisfied with the implementation of social investment during this second phase? In their analyses of EU social investment, Caroline de la Porte and Bruno Palier found that the 2011–2014 phase represented a reinforcement of what they identified as the German productivist model, which was reflected in the strengthened governance of the economic aspects of social policies; they also doubted that their enlarged notion of social investment had really been strengthened during 2014–2019.[74] They found that, even during this phase, the content of the EU's social investment agenda was skewed toward a limited interpretation of social investment to boost productivity and growth and that economic actors dominated the European Semester, with the more social elements of social investment being implemented only via soft law. The fact that some of the most strenuous policy entrepreneurs of social investment in academia found in the EU's commitment to the social investment agenda an emphasis on boosting productivity suggests not only that the adoption of social investment policies has been selective and partial, but also that social investment EU institutions have used promote a specific political and social framing: the idea that a productive and activated European citizen is morally virtuous.

Summary

In his first interview after Greece's second bailout, Mario Draghi, president of the European Central Bank at the time, affirmed: "You know there was a time when [economist] Rudi Dornbusch used to say that the Europeans are so rich they can afford to pay everybody for not working. That's gone, backtracking on fiscal targets would elicit an immediate reaction by the market."[75] In his words, and in quoting Dornbusch's vision of an overly generous European welfare state, Draghi acknowledged that the functions of European welfare states had shifted, due to a supposed lack of public interest in supporting passive income schemes.

The move toward insecurity is often conceptualized as an inevitable and inescapable consequence of the economic shift toward neoliberalism. Because of the conceptual stretching behind the use of neoliberalism, it is more precise to characterize and define the process I have described as a desecuritization of the welfare state.[76] The rise in insecurity is the product of political and institutional choices to reduce, materially and symbolically, the objective of sustaining people's socioeconomic security through social policies. Institutions have implicitly accepted that a certain level of insecurity will emerge from the enhanced dependency of individuals on the cyclical fluctuations of the market, that societies will be socially affected by it, and that the state will equip individuals to navigate this bumpy ride through interventions aimed at making them more competitive in respect to other individuals (the social investment agenda).

At the national level, the desecuritization of the welfare state means that the state intervenes to compensate only those out of work and the poorest, while the shift toward active policies implies a direct intervention in job insecurity, generating a trade-off between job creation and job quality. The EU's response to the Eurocrisis has contributed to the enhanced climate of insecurity. The austerity phase consisted of an insecurity shock at multiple levels (content of policies, discourses, and governance), while the second phase changed the discourses but did not result in a substantial change in policy and content to address the increase in insecurity of the previous years.

In countries that have made welfare state interventions a central pillar of their security regime—such as Sweden, Germany, and the Netherlands—the transformation in welfare provisions has had qualitative repercussions. The use of strictly assessed, insufficient, and highly stigmatized state sources to buffer security has increased the insecurity of welfare claimants, as well as other citizens who had a potential cushion to fall back on. Security in Europe, as stressed by the economists Alberto Alesina and Francesci Giavazzi, "was a material, as well as an emotional, state of collective well-being that was socially solidaristic, economically redistributive and international."[77] The slow move toward a material and emotional state of insecurity was accompanied by a Europeanization process that was imbued with an individualistic approach to navigating the new market-state mix rather than regulating it. Because of the implicit selectivity of the system and its preference for conditionality, targeting, and deservingness, institutions are set up to offer security to deserving individuals with the productive potential to be (re)activated. Hence, the new welfare-state system creates a societal dynamic whereby the presence of insecurity is more normalized, but also one in which—institutionally—individuals are placed against one another along oppositional lines in a societal fight to be deemed deserving of protection from the very institutions that have been politically created to protect them and in a climate in which support is targeted and limited. What sort of political reaction can emerge in a society where the institutional political script postulates that job and financial security are inextricably attached to productivity?

CHAPTER FOUR

Demand and Supply in the New Politics of Insecurity

"POPULISM" IS A TERM that tends to attract polarizing views in public debate and at times also in academia. On the one hand, it is criticized and avoided for holding a negative connotation of those who support populist parties.[1] On the other, the term has been critiqued for reducing the rise of the far right to a euphemism and diminishing its proponents' attempts to normalize xenophobia and racism in the public discourse.[2] Those who take the latter stance argue that liberal thinkers have used populism instead of talking explicitly about the rise of the far right in order to tactically bring everyday racism into the political debate.[3]

Equating the phenomenon of populism with the populist right, or with racism, is reductive at best and misleading at worst, as it places the focus on one of the manifestations of insecurity instead of analyzing the broader societal roots of populist support. It provides no insight into why, in the French national elections of 2024, the inevitable surge of the far-right National Rally (NR) was in part counteracted by the surprising rise of the New Popular Front (NPF), a left-wing alliance led by the populist left leader Jean-Luc Mélenchon. Therefore, using a minimalist definition of populism is, for part of the scholarship, a deliberate intellectual choice to try to understand populism from the perspective of voters and not simply from that of populist parties or the political discourses used by the elites, as well as to account for the various directions that populism takes and for the existence and rise of the populist left.[4] The ideational definition of populism that I use here provides a broader analytical framework to understand populism that goes beyond the manifestation of right-wing populism or the focus on parties' politics and explores the root of what generates an alignment between people's sentiments and existing political agendas.[5]

In this chapter I provide a political sociological framework that sets out what links insecurity to populism, and I examine how party politics present various political agendas that respond to insecurity. In doing so, I rely on the idealist definition of populism introduced earlier, because it takes as its basis the perspective that voters hold, rather than being concerned with populist parties. In its minimalist terms, populism is understood and empirically investigated through two core beliefs that individuals have: the belief that people must be central in politics, which is accompanied by the understanding that they are not; and the belief that politics is characterized by an opposition between "the people" and the economic, intellectual, and media elites. A third, albeit derivative, belief is what is called the Manichean outlook—namely, a sharp and dualistic vision of reality as divided between good and bad. How can insecurity explain the development of a populist outlook, which is defined as holding these three beliefs?

Linking Insecurity to Populism: An Enlarged Framework

The impact of insecurity on populist voting is ubiquitous, as it affects, at one level, voters, who are influenced by insecurity in their choice to go to vote and in how they vote, but also molds, at another level, the formation of parties' agendas. Using a common division in political science, I simplify this distinction by referring to the first level, the voters, as the demand and the second level, the parties and their agendas, as the supply. I use a framework that is an alternative to rational choice theory, which remains the most popular theoretical framework in the study of politics,[6] as I do not presuppose a process that rationally links the choices that people make and the solutions they are presented with. The political sphere is not an economic market, and voters are not simply political consumers who pick and choose a party to maximize their utility.[7] I believe that it is more correct to consider the relationship between voters and parties as a dual phenomenon, with the new politics of insecurity emerging from the constant interplay between how institutions and political actors—through policies and political actions—produce narratives and discursive frames that enter the public and political culture of a society, in addition to offering political solutions to it.[8] This creates a constant dialogue between the supply of discursive frames—which legitimate or deny the existence of insecurity, and which propose to address it or choose to ignore it—and how "the people" would like to see insecurity both acknowledged and addressed. What makes the process even more complicated is that the likelihood of a discursive frame on insecurity resonating with the beliefs of "the people" depends not only on congruence (what political scientists call the fit between the supply and the demand) but also on the socioeconomic context.[9] In other words, the political landscape resembles tectonic plates that keep moving according to what resonates with "the people" and what the political sphere has to offer, which is mediated by the context of rising insecurity.

The analytical framework I propose in figure 4.1 summarizes the sociological process of the new politics of insecurity and shows how the direction of populism—both why individuals tend to vote for RPR and RPL parties and the specific form that populism takes, as right or left populism—is profoundly shaped by socioeconomic and cultural factors. When trying to explain the political support for populism, classic political science theory privileges explanations that are strictly political (i.e., party supply) and relate to a restricted set of cultural attitudes. In other words, according to this theory, individuals are more likely to vote for RPR parties if they have authoritarian values, or specific cultural values regarding migration, gender, and LGBTI+ equality, while RPL voting is more associated with opposing views on these areas. The risk, using this type of framing, is to make the explanation circular, as these are not simply opinions or attitudes associated with RPR or RPL voting: They constitute the content of parties' agendas and define what it means to be an RPR or an RPL voter. Instead, the process I illustrate contains a broad set of sociological factors that are not included when insecurity is understood simply as an economic factor, such as the changing role of the security providers (market–state–family), the individual experiences of work and financial insecurity, and the influence of the dominant cultural narratives and the symbolic boundaries they create.

The first tangible consequence of the political effects of insecurity is the declining support for the mainstream or established parties that have dominated politics since the end of the Second World War, in particular the two main blocks, made up of center-right parties (Christian Democrats) and center-left parties (Social Democrats) (in certain contexts, this declining support has also encompassed the liberal parties). The new politics of insecurity plays a role in explaining the pull away from the established parties, as much as it helps to explain the pull in toward new populist forces. In terms of the pull away, mainstream and established parties have supported agendas that, as discussed earlier, have resulted

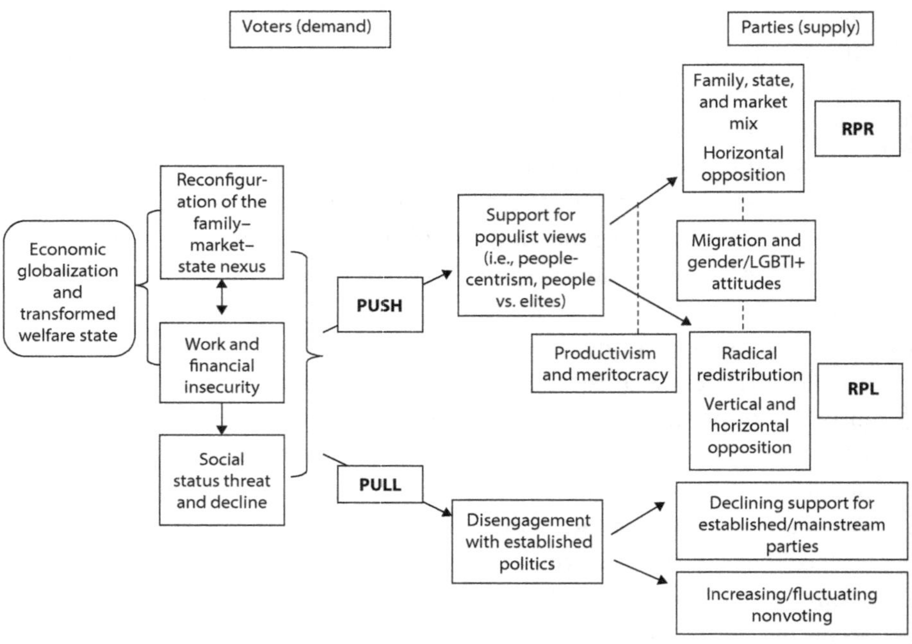

FIGURE 4.1. Demand and supply in the new politics of insecurity.

in a squeeze in how the market–state–family mix can address insecurity. The Social Democratic parties adopted a pro-market, flexible labor-market agenda from the 1990s, which intensified after the 2008 crisis, geared toward the normalization of a postsecurity polity.[10] The agenda of the Christian Democrats—who have traditionally been tepid supporters of social-protection policies—has become more centered on competitive and procompetition labor market policies, and both centrist groups have adopted a post-social-capitalism agenda.[11] On top of this, all centrist blocks, including the liberal parties, have positioned themselves as strongly pro-European and aligned with the EU project. In this context, the Euroskeptic agendas proposed by populist parties from both ends of the political spectrum, and their opposition to the EU project, can be understood as a way for populist parties to distance themselves from institutions that have contributed to the insecurity shift. For this reason, Berezin, who was investigating the political rise of insecurity in Europe before the 2010 crisis, perceived the rising Euroskepticism in the early 2000s to be a direct result of the political normalization of insecurity.[12]

A number of scholars have theorized and empirically shown the link between social status and RPR support, arguing that there is a symbolic connection between feeling that one's status has declined in relation to the other members of a society and sympathizing with antiestablishment parties or political newcomers. They also seem to suggest something more fundamental that explains the decline of social status in the first place, which has to do with the structural rise of insecurity in society and its effects at the micro level.[13] Existing theories are unhelpful in explaining the process behind the decline of social status and its relation to insecurity. Is it insecurity that leads to a perceived decline of social status, or is it status threat that results in higher perceived insecurity? Social status is usually conceptualized and measured as an assessment of one's position in the social hierarchy in relation to others, but it does not contain any reference to the causes of one's perceived decline.[14] Hence, we can hypothesize that the decline of work and financial conditions for a large portion of individuals could generate a loss of perceived social status among individuals from different social classes (e.g., working classes and lower middle classes). Insecurity and social status interact with each other and represent the conditions that bind the people together in opposition to secure elites in respect either to everyday conditions (insecurity) or to the outcome of their changed conditions (social status). The conceptualizations of social status and populism contain a competitive element and a bonding factor: People perceive their status to have declined in relation to most secure members of society, and this feeds into the vertical opposition between the people and the elites and the horizontal opposition between who belongs to the people in the first place. At the same time, insecurity—and the decline in social status that results from it—is the bonding factor that serves to construct a notion of the people that combines in-group and out-group dynamics. This process is influenced by the presence of symbolic boundaries, namely, by the conceptual tools that individuals and groups use to categorize themselves and others and, in this case, define who enters in the solidaristic notion of the people based on worth and other moral distinctions and who is excluded from it.[15]

Until recently, research tended to focus only on the exclusionary element of populism, particularly in relation to RPR populism. RPR and RPL populism both contain exclusionary elements but also engage actively in proposing solutions to insecurity. Examining the combined use of exclusionary and security-fixing elements in RPR and RPL agendas helps us to avoid viewing populism in terms of the two extreme and somewhat naive positions that these parties propose—in other words, as purely welfare chauvinist or welfare expansionary. A core narrative and discourse frame of RPR parties is based on a horizontal exclusion regarding who constitutes the category of the people and who is excluded from it, based on racial and ethnic distinctions (defined in chapter 1 as a horizontal oppositional frame).

This oppositional framing is also articulated through the provision of a key source of security: the welfare state. Almost all RPR parties in Western Europe have in the past decade changed their position on the welfare state from supporting a minimal vision of the welfare state to endorsing a comprehensive welfare state that is dualized according to the insiders and the excluded outsiders.[16] While the emphasis in the past was on how RPR parties mobilized support around cultural issues, evidence is mounting on how they attract support through a chauvinist view of welfare-state access.[17] More generally, RPR parties have attempted to provide a solution to a gap in security provision left by established parties through both a welfare-state agenda that is protective of insiders and an exclusionary agenda that conceives access to welfare as something that is deserved either via citizenship or, even more profoundly, through one's racial and ethnic proximity to the majority. This second trend does not simply reflect a cultural position but also constitutes a response to a gap in the political provision of security, which has basically seen socioeconomic security disappearing from the political debate in favor of a domestic notion of physical security.[18]

In addition to presenting horizontal exclusionary frames whereby race, ethnicity, and citizenship are mobilized as sources of horizontal opposition between individuals, the agendas of European RPR parties contain a form of social populism based on societal hierarchies that exist between deserving individuals and undeserving ones. RPR parties often mobilize market-centered logics of deservingness and merit because productivism is now a hegemonic cultural script in European societies. A recent study investigated the diffusion of "producerism" among citizens in Europe (i.e., how much people believe that one has to be productive to have value in society), finding that, first, European citizens have become strongly in favor of producerism, to a level that is equivalent to their American counterparts; and, second, that those with a producerist viewpoint in Europe are more likely to support RPR parties.[19] This suggests that RPR parties have been able to politically mobilize the emphasis on being productive during the political shift toward a modernized welfare society described in chapter 3.

As mentioned, the ideational definition conceptualizes populism as based around two core ideas: the centrality of the people and the opposition between the people and the elite. The construction of "the people" implies a form of othering and categorization that is shaped by the socioeconomic and moral values in society. A society that strongly believes in meritocracy and productivism will include in the category of the people those who are deserving and will create discourses to exclude other individuals who are not considered deserving of belonging to a solidaristic vision of the people, such as welfare claimants. RPR parties are not the only ones—or even the first ones—to have politically mobilized economic-based notions of worthiness. Established parties on both the center right and the center left have done the same by encouraging welfare reforms that enhance individual competition and deliver state interventions based on deservingness. One could argue that RPR parties have surpassed the first political proponents of producerism in Europe (i.e., mainstream parties) in terms of how to politically mobilize the moral standard of productive members of society to create divisions or bridges between "people like us" and members of society with different perceived levels of social worthiness based on race, ethnicity, or economic productivity.[20]

Their newcomer status affords them the freedom to formulate even more extreme narratives than established parties, targeted at gaining political support by making cultural distinctions based on worthiness. As Bonikowski described in relation to the United States, in Europe, too, "insecurity and resentment toward those who are seen as receiving higher levels of government assistance" have fed into a rise in RPR support.[21] Working-class individuals and emerging insecure groups from the lower middle classes who compete to sustain their security in a climate of scarce resources have therefore become the ideal target audience of a political discourse based around deservingness.

In addition to the *pars destruens* of these RPR parties, and the role of such arguments in creating and reinforcing hierarchical positions and exclusionary frames, there is an evident *pars construens* that RPR parties offer by proposing new solutions to stop the squeeze of resources to address insecurity from the state–family–market mix. After all, as Kirk Andrew Hawkins et al. suggested, "populist attitudes will not translate into political behavior without activation."[22] Individuals do not necessarily turn up at the ballot box to vote for populist parties, even though they might sympathize with how populist parties oppose the elites and aim to put people at the center. Indeed, another phenomenon that characterizes the current political environment is the existence of a stable and not insignificant portion of nonvoters, which has led to the identification of mainstream voters, populist voters, and nonvoters as the three core constituencies of contemporary politics in Europe.[23] What does generate an activation toward voting for RPR parties?

Activation does not occur only by mobilizing voters around opposition to others, but also by reintroducing voters' own insecurity in parties' agendas and narratives. On top of reestablishing the role of the state as a security provider, albeit in an exclusionary way and often by embedding a market-based logic, RPR parties become providers of security by advocating for the reestablishment of the role of the family.[24] In a context where insecurity is widespread, proposing a higher role for the state or the family in providing security is likely to resonate with voters.[25] The use of the family in RPR discourses does not simply represent a moralistic choice, in terms of supporting the traditional role of the family, because RPR parties refer explicitly to the role of families as providers of socioeconomic security, whom they attempt to facilitate via familistic state interventions, in stark contrast to an atomistic and individualized vision of the transformed welfare states endorsed by established parties.[26] While much emphasis is placed on what RPR parties oppose, it is important to stress that such parties have also an ability to inject discourses and cultural frames of reference that are lacking in the mainstream debate, in this case through an agenda that provides proposed solutions to restore microlevel security.[27]

Scholars have also noted that European RPL parties, which present themselves as an alternative to the moderate positions of the center left vis-à-vis the welfare state and labor-market policies, have moved even further left as promoters of social populism.[28] In practice, this has meant that RPL parties have argued for the reinstatement of the state as a security provider for individuals and their families. Part of the success of these parties in Europe post-2008 has to be ascribed to the gap in the political scene that the austerity agendas of mainstream parties on both sides created, which has been filled by an even more extreme realignment of RPL parties toward radical redistribution.[29] The *pars construens* of RPL parties, capitalizing on the public debate on the perils of wealth and income inequality in Europe, consists of proposals to redistribute resources from the economic elites to the people. RPL parties' identification of the "people" also contains implicit exclusionary elements, which mostly emphasize the vertical hierarchies that exist between the people and the economic or cultural elites. However, RPL parties have also flirted with forms of patriotism that imply horizontal oppositional frames that exclude noncitizens. Two cases of this are the acceptance of a citizens-oriented narrative of the Brexit Referendum by Corbynism and the reference to patriotism in the discourses on welfare interventionism by RN/FI in France.[30] This suggests that in order to make the opposition to the others more intelligible in a political climate characterized by ethno-racial social distinctions, RPL parties can also draw from exclusionary framings.

In the framework I propose, the shape that the oppositional hierarchies take—as vertical or horizontal forms of opposition—is influenced by two processes that I have alluded to and will examine further in the next two sections: the role of insecurity in making migration attitudes a dominant horizontal hierarchy, and the influence of productivist and meritocratic narratives in making Europeans receptive to horizontal oppositional frames.

THE ROLE OF INSECURITY IN MAKING OPPOSITION TO MIGRATION A KEY OPPOSITIONAL FRAME

In contrast with the operationalization of antimigration attitudes as purely cultural, and beyond the framing of migration as a simple economic risk, studies in migration attitudes have empirically confirmed an interplay between economic and cultural factors in the development of migration attitudes.[31] Attitudes and views toward migration have been found to be influenced by the native-born population's skill level, the perceived skills of the migration population, whether the migration is occurring in a strong or a weak economy, and the size of the racial or immigrant group, as well as the overall context of socioeconomic insecurity present in a society.[32]

Research conducted in the United States has indicated that perceived immigrant job threat tends to increase in settings with economic stagnation, where labor unions are weaker and there is a rise of work insecurity resulting from corporate restructuring and low wages.[33] Furthermore, perceived job threat is fueled by labor market deregulation: States that have experienced higher declines in union density over the previous decade tend to show higher levels of perceived job threat, while states with higher minimum wages show lower levels of perceived job threat. The presence of state interventions acts as a form of safety net for both native and immigrant workers, "thus removing a key source of conflict in the labor market."[34] In this context, the welfare insecurity shift illustrated earlier exposes countries and immigrants in particular to potential nativist threats. The perceived job threat that individuals report is hence dramatically shaped by the general socioeconomic environment of insecurity, which is directed against the migrant workers.

Studies on competitive threat in Europe have confirmed that migration attitudes in Europe have been profoundly shaped by the rise in insecurity, particularly after the Great Recession. Research by Joakim Ruist found that negative attitudes toward non-European immigrants from poorer countries were 40 percent higher than they would have been if conditions in 2012 had been as good as in 2006, indicating that the rise in socioeconomic insecurity that occurred between 2002 and 2012 had an effect on attitudes toward migration.[35] A study examining the effect of the economic crisis on attitudes to migration reported that the Great Recession increased perceived immigrant threat (PIT) in twenty-two countries in Europe.[36] Reaching a similar conclusion, research that tested competitive threat theory among the various theories on intergroup relations in the context of the economic crisis in Western Europe found that anti-immigrant sentiments increased in countries in which perceptions of economic insecurity also rose.[37] A similar study conducted during the crisis revealed that individuals' financial distress is statistically associated with negative attitudes toward immigrants in both a direct and an indirect way, as even native citizens who have not been directly hit by the economic recession tend to have a lower perception of the national economy, which shapes their attitudes toward immigration in a negative way.[38]

To sum up, the studies that have investigated both insecurity and migration have shown overwhelming evidence of the connection between the potential and effective rise of socioeconomic insecurity in Europe and the development of antimigration attitudes. Furthermore, they have suggested that it is not purely the presence of individual economic insecurity that is associated with the opposition to migration, but also the existence of insecurity in societies coupled with a reduction in the mechanisms to address it through welfare interventions. To understand why people living in Europe are so receptive to the framing of antimigration attitudes in such an oppositional way, we need to delve deeper into why oppositional horizontal frames are so popular in Europe in the first place.

US VERSUS THEM: THE POPULARITY OF HORIZONTAL OPPOSITIONAL FRAMES IN EUROPE

The previous section referred to the existing research on how migration attitudes are formed to show that antimigration attitudes are not purely the product of a cultural backlash but a resonating frame in a climate of insecurity. This section broadens this perspective by showing that migration attitudes are just one type of horizontal oppositional resonating frame among others that have emerged in Europe in a climate of insecurity.

As I hinted at earlier, mine is not simply an economic argument, as the new politics of insecurity emerges from the connections between economic, cultural, and political factors, with national and European institutions contributing to the creation of a postsecure polity. The economic competitive threat becomes a resonating frame due to a cultural and material climate of postsecurity in which security is no longer a given; rather, it is something to be obtained through competition for scarce resources and is dependent on deservingness. The rise of antimigration attitudes represents a specific configuration of a horizontal oppositional frame, but there are other visible cases of the exacerbation of in-group/out-group distinctions in European societies.

The evolution of attitudes toward welfare use in Europe constitutes another key area that allows us to appreciate the existence of out-group dynamics and the horizontal oppositional frames they generate, as welfare has had a bonding function in European societies that, historically, has produced horizontal solidaristic frames; furthermore, negative welfare attitudes do not apply specifically, or exclusively, to migrants but to the broader spectrum of undeserving citizens. As far back as 2012, Tim Reeskens and Wim van Oorschot found that the development of negative attitudes against migrants who used welfare reflected a more general trend of limiting undeserving citizens' access to welfare. They suggested that this was the result of nations having made welfare access more targeted and residual through the transition to the transformed welfare state, as described in chapter 3. Placing migration within this more enlarged welfare context characterized by scarcity, they found that "symbolic boundaries between 'us' and 'them' are more outspoken when a scarce pool of welfare resources is at stake among those who are the most vulnerable."[39] The category of the most vulnerable is not inclusive of all citizens: As indicated, Europeans place an increasing emphasis on productivity and deservingness in shaping access to social citizenship, and such value formation intersects with other distinctions of worth based on race and ethnicity.

As mentioned earlier, populism does not only express itself as RPR support but can also take the form of attitudes against the economic elites, which are more likely to be associated with RPL support. In a context of growing inequality and insecurity, one would expect voters to turn against the economic elites and develop vertical oppositional frames. The lack of a political articulation of vertical hierarchies can be directly linked to the popularity of the meritocratic frame, which serves as a justificatory script for the existence of inequalities. Investigating why the rise in inequality has not resulted in support for redistributive interventions, Jonathan Mijs found that this is explained by the meritocratic frame, which reinforces the belief, in Europe as well as in the United States, that individuals are solely responsible for their own fate.[40] In addition to resulting in a higher sense of responsibility for themselves, meritocratic attitudes tend to underpin a belief in how others are responsible for their own conditions, thereby limiting the potential solidarity among social groups affected by similar issues and generating particularly strict moral judgment against individuals who are in social proximity to us and yet lack the characteristics that would make them as deserving as we are. In this way, we refuse even to acknowledge the political responsibility of the distant economic elites, who are also too morally protected by their economic success to become the source of our political opposition. Given the stickiness of economic-centered scripts based on merit and productivity, which are also reproduced by the transformed welfare state, it is unsurprising that horizontal oppositional framings—whether against migrants or against other supposedly underserving citizens—remain so successful in politics.

Oppositional horizontal frames are very visible in countries that adopt exclusionary practices in the articulation of policy solutions to security, such as liberal welfare regimes, as analyzed in chapter 2. In addition to the moral-underclass discourse that has stigmatized the most financially insecure since the Poor Laws, the UK has adopted an exclusionary notion of social citizenship that is conditional to participation in the labor market, a perspective that began to be pushed in the 1980s and was normalized by the left in the 1990s.[41] The productivist form of social citizenship developed in the UK is characterized by a normalization of financial and work insecurity in society, accompanied by the heavy use of cultural repertoires of deservingness and nativism in mainstream politics to cover up the political responsibilities for the postsecurity shift. The political reliance on horizontal oppositional frames is also visible in other European countries. Activation policies and policies geared toward individual responsibility, described in chapter 3, have even made voters in the Netherlands, one of the frontrunners of active-oriented reforms, more receptive to political frames centered on deservingness.[42] As I will discuss in the following section, parties contribute in determining which oppositional frames are dominant via the political solutions and discourses they formulate to fix the rising insecurity.

The Political Supply of Security Across Regimes

A traditional way to apply insecurity to the study of party politics would be to use cleavage analysis to examine whether parties represent the political interests of the precariat, and to test whether people experiencing insecurity are more likely to support populist parties in return. As mentioned, insecurity and precarity are not identity-based categories but shared conditions used to investigate the dynamic reconfiguration of social cleavages. Aligned with this, the analysis that follows aims at understanding how insecurity enters the agendas, strategies, and discourses of populist parties in relation to the dominant political agendas within each case study.

The following focuses on the case studies introduced in chapter 2, divided according to the same security regimes, under the assumption that the regime division I used to investigate the evolution of insecurity is also valid to analyze security politics: the UK (the liberal regime); Italy and Spain (the Southern European security regime); the Netherlands, Germany, and France (the continental security regime); Sweden (the Nordic security regime); and Hungary and Poland (the Eastern European security regime). The case studies incorporate a variety of populist parties from the left (e.g., Podemos, Die Linke, La France Insoumise) and the right (PVV, the Sweden Democrats, Rassemblement National), as well as those that have been in government (Italy, Hungary) and those that have only been in opposition (Spain, France) (see the full list of parties in the methodological appendix). Several classifications have been elaborated to identify populist parties, which at times differ in how they evaluate borderline parties.[43] These evaluations tell us if parties are populist or not on a binary scale, but they don't tell us how a party articulates and uses populism to gain support. Analyzing the offer of populist parties across countries helps to explain why the demand for populism and the votes for populist parties take different forms across the case studies. However, demand and supply in populism are not entirely distinct concepts, as the use of a market language would suggest, and it is important to capture the constant exchange between what parties do, what the voters express at the ballot box, and the external context of insecurity. Three trends emerge in how political insecurity influences party politics and parties' realignment.

First, support for populist parties often takes the shape of a relevant but not majoritarian portion of the electorate. Obtaining a fourth, or even a fifth, of the total vote does not constitute a dramatic populist surge, but in the current political climate it is enough to lead to a profound shift in party politics—one that has disrupted the domineering role that mainstream and centrist parties have had since the postwar period. Populist parties have not disrupted party politics in Europe by becoming take-all parties but through their capacity to fragment mainstream support. In proportional systems, their main role has been in facilitating the end of bipartisanship and in making it more difficult for established parties to be in government without having to form coalitions. While this goal is much harder to achieve in systems that are bipartisan as an effect of their electoral system, even in the UK—a first-past-the-post electoral system that inherently rewards the two biggest parties, one on the center right and the other on the center left—the presence of RPR parties such as the Brexit Party and Reform UK, together with RPL-friendly independent candidates, has fragmented the vote within each constituency, leading to a loss of safe seats for Labour and the Tories (e.g., Reform UK won five seats in the 2024 general election).

Second, populist parties are in a symbiotic, if antagonistic, relationship with mainstream established parties, because the latter represent part of the political elite that populist parties oppose and are central to how successful parties are in framing their agendas as innovative or an alternative to the status quo. As I will show, offering an agenda that provides security to voters is also a way for populist parties to distance themselves from the insecurity-enhancing agendas promoted by mainstream parties since the 1990s. As some of the populist parties that have been in government are aware (e.g., the League or the Five Star Movement in Italy), populist parties have to walk a fine line: They strive to become popular but without having their agendas and frames becoming too established or mainstream.

Third, populist parties will not necessarily retain support once they enter established politics. Despite their lack of continuity when in a coalition or in government, they have a medium-term impact on party politics as agenda reminders or as catalysts that move the agendas of established parties back where they were before the insecurity shift. They have a role in proposing solutions to address insecurity through horizontal (RPR) or vertical (RPL) oppositional frames and through the reestablishment of the market–family nexus in offering security.

In the following section, I analyze the frames and positions of the main populist parties vis-à-vis established parties within each case study. I also show, through figures available for three cases of the first three security regimes (Spain, Sweden, and Germany), the results of the analysis of the Manifesto Dataset I conducted with Jan Philipp Thomeczek that examined the saliency (namely, the frequency in which certain political terms are used in parties' manifestos) of commodification and redistributive security between 2000 and 2021, measured as agreement to welfare expansion, union role, and equality (see details in the methodological appendix).[44]

THE SOUTHERN EUROPEAN SECURITY REGIME

Southern Europe is a textbook case of insecurity and the rise of populism, to the extent that some scholars have called it the Mediterranean populist regime.[45] In his analysis of antisystem politics, Jonathan Hopkin discussed how the rise of populist support consisted of a double move against austerity and in favor of nationalism in Spain, while it materialized in an incoherent critique of austerity through support for center and right-wing populism in Italy.[46] Hopkin's argument is underpinned by the belief that there is a logical and coherent response to austerity for the electorate through populist *left* support. As previously outlined, populist viewpoints do not automatically take the form of populist left political support due to the presence of existing horizontal oppositional cultural frames that resonate with the average voter. More than a reaction to austerity, we can interpret the continuous support for various forms of populism in Spain and Italy as the result of a rise in socioeconomic insecurity in their societies, accompanied by the use of oppositional political frames that were vertical in some brief instances but generally overwhelmingly horizontal.

In Spain, the popularity of populism started with support for an RPL party in the form of the movement-turned-party Podemos, which is often cited as an exemplary case of an articulation of left-wing populism as a collective way to address insecurity (see chapter 1). The early support for Podemos can be understood as a logical realignment of voters' support for redistributive welfare security and less market-based orientation, based on an analysis of the party's insecurity agenda via its manifesto data. Figure 4.2 shows that the position of Podemos in 2019 was substantially more prosecurity than the established Social Democratic party of that time (PSOE), as well as more prosecurity than PSOE in the earlier period. Podemos rose to prominence organically, obtaining 8 percent of the vote in 2014; becoming the first party in 2015, with 21 percent of the vote; and then getting 12.9 percent in 2019, when it formed a coalition government with PSOE. After this point, the support for PSOE stabilized, and Podemos lost its traction as a political force that was alternative to the mainstream.[47] As Podemos's popularity started to dwindle, another populist party, the RPR party Vox, gained more support. Often compared to the Sweden Democrats, Vox's agenda, based on analysis of Manifesto Data between 2000 and 2019, is procommodification and appears to have a relatively limited stance on redistributive security, though interestingly it is positioned to be more prosecurity in redistributive terms than the main center-right party was in 2000. If the popularity of Podemos in Spain

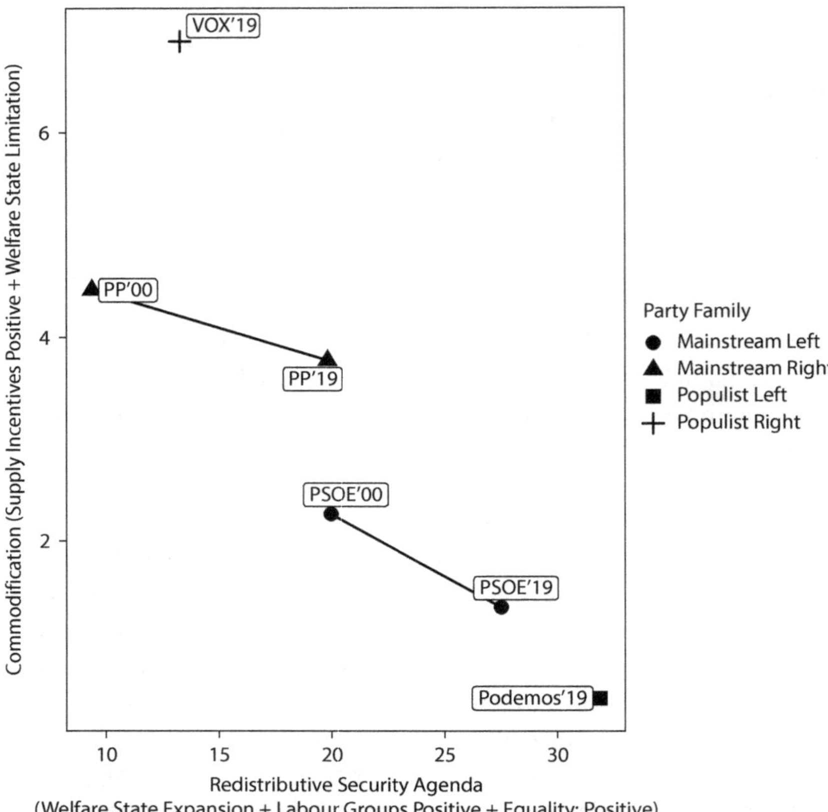

FIGURE 4.2. Salience analysis of commodification and security agendas of the main parties in Spain based on Manifesto Data.

represented a bit of an exception, the rising support for Vox reflects the dominant approach of addressing insecurity via horizontal oppositional frames against migrants and by proposing a combined role of the state and the family in providing security.[48]

The popularity of populism in Italy precedes the most recent populist momentum: In the 1990s Italy was defined as the "paradise" of populism.[49] Berlusconi and his party (Forza Italia, or FI) can be considered as a precursor to the recent rise of populism in Europe: FI switched its positioning in the political arena and, at times, made itself part of the establishment, but it was one of the first parties to have popularized populism in Western countries using the centrality of the people to gain political support. The rise of right-wing populism in Italy in the 1990s—through FI, but also via its allies AN and the League—was symptomatic of an increase in socioeconomic insecurity following the entrance into the Eurozone, which had injected market-based forms of instability and destabilized some of the sources of security that Italian society had enjoyed since the postwar period.[50]

What occurred in the late 2010s was an acceleration of this trend, with newcomers appearing and old parties, like the League, realigning to take an even more explicit prosecurity agenda. The first actor to have benefited politically from the climate of insecurity is the Five Star Movement, a party that is decisively populist in its nature but not easily placed on the right or left spectrum, due to its mix of various prosecurity agendas: pro-redistributive stances, horizontal opposition to migration, welfare chauvinism, and vertical opposition to elites.[51]

The other two populist parties that have increased their political support (the League and Brothers of Italy) can be more easily placed in the RPR box, as, despite their welfare chauvinist positions, they are more classically and markedly positioned as antimigration parties. In addition to being parties that articulate horizontal oppositional divisions, they offer solutions to rising insecurity. For example, the League supports welfare-state expansion in healthcare, pensions, and labor policy, while also articulating a political script centered on deservingness that makes social security extremely selective, while at the same time placing at the center of its agenda the family, not just as a cultural actor, but as a key provider of socioeconomic security.[52] The idea of proposing different forms of horizontal exclusions, coupled with an emphasis on the state and the family as providers of security, was pushed even further by Brothers of Italy. BoI's agenda is a mix of market-fueling proposals, meritocratic discourse, and exclusion of noncitizens. Through its leader Meloni, BoI has developed the most comprehensive horizontal and vertical exclusionary agenda in Italy, as it exploits several forms of opposition, such as "the opposition between natives and immigrants, deserving and non-deserving, people and (economic) elites."[53] At the same time, similar to Vox, Meloni has put forward a positive, security-addressing, populist-right agenda based on the combined role of the traditional family and the strong state as a way to address the insecurity emerging in Italian society.

THE NORDIC SECURITY REGIME

Right-wing populism in Sweden has a long-standing history: The Center Democrats of Sweden have been active since the 1970s, while the populist-right party New Democracy (NyD) received 6.7 percent of the vote in

1991.[54] However, none of these early right-wing populist successes compares to the rise of the Sweden Democrats (SD). For many years, Sweden was described as an exceptional "negative" case of populism due to the absence of electoral success of radical right-wing parties in the country. Originating from a far-right party (the Sweden Party), SD increased its support from 5.7 percent of the vote in 2010 to 12.9 percent in 2014, before becoming the second largest party in 2022, with 20.6 percent. How can we explain the rise of populism through insecurity in the land of welfare security?

If we were to ignore insecurity, the rise of the populist right in Sweden could be interpreted as a reaction to migration and a sign of the cultural closure of Nordic societies. However, the SD agenda developed around two concepts: the notion of *folkhem* (literally translated as people's home and referring to a sense of belonging in the wider society) and the concept of *trygghet* (see chapter 1), used to describe a collective sense of socioeconomic security. Like other RPR parties, SD relied heavily on the notion of welfare chauvinism—that is, the idea that Sweden should provide generous welfare support to those who are ethnically Swedish, thereby excluding migrants and nonethnic Swedes. This is because the existence of a societal sense of home and belonging in Sweden is historically intertwined with the provision of security (of *trygghet*) through welfare state policies;[55] hence, the solution that right-wing populists propose to defend individuals from a loss of socioeconomic security through ethno-nationalism is inevitably attached to welfare. While Swedish sociologist Jens Rydgren described the rise of SD as an example of postclass politics, this does not mean that the increase in the party's popularity is postsecurity or postmaterialist.[56] Instead, SD proclaims itself to be a defender against a rise in socioeconomic insecurity or a restorer of a previous state of *trygghet*, which has clear material connotations and cultural implications. Its manifesto states: "The feeling of belonging is not founded on class solidarity but rather on national affiliation and identity, in which all citizens are guaranteed a physical, economic and social security."[57]

In addition to its specific agenda, what has made SD's support relevant for voters is its position relative to other parties and the timing of the shifts in parties' agendas. Between 1988 and 1998, the Swedish Social Democratic Party (the Social Democrats), the main center-left party, became substantially procommodification and distanced itself from the redistributive prosecurity agenda that characterized its previous period. When the Social Democrats abandoned the idea that the state had to play an active

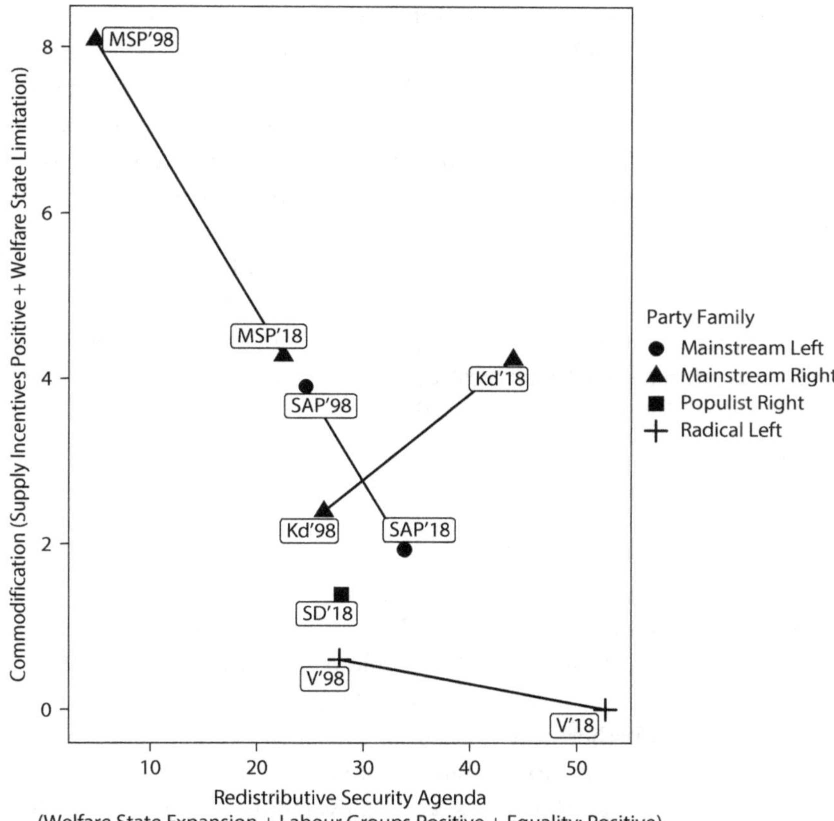

FIGURE 4.3. Salience analysis of commodification and security agendas of the main parties in Sweden based on Manifesto Data.

role in providing security, a space was left in the political system for a party that was prepared to address how security should be provided to Swedish citizens, and that has been taken by SD.[58] The gap that mainstream parties had left became evident during the 2018 elections, when there was a public discussion on the lack of *trygghet* and the presence of insecurity (*otrygghet*). Using the Manifesto Data (see fig. 4.3), in 2018 SD appeared a bit less pro-redistribution as a means to address security than the Social Democrats but also, remarkably, less procommodification than the Social Democrats. However, SD had the capacity to address insecurity with a chauvinist agenda and one that reestablished the role of the state. The gap left in the security agenda has also been taken by the Christian Democrats, who seem to have moved toward a more pro-redistribution agenda.

Why has support in Sweden not swayed to the left? While official classifications of populist parties do not identify a populist-left party in Sweden, the major radical-left party, V (the Left Party), expressed populist orientations in the international sphere in 2018 when it joined the European political movement "Now the People!," which was established by leaders of the populist left in Europe, including the founders of the Portuguese Left Bloc, Podemos, and La France Insoumise. However, the support for this party has been relatively minor, indicating that the success of the populist right in Sweden might be due to the RPR's adoption of an exclusionary political language in relation to welfare support, as well as the diffusion of meritocratic scripts in the country, which pushes people toward populist solutions that emphasize horizontal forms of opposition.

THE CONTINENTAL SECURITY REGIME

France is a continental case study in which, as we saw in chapter 2, insecurity has increased and has been politically channeled toward support for RPR (National Front, now Rassemblement National) and RPL (La France Insoumise) parties, while also influencing the agendas of established politics. Furthermore, insecurity has been explicitly attached to political expressions of anti-establishment politics in France even beyond party politics through the Yellow Vests movement. This movement has been described a form of political revolt against budget cuts and has been sociologically investigated as a social group characterized by evident forms of both job tenure insecurity and financial insecurity.[59] Insecurity has entered the French mainstream political debate even beyond the most extreme forms of politicization of precarity expressed by the Yellow Vests.

The 1990s and 2000s were years of profound transformation in terms of how mainstream parties used welfare and security to gain political support, with a realignment of the established parties toward more market-oriented agendas. Responding to this, the National Front shifted its agenda around an expansionary notion of social citizenship centered on national socioeconomic issues.[60] As discussed in chapter 3, the low economic growth of the 1980s was followed by a series of policy responses in the 1990s that diverted from the principle of solidarity in sharing resources to address insecurity; during this period, mainstream parties moved from a notion of shared solidarity to address insecurity to an individualized one, in a move that dramatically affected the French welfare state.[61] It was during the 1990s that the National Front started to adopt a more pro-interventionist social policy agenda, initially through a simple welfare chauvinist approach that aimed at prioritizing citizens to increase voters' security, as well as allowing the state to have a more interventionist role compared to what was proposed by mainstream parties.[62] From the 2000s the National Front/National Rally (NF/NR) began to become much more critical of market solutions, particularly in areas characterized by work insecurity—e.g., supporting "dignity of work" over "excessive deregulation of the labor market"—while also reestablishing the role of the family as a provider of security. During the 2010s NF/NR made even more explicit use of exclusionary welfarist positions in all policy fields and hence used more explicitly horizontal oppositional discourses that targeted migrants.[63] This, in turn, contributed to the realignment of the Republican party toward the right, particularly through the use of horizontal exclusionary frames against migrants.[64]

La France Insoumise (FI), led by Mélenchon, represents an RPL solution that has gained considerable support in reaction to the normalization of insecurity in mainstream politics. FI received an increasing number of votes in the parliamentary elections in 2017 (11.03 percent) and 2022 (13.82 percent), and Mélenchon's candidacy for the presidency received 19.58 percent in 2017 and 21.95 percent in 2022; in 2024 the left group (the New Popular Front) led by FI won more seats than any other group in a very fragmented general election result. Insecurity has featured heavily in the agenda proposed by Mélenchon since the very start. The first chapter of the 2012 Left Front's manifesto (the precursor of FI) was titled "Sharing the Wealth and Abolishing Social Insecurity" and established a clear political link between addressing insecurity and redistribution, while the FI manifesto in 2017 had an entire chapter on "The Social Emergency. Protecting and Sharing," which referred explicitly to socioeconomic insecurity. When talking about those affected by insecurity, Mélenchon does not refer just to the working classes. His discourses mention "a new urban 'multitude' composed of the traditional working class, 'the poor and the precariat,' other non-employed middle-lower strata and parts of the so-called 'middle classes,' which 'may easily identify with the people as events unfold.'"[65] With respect to class cleavages, FI demonstrates an in-depth understanding of the dynamic reconfiguration of insecurity and does not try to appeal to single or specific social classes but to all social groups that experience insecurity. Its manifesto also uses vertical oppositional frames and suggests that the secure economic elites contribute to the generation of the insecurity that people experience, and hence FI supports radical forms of redistribution and economic planning.[66] RPR and RPL parties in France have not just proposed new political agendas to address insecurity; their agendas have also contributed to a realignment in terms of how established parties talk about insecurity. The main center-right party (the Republican Party or LR) has borrowed from the NF a more distinctive horizontal oppositional framing against migration in recent years, partly also as a way of distinguishing itself from the mainstream liberal agenda of Macron's En Marche. Conversely, the main center-left party (the Socialist Party) moved progressively closer to FI's positions, ultimately forming a coalition with group for the 2024 election.

While the popularity of populism in France might not be considered that shocking given the rise of *précarité* in the country, the growing support for populism in Germany is more surprising. Although Germany is commonly viewed as a stable and secure country, we saw in chapter 2 that insecurity is slowly creeping into German society and its politics. This is evident, for instance, by looking at the rising popularity of AfD (the main German RPR party) in Eastern Germany—an area that is characterized by more insecurity than its more secure Western counterpart.[67] It would, however, be a mistake to consider the rising support for RPR parties in Germany to be limited to the East, and not to be a consequence of a reconfiguration of politics that concerns German society as a whole.

As in the other countries, the story of populist support in Germany begins in the 1990s and 2000s. The adoption of a pro-insecurity agenda by the Social Democratic Party (SDP) during the 2000s introduced market instruments and logics in the provisions of welfare and resulted in a more pronounced use of productivist frames in addressing insecurity.[68] SDP has progressively lost support in favor of the Christian Democratic Union, first, and most recently the main RPR party, AfD. The analysis from the Manifesto Data based on saliency (fig. 4.4) shows a clear move toward agendas that are less prosecurity and a dramatic shift toward procommodification by both center-right and center-left parties in Germany. In the figure, AfD does not appear to be more in favor of redistributing to increase security than center-left and center-right parties, though it appears to be remarkably less promarket than the center left and center right. How does the AfD's agenda on socioeconomic insecurity explain its political gains?

On the one hand, AfD believes in the capacity of the market to award the best and proposes a strong state that allows the market to flourish (ordoliberalism).[69] On the other, AfD has adopted elements of social populism, particularly since 2017, which have established a role for the state in providing benefits to citizens, albeit in a welfare-chauvinist fashion.[70] Hence, in comparison with the other parties, AfD is actually less

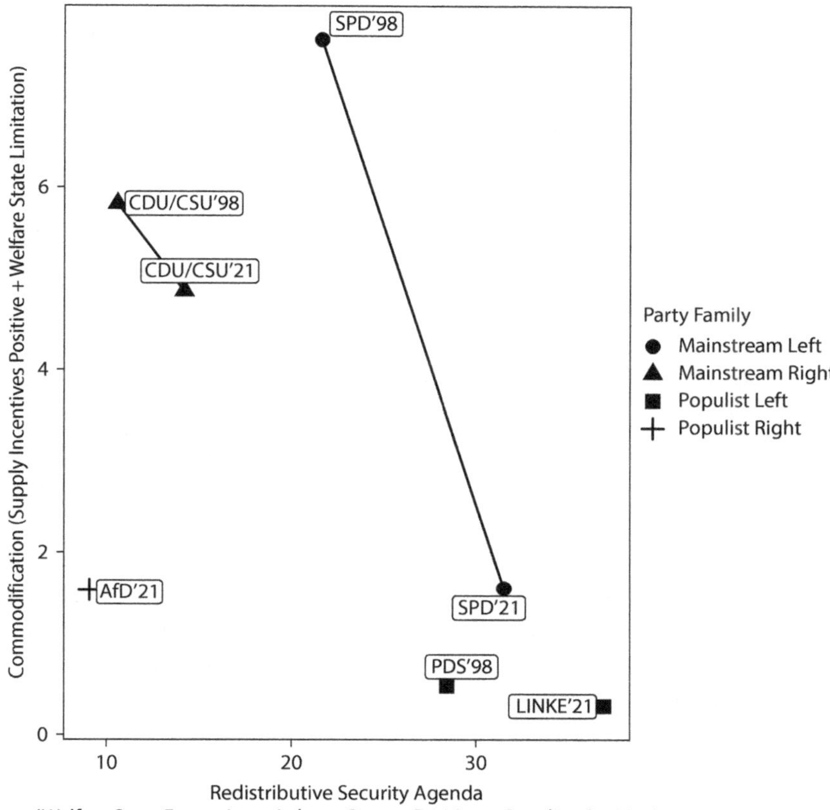

FIGURE 4.4. Salience analysis of commodification and security agendas of the main parties in Germany based on Manifesto Data.

promarket than it would immediately appear. Initially, AfD support was thought to be concentrated among working-class voters, but most recent studies have tended to stress the support it has received from the middle classes. AfD supporters are motivated by socioeconomic concerns but not necessarily in a redistributive way: They are particularly critical of programs that are perceived to benefit immigrants over citizens and of welfare programs that are directed toward the lowest social strata. Indeed, confirming the meritocratic and individualized approach used by right-wing populists to provide security, "AfD sympathizers are not only pronounced welfare chauvinists, but they are also highly critical of class-based redistribution via welfare and taxation."[71] In other words, AfD combines a strong component of horizontal opposition with the idea that both the market and the state can address insecurity.

The popularity of horizontal oppositional frames has drawn populist support away from Die Linke, the main RPL party. Over the 2000s, Die Linke gained substantial support from those who had previously voted for SDP, but its success in recent years has been more mixed.[72] Die Linke's agenda, aimed at reducing insecurity via redistribution, has proved to be less successful than horizontal oppositional agendas, possibly because the concentration of insecurity in Germany means that vertical oppositional agendas do not resonate with large segments of the population.

Similar to Italy, the Netherlands was a precursor of the populist rise that has occurred in the rest of the continent and a multiplier of populist options. The two major centrist parties (the Christian Democrats and the Social Democrats) moved away from supporting welfare as a way to provide socioeconomic security during the 1990s and 2000s and have contributed to a normalization of a political script centered on deservingness in politics.[73]

The Party for Freedom (PVV), one of the main RPR parties, has center or even left stances on welfare and social policy, as the party adopts welfare-chauvinist positions that are aimed at addressing the increasing insecurity among individuals as an effect of an infusion of market logics in Dutch society. On the other side, the other right-wing populist option in the Netherlands, the Forum for Democracy (FvD), adopts more ordoliberal stances, similar to its populist-right German counterpart. The Socialist Party, classified as populist left, has offered a more pro-welfare stance, although, similar to the political situation in Germany, it has failed to gain much support, possibly due to the above-mentioned prevalence of productivist and meritocratic attitudes in the Netherlands.

THE LIBERAL SECURITY REGIME

The first-past-the-post electoral system in the UK represents a natural barrier that prevents newcomers—populist parties included—from gaining political representation and eroding mainstream representation. In practice, populism has entered UK politics in multiple forms, notably with the Brexit referendum, when even moderate voters, who usually supported the mainstream parties, were drawn to populist rhetoric.[74] In general, while RPR support (particularly in the shape of Reform UK) remains relatively marginal, populist rhetoric and populist agendas have profoundly reshaped the agendas of mainstream and established parties in the country.

The bond that already existed between the Conservative Party and the UK Independence Party (UKIP), for example, became even more evident after Brexit, particularly when Boris Johnson's success in the 2019 elections was crucially linked to the adoption of right-wing populist discourses.[75] The analyses of the party manifestos from the 2019 elections indicate that the Conservative Party has realigned itself as a right-wing populist party in several respects, which include its adoption of a strong antimigration agenda.[76] As we have seen, the UK is a clear example of a rise in insecurity accompanied by an increase in pro-meritocracy and individualized attitudes, which has resulted in overwhelming support for agendas that address insecurity by using horizontal oppositional frames targeted against migrants and undeserving citizens.

An alternative to the rising support for right-wing populist frames was the short-lived affirmation of left populism during Jeremy Corbyn's tenure as leader of the Labour Party. Corbyn features heavily in Chantal Mouffe's *For a Left Populism* alongside Podemos, given his emphasis on the centrality of the people. While the Labour Party under Corbyn was not officially classified as an RPL party due to its broad political membership, scholarship has remarked on the presence of populist discourses within the Labour Party at that time.[77] Furthermore, the agenda and movement around Corbyn, which came to be known as Corbynism, contained an explicit attempt to address insecurity through economic measures. The 2017 Labour manifesto contained several policies intended to address the insecurity of emergent service workers and the educated precariat, such as removing tuition fees, raising public sector pay, making housing more affordable, increasing public spending, and nationalizing public services. In response to the prosecurity agenda, the support that Labour gained during the 2017 elections included both working-class and professional voters, and the agenda was extremely popular among young voters, who are among the most precarious.[78]

In 2019, however, the Labour manifesto, which showed a quiet complacency with horizontal oppositional framings in respect to Brexit, was not able to offer an alternative narrative to the horizontal opposition against migrants that the Tories proposed under Johnson's leadership. The analysis of Conservative Party discourses during and after Johnson indicates that populist-right discourses based on horizontal oppositional frames were normalized in British politics during this time. The influence of right-wing populist discourses on the mainstream is also evident in the quiet positioning of Labour's current leader Keir Starmer and his use of patriotism.[79] The result is a political agenda to address insecurity that is heavily based on horizontal oppositional frames against migrants, even in mainstream politics.

THE EASTERN EUROPEAN SECURITY REGIME

Postcommunist Eastern European countries pose a challenge in respect to determining which parties are populist and which parties are nonpopulist.[80] In Poland there are two main RPR parties (Law and Justice, or PiS, and the more recently formed Kukiz), while Hungary has six parties in the RPR classification. In both cases, two major RPR parties have been in power: Fidesz was in power in Hungary between 1998 and 2002 and has ruled continuously since 2010, and PiS formed a coalition government in Poland from 2005 to 2007 and was in government with a strong majority between 2015 and 2023. Socioeconomic interventions to address insecurity have a potentially unique political meaning in Eastern Europe: RPR parties might not be able to gain political support for an agenda that addresses socioeconomic insecurity via state-based welfare chauvinism, as they do in other countries, due to the post-Soviet skepticism toward state interventions (see chapter 2).

Such skepticism might explain why the main RPR party in power in Hungary, Fidesz, does not adopt a classic welfare-chauvinist approach to address insecurity and relies heavily on a mix of the state and the market to relaunch the Hungarian economy. Insecurity features prominently in Fidesz's agenda in respect to the securitization of migration: Migrants are mobilized by the party mainly as a cultural threat, though their initial agendas referred to the socioeconomic threat migrants pose in terms of stealing citizens' jobs.[81] The party's focus is not on microlevel insecurity as experienced by citizens but on the positional insecurity that Hungary faces vis-à-vis the rest of the world, and the party adopts a market-oriented agenda centered on mobilizing horizontal oppositional frames that does not make explicit reference to socioeconomic insecurity.

A dissatisfaction with mainstream and established parties, partly due to socioeconomic concerns and the rise in insecurity in Eastern Europe described in chapter 2, is one of the key factors behind PiS's ascendance to power in Poland in 2015.[82] The PiS agenda can be considered welfare expansionary and welfare chauvinist, as it responds to the dual system present in Poland (see chapter 2), which offers high protection for insiders and low protection for outsiders. Indeed, PiS was able to gain support in 2015 in part due to the mobilization of low-educated people and women in rural areas, who usually did not vote, through an agenda that aimed at reducing the precarity of outsiders.[83]

After 2015, PiS performed a dual shift: On the one hand, it moved politically to the right by absorbing the League of Polish Families, an ultra-Catholic group, while, on the other, it became more expansionary in its social policy.[84] To be specific, the model of social policy pursued by PiS is a welfare familistic model. In 2019 the party published a manifesto entitled "A Polish Welfare State Model," which aimed at replacing a market-based approach with a model of welfare based on social transfers but also giving a central role to the family. Hence, similar to other RPR parties in Southern Europe that I have already discussed, PiS pursues a security agenda that has both a cultural component (centered on nationalism, a traditional vision of society, and an ideology against women's reproductive rights and LGBTI+ rights) and a socioeconomic one, as it reestablished the role of two central sources of security: the family and state interventions. Confirming that addressing insecurity via welfare-state interventions does not pay off in Eastern Europe, in 2023 PiS lost its majority to established parties, although it remained the main party in parliament. As noted by an analysis conducted after the elections, PiS's welfare-state interventions contributed to creating a small middle class that is less supportive of state-led redistributive policies and that was no longer in the party's target socioeconomic groups.[85]

Summary

The rise in insecurity constitutes the cultural and material force behind the pull in toward populist parties and the pull away from established parties and pervades the analytical framework illustrated at the level of voters and parties. The insecurity shift has not resulted in the adoption of uniform or univocal political agendas, as voters' support for parties is mediated by the oppositional and constructive frames that these parties use to connect with their potential voters. The direction of the populist support is influenced by parties' political use of cultural repertoires of worth and productivism and by the solutions they propose to address the loss of security in relation to the family–market–state nexus.

RPR parties generally adopt discursive and strategic frames that reproduce and reinforce the social hierarchies that already exist in European societies between citizens and migrants, native individuals and those with racially and ethnically distinct profiles, deserving and undeserving citizens, and hardworking and lazy citizens (horizontal oppositional frames).

They also, based on the security regime they operate in, propose solutions that will enable individuals to be more secure through the state–family nexus (as in the Southern European regime) or through the state–market nexus, particularly in core countries (e.g., Sweden, Germany, the UK, and the Netherlands). In certain cases, RPL solutions—which are based on a vertical opposition against the elites and rely on the state as a security provider—can be successful, as proved by the short-lived support for Podemos in Spain or by FI/NR in France. Furthermore, populist parties, even when not in power, can substantially shift the pendulum in a country, as demonstrated by the British move toward right populism.

Horizontal oppositional frames remain popular due to the pervasiveness of meritocratic and productivist narratives and discourses, which are, in turn, the result of productive-oriented reforms to welfare interventions. The new politics of welfare-state interventions has therefore generated a toxic environment: How can voters move away from a sociopolitical script centered on deservingness and merit-based worth that is reproduced by institutions themselves and that even mainstream parties adopt? I will return to this impasse in chapter 6, after discussing and empirically demonstrating the link between insecurity and different forms of populist support.

CHAPTER FIVE

From Insecure People to Populist Voters

FROM DANI RODRIK to Thomas Piketty, economists have made several influential contributions to the debate on populism. Rodrik revived the globalization-losers-versus-globalization-winners argument, suggesting that the rise of populism is a reaction by globalization losers, while Piketty applied his focus on inequality to populism and found that opposing political positions were taken by the uneducated wealthy class, which supports the right, and the educated class, which votes for the left.[1] In 2018 a group of influential economists led by Tito Boeri published an imaginary dialogue between an economist and a populist candidate. In the conversation, the populist challenges the economist to explain a puzzle: Why are populists winning if the economy is not going so well? The economist replies first by using the classic Heckscher-Ohlin economic model that all economics undergraduates study at university (as I did myself), discussing its effect on the generation of economic winners and losers. The populist is not convinced that this can explain the specific direction of the vote and wants the economist to add more political explanations. As a result of the exchange, the model becomes more complex. The economist adds a few other variables, such as gender, education, unemployment, and an interaction effect between unemployment and trust suggested by the populist, before concluding that "economists and populists may be in consonance after all!!"[2]

This conversation might be purely imaginary, but the assumptions and variables discussed in it reflect the employment-focused and binary conceptualization of how socioeconomic disadvantage influences populism, which, due to the influence of economics, also underpins a large proportion of political science research.[3] At the individual level, the model considers extreme forms of financial disadvantage while operationalizing unemployment as the main socioeconomic trigger of populism.[4] Numerous influential studies in political science reproduce a similar conceptualization of how socioeconomic variables relate to populism by equating socioeconomic disadvantage with the experiences of the so-called outsiders of the labor market (namely, unemployed people and those with temporary contracts) and assuming that the voting patterns of the majority of labor market "insiders" (individuals in full-time permanent work) are not affected by socioeconomic concerns.[5] Furthermore, the connection between the economy and politics that underpins the initial question (that if the economy is going well, voters should not have any major discontent) is assumed to be rational and automatic, while, as discussed in chapter 4, this link is mediated by several dominant cultural mechanisms. Overall, we lack multidimensional measures of security that allow us to measure and test the impact of economic variables in people's lives beyond their employment status, such as their work conditions or the multidimensional experience of financial security, and, more broadly, their subjective feelings about how they are experiencing an economy that is supposedly going well.[6]

In all fairness, the limited number of socioeconomic variables investigated in studies of populism often reflect the lack of multidimensional measures of socioeconomic disadvantage in the probability sampling datasets used in the research.[7] This leaves scholars unable to test the types of explanations that we conjecture from our theories using existing datasets. In this chapter, I illustrate the empirical work I have conducted with a team of collaborators since 2015 to expand the socioeconomic explanations of populist voting using three techniques: surveys with ad hoc items and measures of insecurity that I selected and/or designed; data-matching techniques that allow different datasets to be combined, thereby producing a larger array of socioeconomic variables; and, finally, an analysis on a longitudinal online dataset that follows the changes to financial and work security during Covid-19 among the same panel of populist/mainstream voters and nonvoters.

The findings are presented in the order in which the analyses were conducted. The first section discusses how disadvantage was used to explain the decision to vote for Brexit and how the framing of disadvantage was expanded to the category of the squeezed middle class to consider the rise of insecurity. The second section covers the empirical investigation of the links between insecurity and populism by using ad hoc measures of work and financial insecurity in the European countries discussed in earlier chapters. In the third section, the findings of a study that explored the gendered impact of insecurity on populist voting are discussed. This study overcame the issue of limited variables by using statistical matching to combine two existing datasets introduced in chapter 2, the EWCS and the ESS. The last section presents the results of an investigation on the effect of work and financial insecurity during Covid-19, which revealed the connections between populist voting and nonvoting.

Populism and the Insecure Middle Class

In the aftermath of the Brexit vote, a consistent body of scholarship interpreted the result—and, by extension, the election of Trump that followed—as the sign of a revolt by the left-behind. This group of people was defined by an early analysis of the Brexit vote as the working classes or historically disadvantaged segments of the population living in low-skilled areas of the UK and having lower levels of formal education.[8] The "Leave" vote presented a puzzle to social scientists. It was a result that reflected a widely felt socioeconomic malaise and could not be interpreted as the voice of a socially homogenous group given the number of people who voted Leave. Yet, the idea that the propensity to support populism derives from a condition of absolute disadvantage—which was conveyed in the imaginary conversation between the economist and the populist—characterized several influential studies that investigated the socioeconomic roots of the Brexit vote.[9]

In 2017 I led an analysis of post-Brexit individual-level data that challenged the dominant narrative of the Brexiter as an angry and left-behind individual.[10] The article I published with my team argued, instead, that a core part of the vote was the intermediate group whose position was declining due to the increasing insecurity they were facing, whom I described earlier in this book: the squeezed middle. The decline of the middle class can be explained partly by the exogenous effects of globalization, but also by the specific dynamics of austerity, which had affected many of those who had voted for Brexit.[11] Given that austerity had negatively affected a wide cross-section of the population, the research hypothesized that the emerging group of disadvantaged people—those with a declining economic position—was even more significant in driving the Leave vote than the "traditionally left out" working class, who had been the focus of prior studies on Brexit.

To expand the potential factors behind and thus explanations of the vote, the study proposed a different notion of disadvantage. In relation to voting, disadvantage has been conceptualized in an extreme and static form; this needed to be broader in order to capture the declining position of individuals in UK society. Subsequently, the first hypothesis was that the probability of voting Leave was high not only among those with low levels of education, but also among those with intermediate levels, especially if combined with a reported negative dynamic in personal finance. The second hypothesis concerned the psychosocial elements behind voting for Brexit. By using a number of questions that related to feelings—in particular, anxiety, anger about whether life had become complicated, whether the respondent felt left out of society, and whether what they did in society had any worth—the research was able to explore Leavers' social malaise and exclusion. The study hypothesized that a person's anxiety about their life could have contributed to their decision to vote Leave, in particular in the context of a declining financial situation. These novel theories were tested through new indicators, including a variable that measured their perception of changes to their financial situation (i.e., whether it had stayed stable, improved, or worsened) in addition to their education. Finally, a small sample of voters had replied to questions asking about their income, which meant that it was possible to empirically test how low- and middle-income groups had voted.

The model predicted that the highest proportions of Leave votes were cast by segments with high GCSE grades and with A levels (an intermediate level of education in the UK), rather than those with no qualifications or low grades at GCSE. Therefore, there was little evidence that those with the lowest levels of education would be more likely to vote Leave than "Remain." The model also revealed that some of the education effects were mediated by a perception of worsening financial conditions among Leavers with A levels (an intermediate level of education) (fig. 5.1).[12]

Another major contribution of this study concerned the psychosocial profile of the Brexit voter, who, in social narratives of the Brexit vote, was described as being a society outsider and experiencing angry feelings.[13] The analysis did not find that voting Leave was associated with such feelings. However, it was associated with a specific negative emotion: feeling worthless. The analysis also found that Brexit voters felt that life had become more complicated. Those experiencing feelings of having been left out of society were more likely to vote Leave, but only when they felt that they had experienced worsening financial conditions over the previous years. Furthermore, in the model only the top income quantile slanted significantly to the Remain side, and the analysis did not find evidence that intermediate voters were more likely to choose Remain.

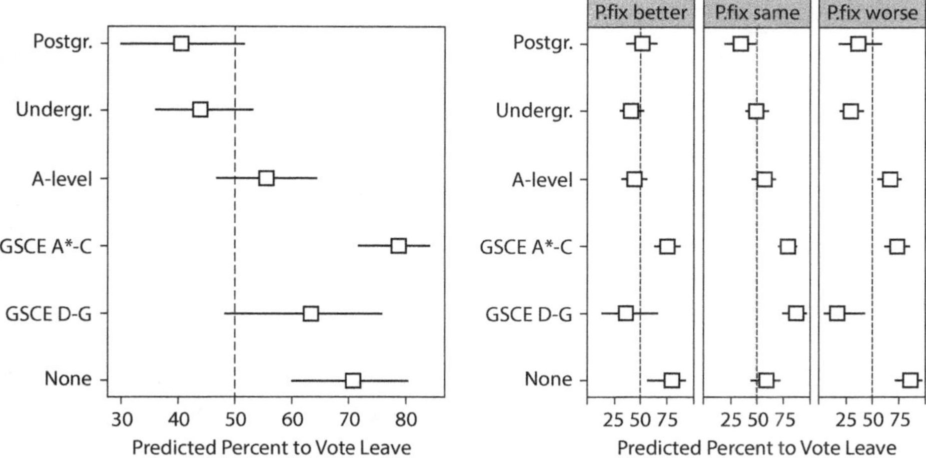

FIGURE 5.1. Predicted probabilities by education (*left panel*) and perceived change in financial situation (*right panel*). *Source*: Lorenza Antonucci et al., "The Malaise of the Squeezed Middle: Challenging the Narrative of the 'Left Behind' Brexiter," *Competition & Change* 21, no. 3 (June 2017): 281.

Overall, therefore, these findings highlighted the combined effects of psychosocial feelings of worthlessness, feeling left out, and feeling that life had become complicated, and experiencing the realities of insecurity. The findings proposed a new approach to disadvantage in the discussion of Brexit and populism more generally. Contrary to the interpretation of Brexiters as a crystallized and left-behind social group, the study suggested that Brexit was in fact capturing a perceived decline in financial conditions that combined subjective and objective elements. Instead of being someone who had been permanently left out of society, the Leave voter appeared to be an individual with a worsening social position who was increasingly struggling—and hence a member of the intermediate middle class and the wide group of people who experience insecurity.

Following the study, several scholars used the argument of the squeezed middle to test populist support. Their research suggested that for populist voting in Europe more generally, the vote was driven not just by the left-out and outsider groups, but by a broader segment of the population that included the squeezed middle.[14] These findings raised other questions. Why is the squeezed middle turning toward populism? What are the changes to these segments' work and financial conditions that explain this choice? Based on the first study on Brexit and the items on the changes to financial conditions, the hypothesis of my next research

Table 5.1. Measures of Tenure and Work Precarity

Precarity of tenure	Precarity at work
1. "I fear I might be dismissed in the near future."	4. "I usually get paid if I miss a day of work."
2. "I fear I am not working enough according to my managers."	5. "I am autonomous in my work decisions."
3. "My total hours of paid employment are likely to decrease in the next six months."	6. "It would be easy for me to find a job with another employer with approximately the same income and benefits I now have."
	7. "I have satisfactory opportunities for career advancement."
	8. "My work–life balance is satisfactory."
	9. "My salary is appropriate for my responsibilities."

was that insecurity, particularly in work conditions and finances, might be behind support for populism. As existing datasets contained limited variables to investigate insecurity, I worked on transposing existing indicators, which are used to measure precarity in the job quality literature and studies on deprivation (see chapter 1), to the realm of political sociology, in order to expand the possible socioeconomic explanations of populism.

The Associations Between Insecurity and Populist Support

The first opportunity to investigate and test new indicators on work security was a study I coauthored on the 2017 elections in France and the Netherlands.[15] In that year, both countries experienced a decline in support for established parties and a rise in support for RPR and RPL parties. As we saw in chapter 4, France and the Netherlands represent examples of the continental security regime. This regime, as illustrated in chapter 2, is more secure than the others, but both countries had experienced a crippling rise in work insecurity, with France showing the biggest decline of security in work conditions and rising job tenure insecurity, and the Netherlands presenting a moderate decline in insecurity in work conditions.

In line with the attempt to broaden the measures of subjective insecurity in relation to voting,[16] I compiled a list of items that captured the different aspects of work-related insecurity discussed in chapter 1 (see table 5.1). Through theoretical development and via exploratory factor analysis, these items were grouped into two categories. The first, precarity or insecurity of tenure, represents the classic item to capture insecurity about keeping a job, namely, the fear of losing one's job and the threat to one's tenure. As discussed in chapter 1, this dimension of work insecurity offers a limited understanding of work-related insecurity because it only captures insecurity related to the tenure of work or the possibility of losing one's job and does not investigate insecurity in work conditions. Broadly, this measure reflects the position of labor market outsiders, who had been the focus of research on job insecurity and voting up to this point.[17] To remedy this, the study added a second factor, designed to capture the insecurity that working voters experience in relation to their work conditions (work security, autonomy at work, cognitive employment insecurity, job security as upward mobility, work–life balance, and income insecurity); this dimension was labeled "precarity at work" (or insecurity at work).

This study aimed to understand not only if insecurity was behind populist voting (RPL and RPR), but also if its presence could explain the move away from mainstream or established party voting. Importantly, the two main types of radical populist party support were available in the two case studies, offering an opportunity to test whether insecurity was associated with both RPR and RPL (see the methodological appendix for the full list of parties).

The first hypothesis, which posited that voting for established parties—social democrats and Christian democrats—was negatively associated with precarity of tenure and/or precarity at work, was confirmed in the two countries. The study found that insecurity at work significantly reduced the odds of voting for established parties in the Netherlands, while in France tenure insecurity appeared to be the most significant factor in reducing the odds of voting for established parties. Both precarity of tenure and precarity at work were associated with voting for the political extremes, evidencing that perceived precarity at least partly explained why people were less likely to vote for established parties in these countries. The estimated marginal impact of precarity at work on the probability of voting for established parties in the Netherlands ranged between −5 and −10 percentage points, with the confidence interval consistently below zero (which would denote no marginal impact). Broadly the same range of values was found for the marginal impact of precarity of tenure on the probability of voting for established parties in France. The results confirmed that subjective insecurity, in general, pulls voters away from establishment parties.[18] In France, precarity of tenure was more significant in this process, possibly as a result of the contextual rise in temporary employment illustrated in chapter 2. In the Netherlands, the significant association concerned insecurity in work conditions, which could be an effect of the decline in some features of work—for example, the decline in work–life balance in the country, as discussed in chapter 2. Overall, it appears that the political detachment from mainstream parties was attached to the most socially relevant quality of insecurity present in each case study.

The second hypothesis delved deeper, proposing that precarity of tenure and/or precarity at work were positively associated with voting for both the RPR and the radical left (RL) in both countries. (Note that I use radical left rather than RPL here, as, in addition to the major populist left party, La France Insoumise, there are a number of minor yet established radical left parties in these countries—see the methodological appendix for more details.) The analysis showed that insecurity was associated with voting choices, although the "precarity effect" varied across the two countries and depended on the specific dimension of precarity (tenure or precarity at work) and the type of radical support (radical right or radical left). Interestingly, precarity at work seemed to have similar effects on the odds of voting for either the radical right or the radical left: In both countries, the probability increased by a factor of two to three.

Insecurity of tenure increased the odds of voting for the radical right in particular. This effect was particularly pronounced in France, where precarity of tenure (or fear of job loss) increased the likelihood of voting for the radical populist right by a factor of 7.5. The findings were revealing of a relationship between precarity and voting for radical parties, especially in France, where other parties that were aligned with flexible labor market agendas (Macron's En Marche) appeared in the electoral system without attracting the votes of those who experienced insecurity, as voting for En Marche was actually negatively associated with both forms of precarity. Figures 5.2 and 5.3 depict the results, respectively, for RPR and RL voters in the Netherlands and France to illustrate the intensity of the effect of insecurity on voting.

Overall, the research found that in both nations, work-related insecurity was negatively correlated with voting for established parties and positively correlated with voting for RPR and RPL parties. Furthermore, the investigation indicated that insecurity in work conditions was more significant in explaining voting support than the more widely investigated "precarity of tenure," as shown in figures 5.2 and 5.3. In France, both forms of insecurity (tenure and conditions-related) were positively associated with voting for the National Front (an RPR party), while insecurity in work conditions was positively associated with voting for La France Insoumise (an RPL party) in particular. This confirms the idea that the

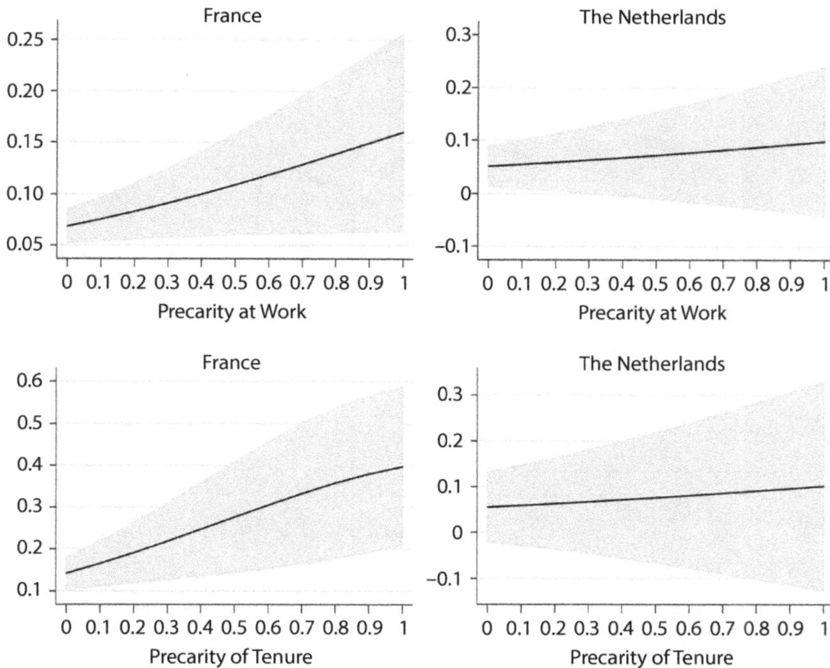

FIGURE 5.2. Association between work insecurity (precarity at work and precarity of tenure) and radical populist right voting. Estimated marginal impact of precarity at work and precarity of tenure on the probability of voting for radical populist right parties in odds ratio. Gray areas indicate confidence intervals. *Source*: Lorenza Antonucci et al., "What's Work Got to Do with It? How Precarity Influences Radical Party Support in France and the Netherlands," *Sociological Research Online* 28, no. 1 (2023): 125.

National Front, through its horizontal oppositional political frame, was able to co-opt support from a broad segment of the population affected by precarity in tenure and work conditions, while the RL attracted support from voters with precarious work conditions. It is also relevant to note that in the Netherlands, only insecurity of work conditions was positively correlated with support for RPR and RL parties, possibly because contracts with nonregular tenure are taken up voluntarily, which results in lower experiences of job tenure insecurity overall (see chapter 2).

This study positioned the rise of populist-right support within the broader framework of voters moving away from establishment-party support and toward radical-party support, whether that was for a left-wing or a right-wing party. The findings indicated that research on insecurity should look beyond labor market outsiders as populist supporters and showed that labor market insiders' declining work conditions explained

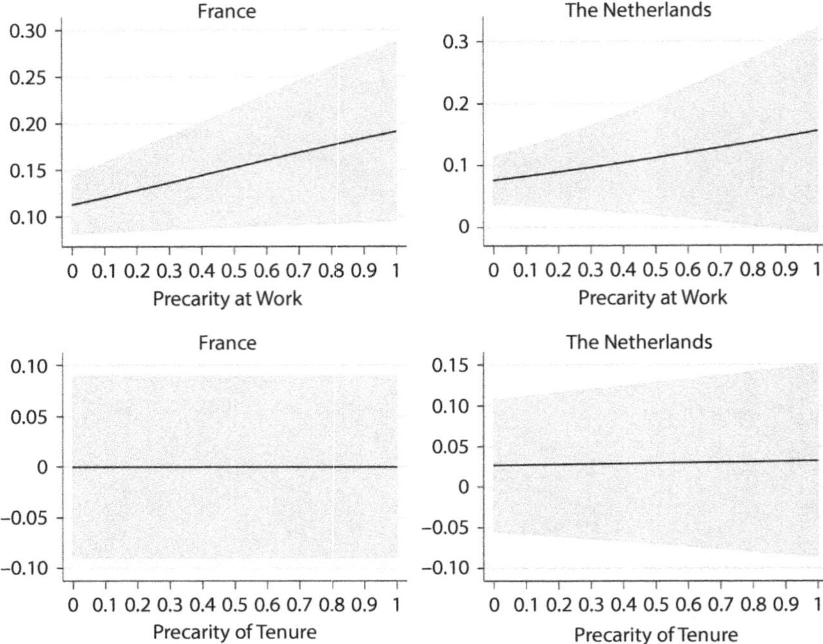

FIGURE 5.3. Association between work insecurity (precarity at work and precarity of tenure) and radical left voting. Estimated marginal impact of precarity at work and precarity of tenure on the probability of voting for radical left parties in odds ratio. Gray areas indicate confidence intervals. *Source*: "What's Work Got to Do with It? How Precarity Influences Radical Party Support in France and The Netherlands," *Sociological Research Online* 28, no. 1 (2023): 126.

populist support more than tenure-related insecurity. This research confirmed, as illustrated in the analytical framework in chapter 4, that work-related insecurity drives support toward not only the RPR but also the RPL—indicating that populism relates to an outlook that cuts across the left and right divide. Furthermore, this study suggested that insecurity also explains the move away from established and mainstream political support: Work-related insecurity is not just leading to rising support for populist parties but also pulling voters away from established parties.

The research left several unexplained issues in relation to the theoretical discussion presented in chapter 4. First, the study did not clarify why the two types of insecurity affected populism differently across the two countries. One could suspect that the different way in which insecurity was associated with voting choices in the two countries reflects the various forms and qualities in which precarity features across them: as insecurity in tenure and work conditions in France, and mostly as insecurity in the work–life balance in the Netherlands, as evidenced in chapter 2. Furthermore—and representing an important limitation of this study—insecurity was only investigated in relation to work, meaning that the analysis of precarity focused on working voters and left out a big portion of our respondents. Second, the study could not shed light on how the presence of populist parties influenced the effect of insecurity on populist voting, as it included only two cases, each with a significant offer of populist parties. What was happening in countries that did not have such a rich offer of populist parties? Were voters still likely to have a propensity to hold populist views in the presence of insecurity?

To address these questions, and generalize the results to more countries, data on voting and insecurity was collected during the EU Parliament elections in 2019 through an online survey called the European Voter Election Study (EVES), round 1. This new study covered ten countries (including eight of the case studies analyzed in the rest of this book)—namely, France, Germany, Hungary, Italy, the Netherlands, Poland, Spain, Sweden, Austria, and Romania—and aimed to test whether the connection between insecurity and populist voting found in the previous study could be generalized across security regimes. The study, which I coauthored with my colleague Andrei Zhirnov, introduced two innovations: First, it investigated financial insecurity in addition to work-related insecurity; and, second, it tested the link between insecurity and populist outlook, in addition to voting, to explore how insecurity was linked to populism regardless of the presence of RPR and RPL parties in the country.[19] Up to this point, the literature investigating insecurity in relation to voting had operationalized insecurity as related to work (whether it was measured as the risk of losing one's job or as insecurity in work conditions) and therefore excluded the potential insecurity experienced by those who are not involved in formal and paid work, such as those in education, retired and unemployed individuals, and those who provide unpaid care work.[20]

A comprehensive list of variables to investigate insecurity was compiled and divided into factors using both theoretical considerations and exploratory factor analysis. The study measured work-related insecurity among the respondents who reported being employed through a multidimensional operationalization of insecurity in work conditions that strongly resembled the one used in the study of the Netherlands and France. These measures included autonomy at work, work–life balance, and perceived adequacy of income (see table 5.2), which, as indicated in chapter 1, represent different forms of work-related security: Autonomy at work is an operationalization of how autonomous the worker is vis-à-vis employers/managers and represents a core aspect of security in the features of work; work–life balance is an indicator of the ability of the worker to engage in nonwork activities during the week and not work during unsociable hours; and perceived adequacy of income features is a proxy of work-related income security. These items capture the multidimensional nature of insecurity in work conditions introduced in chapter 1.

In addition to the two forms of work-related insecurity, this study offered the opportunity to test for the first time the political effect of financial insecurity through an ample array of items that clustered together via factor analysis. The operationalization of financial insecurity was aligned with what I illustrated in chapter 1 to be the main dimensions of financial security in Europe. In particular, the items of financial precarity listed in table 5.2 captured the presence or lack of deprivation in relation to basic needs (e.g., being able to pay for all required dental work); whether individuals were able to cover necessary expenses; whether they could respond to unexpected expenses (e.g., not having the money to repair or replace broken household goods); and whether they had savings that could help in navigating insecurity. These measures could take in a broad range of insecure groups, as they investigate the political effects of financial concerns that may be more prevalent than extreme experiences of poverty and social exclusion. The other advantage of exploring financial insecurity is the possibility of investigating insecurity for the entirety of the sample instead of focusing only on the working voters.[21]

The second important innovation was that, as well as investigating populist voting, the study took account of whether the respondents had a populist outlook, as per the ideational approach to populism. As illustrated in chapter 4, with this approach, a populist outlook emerges from the combination of three populist views—that is, people-centrism, a negative view of the elites, and a dualist view of good and bad (a Manichean outlook) (see the full list of items in the methodological appendix).[22] This allowed us to test the generalizability of the association between insecurity and populism across countries, despite the variation in the number of populist parties in the ten countries considered, as, in addition to investigating the link between insecurity and RPR/RPL voting, the analysis examined the link between insecurity and holding populist views (see the full list of parties in the methodological appendix).

Based on the framework illustrated in the previous chapter, the study tested two hypotheses regarding the relationship between subjective insecurity and populism. The first was that people experiencing work and/or

Table 5.2. Measures of Financial and Work-Related Insecurity

Measure	Items/questions
Financial precarity	During the next year, how likely is it that there will be some periods when you don't have enough money to cover the necessary expenses for your household? (FI1) I don't have savings for unexpected financial expenses. (FI2) I don't have enough money to do all the recommended dental work. (FI3) I don't have enough money to replace or repair broken electrical goods such as a refrigerator or washing machine. (FI4)
Precarity of tenure	How anxious are you about being dismissed without good reason? (PT1) Agree/disagree: I fear I might be fired in the near future. (PT2) Agree/disagree: My total hours of paid employment are likely to decrease in the next six months. (PT3) How likely is it that during the next year you will be unemployed and looking for work for at least a month? (PT4)
Precarity at work	Agree/disagree: I have freedom to take decisions in my work. (PW1) Agree/disagree: I have a satisfactory balance between work and other activities in my life. (PW2) Agree/disagree: My salary reflects my responsibilities. (PW3)

financial precarity were more likely to have a populist outlook (measured as the three attitudes just listed), while the second postulated that people experiencing work and/or financial precarity were more likely to vote for RPR and RPL parties. Work and financial insecurity were both hypothesized to have an effect on voting among workers who had replied to both sets of questions, while only financial insecurity was hypothesized to have an effect on voting among those who were not in paid work and who only replied to the financial precarity questions. In the model, the relationship between precarity, populist outlook, and voting was mediated by political and institutional conditions and included control variables to account for them (see the methodological appendix).

The findings broadly proved these hypotheses and also indicated which forms of insecurity were more relevant for various forms of populism. The study found a strong association between individual financial insecurity and work-related insecurity, and having populist views. In particular, there was a significant positive association between financial insecurity and all three populist views across the countries covered, although this link was somewhat weaker for the dualist view of good and evil. These findings can be explained by the fact that, as postulated in the theoretical framework in chapter 4, the theoretical connection between insecurity and populist views derives from how insecurity bonds individuals together in the social construction of the people as opposed to the secure elites; based on the framework I set, the Manichean outlook is derived from the other two central populist beliefs (i.e., people centrality and opposition between the people and the elites), and in fact this particular populist view was considered secondary when compared to people-centrism and the people versus the elites.

Regarding the relationship between insecurity and populist ideas, while work-related insecurity was significant with respect to populist attitudes, the insecurity of work conditions appeared to have a stronger effect than the insecurity of one's tenure, confirming what was found in the previous study. In general, the findings confirmed a positive and strong association between subjective insecurity (in particular, financial insecurity and precarity at work) and the populist outlook of voters.

Finally, concerning the link between precarity and voting, a clear positive and significant association between precarity and voting for RPR and RPL parties was found in almost all of the cases, as shown in figure 5.4. Financial insecurity was clearly linked with populist voting: The more financially insecure people were, the more likely they were to vote for populist parties of the left and right. While work-related precarity was also associated with populist voting, the results for eight of the ten case studies considered in this book indicated that precarity at work has a greater effect on populist voting than precarity of tenure.

In most countries, the positive association between populist attitudes and precarity translated into a positive association between the populist vote and precarity, except for in the case of right-wing populist parties in Poland and Hungary. How can we explain this difference? As discussed in chapters 2 and 4, the Eastern security regime represents an exception in the political analysis of the postsecurity shift in welfare-state interventions: Welfare politics is not likely to attract political support in post-Soviet countries among insecure voters because of the skepticism toward state interventions. In Poland and Hungary, there are populist parties that have been in power for several years and offered distinct solutions to address socioeconomic insecurity—a welfare chauvinist and familistic one in Poland, and a market-oriented one in Hungary—but whose political discourses in both cases have relied heavily on national security issues. It

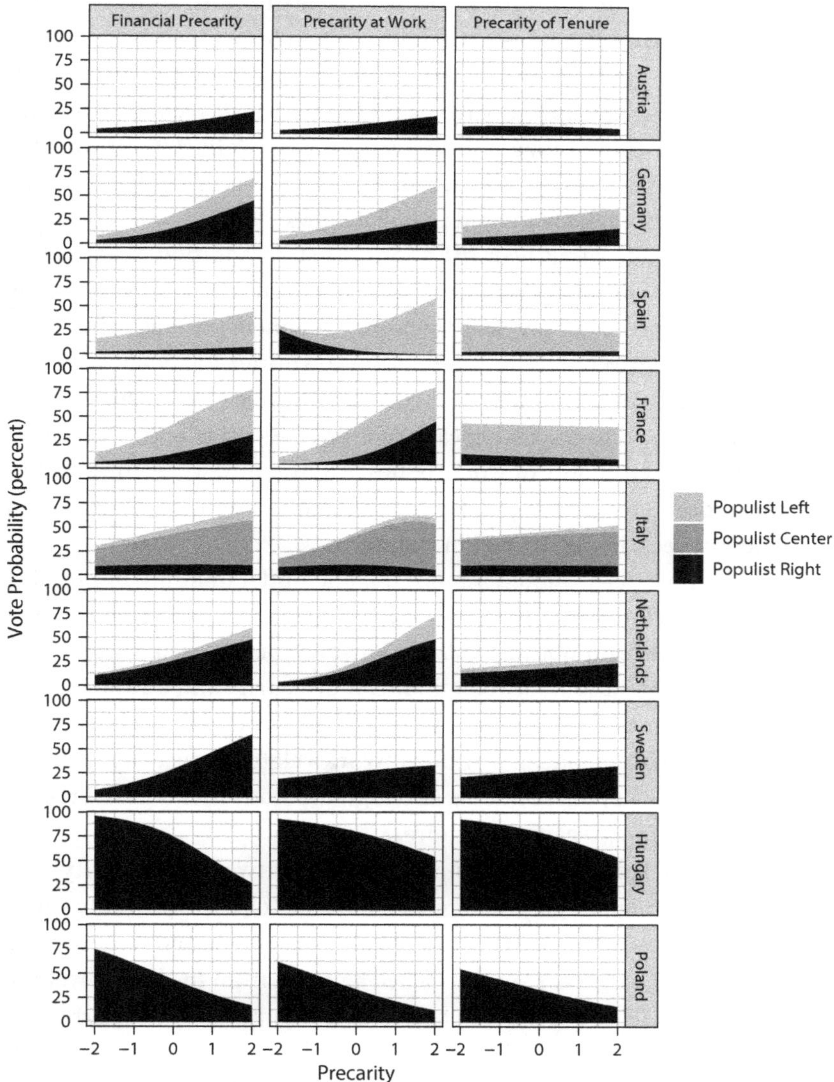

FIGURE 5.4. Probabilities of voting for populist parties based on financial insecurity, precarity of tenure, and precarity at work out of sample predictions of multinomial logit models of the probabilities of voting for populist left and populist right parties. Horizontal axes show the standardized values of the precarity measures: One unit on this axis is one standard deviation in the subsample. All other variables are set to their means or modes. *Source*: Andrei Zhirnov, Lorenza Antonucci et al., "Precarity and Populism: Explaining Populist Outlook and Populist Voting in Europe Through Subjective Financial and Work-Related Insecurity," *European Sociological Review* 40, no. 4 (2024): 714. *Image credit*: Creative Commons CC BY.

is not just a matter of agendas. As mentioned in chapter 4, it is not at all evident that insecure voters in Eastern European countries have a preference for the partially state-based solution to address insecurity offered by, for example, PiS in Poland. Hence, RPR parties' insecurity agendas in the Eastern security regime, perhaps due to its Soviet past, do not offer enough ground to mobilize political support on welfare politics, even though the analysis importantly found that more insecure individuals living there were more likely to hold populist views.

The study made several contributions. First, in addition to extending the two dimensions of work-related precarity used in the previous study (precarity of tenure and precarity at work), a dimension was introduced that had been entirely missing in relation to voting: financial precarity. The introduction of these indicators reflected the need to transpose to the political realm, and test, sociologically relevant issues, including insecurity emerging from the quality of work (issues of autonomy, work–life balance, intensification, etc.) and the independent role of financial insecurity in influencing precarity, as defined in chapter 1.

Second, this study offered a more holistic understanding of populist support that, in line with the framework outlined in chapter 4, considered populist outlook, and not just voting. The analysis showed a significant and positive association between financial insecurity and all the dimensions of populist outlook across the countries considered, with a weaker association for Manichaean attitudes. Work-related insecurity was also associated with a populist outlook, although the study found mixed results on the effect of the precarity of tenure.

Third, this research examined the link between insecurity and populism in a much larger number of countries than the previous study, with significant variation in the types of political systems and welfare-state systems, although the case studies lacked a nation from the liberal welfare regime, as the UK could not be used to examine populist support given its electoral system. The study did generalize the findings from the previous research on France and the Netherlands, and it found a consistent positive association between populist outlook and insecurity, as well as a variation in the estimated effect of insecurity across countries and parties. Insecurity about the tenure of work tends to attract significant interest in explorations of insecurity in populism. However, the results of this study showed that the biggest effects of insecurity in relation to both populist outlook and voting came from financial insecurity and insecurity in work conditions rather than precarity of job tenure, which had been the focus of research on insecurity and populism up to this point.[23] Job tenure seemed to have a conditioning effect on the association between the other two aspects of precarity and populism, but its direct relation to populism was relatively weak.

The research was also affected by an important limitation. The analyses presented were all based on weighted online datasets. These are not probability sampling datasets, but they employ weights to mimic the distribution of individuals in census/probability sampling datasets and are widely used in political science when reliability tests are performed. They allow ad hoc/new insecurity indicators to be tested—something that is not possible with classic probability sampling datasets. On the other hand, probability sampling datasets offer the most reliable distribution of personal characteristics and voting information in the population. As there is a lack of probability sampling datasets that offer both political voting data and data on work and financial insecurity in the way I define it here, the research I will present next proposed an alternative solution: Use statistics to match two datasets.

The Gendered Effect of Insecurity on Populism

The next step I pursued with my collaborators, particularly with Roberta Di Stefano, was to analyze the relationship between work precarity and support for populist parties in Europe by combining two data sources: the European Social Survey (ESS) and the European Working Conditions Survey (EWCS).[24] The ESS contains useful measures on voting and a measure of financial insecurity, while the EWCS, as mentioned in chapter 2, includes several dimensions of insecurity in tenure but also dimensions of insecurity in the features of work, which were used, postmatching, in combination with political variables in the ESS. The procedure for conducting statistical matching was complex and multistage, as, instead of matching the two datasets through average-based imputation, this study used synthetic statistical matching through computational methods to match individuals one by one based on common demographic characteristics (see the methodological appendix).

As indicated by table 5.3, a number of items that are used to measure work pressure (tight deadlines, high-speed routines, and health outcomes) and a series of items that capture job dissatisfaction (which include career prospects, recognition at work, and appropriate pay) were included in the analysis. Job dissatisfaction contains elements (unfair pay, bad prospects, no recognition) that bridge the divide between economic and cultural explanations, to capture not just the material aspects of work, but also the extrinsic meaning and value of work conditions in society. Furthermore,

Table 5.3. Measures of Work-Related Insecurity: High Pressure and Job Dissatisfaction

		Factor
Do you think your health or safety is at risk because of your work?		High pressure
Does your work affect your health?		High pressure
Does your job involve working at very high speed?		High pressure
Does your job involve working to tight deadlines?		High pressure
To what extent do you agree or disagree with the following statements about your job?	Considering all my efforts and achievements in my job, I feel I get paid appropriately.	Job dissatisfaction
	My job offers good prospects for career advancement.	Job dissatisfaction
	I receive the recognition I deserve for my work.	Job dissatisfaction

the ESS contained an item that investigated financial insecurity by asking whether individuals were finding it comfortable, were coping, or were finding it difficult or very difficult on their present income.

The discussion of insecurity and support for populism often brings in the role of gender, particularly in relation to how work conditions, and work recognition in particular, shape resentment among men. Numerous studies have stressed that gender has a key role in the likelihood and direction of populist voting, with men being more likely to vote for RPR parties in particular.[25] Noam Gidron and Peter Hall, for example, found that the rise in right-wing populism was due to a loss of status among men, which they suspected to be the result of an increase in work precariousness among this section of the population.[26] Their economic and cultural understanding of insecurity drew from research by Lamont, which underlined the central role that dignity at work, and work more generally, has in the social construction of working-class men's worth and security.[27]

As men are more likely to vote for populist parties,[28] the role that insecurity plays in driving women toward populist support has gained less attention in the literature. While there is a gender gap in voting for RPR parties, a large portion of women support populist voting: In earlier elections, women constituted around one-third of populist-right voters, while for the most recent populist momentum, they have accounted for 40 percent or more of the votes for RPR parties, and women are also eager supporters of populist-left parties.[29] As so much more attention has been given to men, we have a much clearer idea of which components of insecurity drive populist support among them, whereas we have very little understanding of what motivates women to vote in this way.[30]

In our model, insecurity did not seem at first to be associated with RPR or general populist voting, although a weak association did emerge between job dissatisfaction and voting for the RPL. The results changed when we measured the effects of insecurity separately according to gender. The model run on the matched dataset found a positive and strong significant association between job dissatisfaction and RPR voting and general populist voting, as well as a significant association between high work pressure and RPR voting among men. With the increase in work pressure among men, their probability of voting for populist-right parties increased from 14 percent to 18 percent, while their probability of voting for right-wing populism in the presence of job dissatisfaction increased from 12 percent to almost 20 percent. This indicates that work-related insecurity is associated with RPR voting among men, particularly in the shape of job dissatisfaction, while the effect of more extreme forms of insecurity (high work pressure) is more limited. Most important, the results of the study highlighted the relevance of another dimension of insecurity that is associated with support toward populism among women, while considering (and controlling for) both types of insecurity (work and financial). Women who found it difficult or very difficult to live on their present income appeared to be more likely to vote for populist parties in general, and finding it difficult or very difficult to cope on present income increased women's probability of voting for populist parties (of all types) from 18 percent to 25 percent.

How can we explain this difference? For women, the type of insecurity that is associated with populism might be financial because the financial management of the household and the financially related repercussions of work-based insecurity are highly gendered.[31] Furthermore, for women, work-related conditions might not be as strongly linked with a sense of self-worth, and thus subsequent feelings of insecurity, not least because women are more likely to be in unpaid work than men. Overall, these findings indicate that the political relevance of insecurity to populist voting is likely to be gendered. Work insecurity resonates more with men, possibly due to the role that work participation has in determining men's worth, while women are particularly affected by financial insecurity in their populist voting choices, possibly because they experience insecurity more directly through the pressures on household income.

Insecurity and Alternating Between Voting and Nonvoting

Since 2020 there has been an acceleration in the pervasiveness of insecurity within European societies, fueled by Covid-19 and the cost-of-living crisis. Despite the fact that mainstream governments in power might have galvanized support around sensible and shared measures to combat the pandemic, support for populism remained stable and even increased after the lockdown period. New measures to address insecurity were implemented during the pandemic (see chapter 6), but this phase did not break the pattern of the rising support for populism in the medium term.

However, the economic crisis that occurred during the pandemic did generate some major shake-ups in insecurity. Drawing on the 2018 European Labour Force Survey, an early study attempted to measure the effect of Covid-19 lockdown measures on work. It found that there had been an increase in job tenure insecurity and a decline in work conditions among a group of manual workers (estimated at 10 percent of the total workforce) in sectors with the highest contagion risk (hospitality, personal services, leisure activities) and indicated that those in service sectors would have been less affected by these changes.[32] A qualitative report on remote working during Covid-19 found that—during the pandemic, at least—opinions of the impact of lockdowns on job quality were split between those finding that working from home increased their satisfaction and productivity and allowed for a better work–life balance, and those whose work was affected by isolation, higher work intensity, and higher care responsibilities typical of remote work.[33] Research conducted in Europe among service sector workers suggested that Covid-19 dramatically altered the work–life balance for women and led to a steep decline in work conditions for women with children in particular, with mothers having to change their working hours and hence experiencing changes to work pressure and other elements of work.[34] Other studies on the financial impact of the pandemic in Europe have suggested that, on the one hand, the pandemic had the effect of equalizing income and hence reducing income inequality, while, on the other, it increased socioeconomic inequalities by reinforcing the gap between those with and those without the financial resources to face the pandemic.[35] Furthermore, economic anxiety became much more common during Covid-19 and was as high as health anxiety.[36] Overall, the studies highlighted changes—if not increases—to work and financial insecurity.

Given this reconfiguration of insecurity, and potential further mainstream diffusion of insecurity during the pandemic, having a panel of

Table 5.4. Measures of Work and Financial Insecurity in the Longitudinal Panel

Insecurity of tenure	I fear I might be dismissed in the near future. I fear I am not working enough according to my managers. My total hours of paid employment are likely to decrease in the next six months. It will be easy for me to find a job with another employer with roughly the same income and benefits I have now.
Insecurity of work conditions	I usually get paid if I miss a day of work. My work is constantly controlled by my managers. I am autonomous in my work decisions. My work–life balance is satisfactory. I have satisfactory opportunities for career advancement.
Financial precarity	I am anxious about managing my daily expenses. I can easily meet my current financial obligations and pay my debts. I have enough savings and/or external support to manage a short-term loss of income. I do not have savings for unexpected financial expenses. I cannot have a holiday away from home for one week a year, not staying with relatives. I cannot do all recommended dental work. I do not have enough money to replace or repair broken electrical goods such as a refrigerator or washing machine.

respondents who had answered questions on work and financial insecurity before the pandemic (2018) and after its most dramatic phase (in 2022) permitted an investigation, in a study coauthored with Di Stefano and other collaborators, of how these changes had affected populist voting among nonvoters, voters for established parties, and voters for populist parties (see the methodological appendix for more details).[37] The questions used to investigate work and financial insecurity were very similar to the items used in the previous studies, as illustrated in table 5.4. The operationalization of financial insecurity was even more comprehensive, as, in addition to the dimensions of insecurity reported in our previous study indicated in table 5.3, there was an item on having enough savings to manage a short-term loss of income as well as one for financial anxiety.

The study analyzed the same samples of people across the six case studies discussed previously (Italy, Spain, Sweden, Germany, the Netherlands, and France), representing examples of the Southern European, Nordic, and continental security regimes.

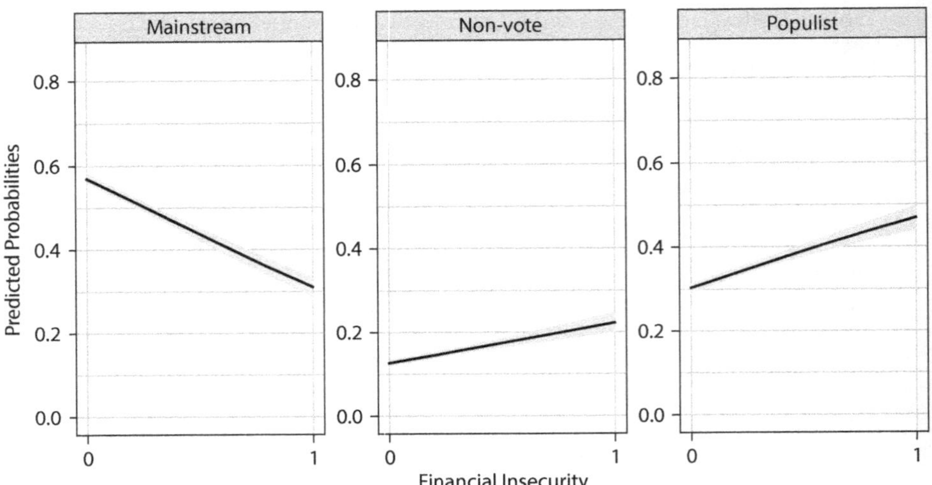

FIGURE 5.5. Correlation between the evolution of financial insecurity and voting for mainstream parties, voting for populist parties, and nonvoting (entire population, no conditions). Predictions of multinomial log-linear models. Horizontal axes show the standardized values of the insecurity measure; vertical axes indicate the predicted probability for mainstream voting, nonvoting, and total populist voting. Gray areas indicate confidence intervals.

Confirming what I reported previously for the prepandemic era, lower financial insecurity, overall, was associated with voting for mainstream and established parties. Importantly, the analysis revealed that those who experienced higher financial insecurity had a higher probability of both voting for populist parties and nonvoting after the pandemic (see fig. 5.5). The second major finding is that insecurity was associated with an intriguing switching of positions: Those who were nonvoting before the Covid-19 pandemic were more likely to vote for a populist party if they experienced financial insecurity during the pandemic, while those who had voted for populist parties before the pandemic were more likely not to vote if they experienced financial insecurity during it.

The model that examined the probability of voting after the pandemic among those who had voted for populist parties before it indicated a positive and significant association with voting for populist parties after Covid-19 in the presence of financial insecurity and an even bigger positive association with nonvoting, as evidenced by figure 5.6. Again, this result indicates that switching between nonvoting and populist voting is particularly driven by financial insecurity.

Did the same apply to work-related insecurity? This phenomenon in both of its forms—higher rates of insecurity at work and fear of losing

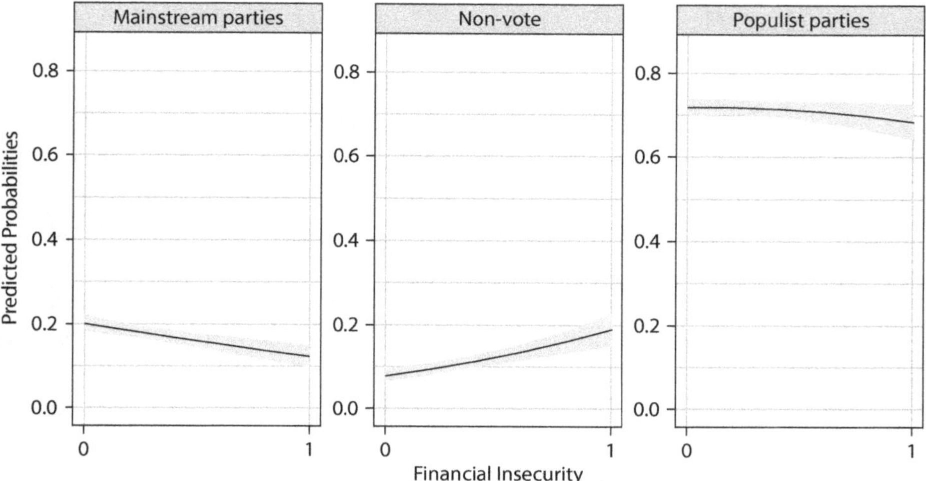

FIGURE 5.6. Correlation between the evolution of financial insecurity and voting for mainstream parties, voting for populist parties, and nonvoting among those who voted for populist parties before Covid-19. Predictions of multinomial log-linear models. Horizontal axes show the standardized values of the precarity measure; vertical axes indicate the predicted probability for mainstream voting, nonvoting, and total populist voting (with the conditional probability that voters have voted for populist parties before Covid-19). Gray areas indicate confidence intervals.

one's job, as discussed in the previous chapter—was in general associated with a greater probability of nonvoting and voting for populist parties after the pandemic and therefore behaved similarly to financial insecurity. Examining the associations between work-related insecurity and populist voting among those who voted for populist parties before the pandemic, significant and positive associations were found between insecurity and voting for populist parties and insecurity and nonvoting, but only in the presence of insecurity of work conditions. This finding confirmed the results from previous research, as, in those studies, too, insecurity at work was a form of instability that was more likely to drive populist voting than the insecurity of losing one's job, while financial insecurity presents the strongest association with populist support. Having used a longitudinal panel of voters, this study established an even stronger association between both types of insecurity (in finances and work conditions) and populist voting. Furthermore, the findings indicated that work insecurity and financial insecurity are likely to cause people to alternate between supporting populist parties and nonvoting.

Summary

Each study presented in this chapter offered a slightly different operationalization of work and financial insecurity, which progressively broadened the way insecurity is conceptualized in relation to voting. The cases demonstrated consistent and pervasive associations between insecurity and populist views, insecurity and total populist voting, and insecurity and RPR and RPL voting. Overall, stronger associations were found for RPR than for RPL voting, although those with the latter were also present and related sometimes to the same dimensions (e.g., financial insecurity), but also to slightly different forms of work-related precarity, such as work pressure.

The findings confirmed the hypothesis that in an environment in which insecurity is highly widespread both at work and financially, individuals who are more insecure are more likely to hold populist views. This makes sense, given that a populist view emphasizes the presence of a uniform mass of (insecure) people versus the secure and protected elites. Indeed, insecurity is associated in particular with populist views/discourses around people-centrism and anti-elitism, regardless of the actual presence of populist parties. The effect of insecurity on populist voting patterns is also gendered: Changes to work conditions and recognition at work are drivers of populist voting for men due to the extrinsic nature of work in our society, while financial insecurity is a driver of populist voting for women, possibly because it has a more direct effect on shaping women's insecurity.

While the insecurity related to the risk of unemployment tends to attract a lot of interest in the debate about insecurity and populism, the results of the empirical analysis consistently indicate that, among all the aspects of insecurity, financial insecurity and insecurity in work conditions present the strongest and most consistent associations in relation to both populist outlook and populist voting. This suggests that the seeds of populist support are to be found not in the growth of unemployment or the lack of a stable job per se, but in voters' everyday experiences of instability in relation to their finances and work conditions. Finally, the research using longitudinal data indicates that in the presence of insecurity, there is a proximity between nonvoters and voters for populist parties, who switch between the two conditions, unsatisfied with what each political choice brings to address their state of uncertainty. If none of the available options (mainstream voting, populist voting, and nonvoting) convincingly appeals to voters who are experiencing growing insecurity, how can the new politics of insecurity offer a viable political response?

CHAPTER SIX

The Future of the Politics of Insecurity

CANVASSING—AN ACTIVITY UNDERTAKEN by volunteers who go door to door to propose a party's agenda to potential voters face-to-face—can be a humbling experience for those who wish to see how their favored party's agenda interacts with the electorate. In 2019 I was canvassing in Dudley, a rundown area on the outskirts of Birmingham that, from Brexit onward, had passed from supporting the mainstream left (Labour) to becoming one of the bastions of antiestablishment politics. Knocking on people's doors and briefly entering their porches, I gathered glimpses of people's housing conditions and the kind of material struggles they were going through. The local party office had asked us to approach potential voters with a progressive macroeconomic plan, which my fellow canvassers and I were not able to dilute into measures that would tackle the sort of concerns we could see right in front of our faces. This left me pondering: Why do progressive political agendas privilege the use of economic-centered agendas over referring more directly to the conditions they are trying to address via their proposed economic solutions?

Not everybody sees populism as a destructive force for politics. For instance, despite recognizing the illiberal threat that populist leaders constitute when in power, Cas Mudde and Cristóbal Rovira Kaltwasser admitted that the rise of populism can lead to a (re)politicization of politics, given the focus on issues that the establishment has overlooked establishment.[1] According to Ernesto Laclau and Chantal Mouffe, it is precisely the lack of polarization and politicization in liberal democracies that has led to the rise of populism in the first place. For Laclau and Mouffe, populism has the positive effect of leading to a reappropriation of politics by the people through an explicit public acknowledgment of the winners and losers of the liberal policies that have been implemented.[2] While the popularity of populism can be considered a useful litmus test to assess the health of liberal democracies in responding to the needs and aspirations of voters, the view of populism as a conductor of inherent positive change is overly optimistic due to the toxic loop that has been set off by the dominant cultural frames of productivism. Due to the resonance of these influential cultural frames among the population, we are more likely to witness populism taking the form of horizontal oppositional politics than horizontal solidaristic populism, even within forms of populism, such as that of the populist left, that refer to vertical opposition.

In this chapter I examine the role that insecurity plays in the formation of the political script based on the assumption that all political actors are subjected to the new politics of insecurity, and I discuss, more prescriptively, how the political script can be directed toward solidaristic frames to overcome the toxic loop that has been ignited. I first look at the latest rise in insecurity through Covid-19 and the cost-of-living crisis, viewing it as a lost opportunity to channel insecurity into more solidaristic political solutions. I then examine the political effects of insecurity. I argue that while insecurity cannot be politically aggregated into a unique self-identified political group (the precariat), it influences politics in three main ways: It recenters politics from macro concerns to everyday lived experiences; it generates connections between material and cultural concerns; and it holds the potential for creating new solidaristic coalitions across class groups and countries. The final section consists of a prescriptive discussion of the two-pronged strategy that would be required to break the vicious circle of insecurity based on horizontal oppositional populism, which consists of a combined effort to introduce new cultural narratives in politics while implementing policy interventions that reduce the squeeze on the providers of security, and hence intervene in the family–market–state nexus.

Covid-19 as a Lost Opportunity to Change the Political Script

The economic crisis that occurred during Covid-19, and the subsequent cost-of-living crisis that is ongoing in Europe as I write, offered a window of opportunity for shifting policies and the potential to review how politics addresses people's socioeconomic uncertainty. Overall, Covid resulted in a new experimental phase of policymaking for many European countries, which either adopted temporary measures to address the rising financial and work insecurity or relaxed the conditions and means-testing criteria of existing policy tools. A few countries introduced new, extraordinary minimum-income schemes or extended existing schemes to address the spike of financial insecurity during the pandemic, given the lack of cash-based transfers in European welfare states. Italy had begun a citizen scheme before Covid-19 targeted at those with low income that was used as the inspiration for a means-tested form of support, which was introduced in 2020 to help households in extreme poverty that were excluded from existing benefits (the emergency income). In a similar way, Greece offered temporary and non-means-tested support for those who could not access long-term unemployment benefits, while extraordinary allowances were also introduced for students/young people in France and children in Austria and Portugal.[3]

Policy initiatives were also adopted to limit insecurity of tenure, which spiked during the pandemic. Seventeen countries in Europe instituted job retention schemes—namely, short-term work schemes that subsidized hours not worked, and wage subsidies that provided a subsidy for the hours worked or topped up the earnings of workers on reduced hours.[4] These measures were able to maintain work security and limit financial insecurity for households, and they filled some of the gaps for those who could not access the existing schemes. While this was a phase of emergency-led experimentation that introduced temporary policy tools to address insecurity for European states, the pandemic did not result in a more fundamental rethinking of the political script in relation to the role of the market and the state in addressing insecurity.

The new temporary schemes and wage subsidies were generally funded exclusively by the state, in contrast with preexisting furlough schemes, which were funded through unemployment insurance funds (publicly managed, but from a mix of funding from the state, employees, and employers), and hence did not fundamentally lead to a rebalance of the state–market mix.[5] The choice governments made to subsidize temporary schemes and wage subsidies through state funding and without asking for support from companies themselves reveals the double function that job retention schemes had during Covid-19: They did not serve just as a form of protection in favor of workers to limit work insecurity, as they also aimed to protect the market from potential losses that could generate a chain of bankruptcies and a possible recession spiral. Though the balance between the economic and social focus varied across regimes, the continental and Southern regimes placed a market logic at the center, and liberal countries used both logics, while only the Nordic countries put the social logic first.[6] Hence, job protection schemes—even if they appeared to be a new, experimental way of providing social protection—reflected the logic of the state operating as a mechanism of security for markets and supporting individuals because doing so stabilizes the market, as discussed in chapter 3. The adoption of job retention schemes was followed by a debate on their potential misuse by companies, though only a minority of countries put a ban on the use of such schemes in the presence of profit-sharing and an increase in bonuses.[7] To sum up, the strategy to address insecurity in European countries remains overall one based on corporate welfare.

If countries reproduced the same policy script during the pandemic, did the Covid-19 phase lead to a dramatic shift in the logic and practices of EU policies? During 2010–2014, as discussed in chapter 3, new governance procedures, new discourses, and new EU strategies and recommendations led to the spread of financial and work insecurity across Europe, while the second phase of EU policies (2014–2020) did not introduce radical changes. As a result of the complex economic shocks generated by Covid-19, the EU used two new flagship instruments to address the socioeconomic issues from the crisis: SURE and NextGenerationEU.

Designed to support the endeavor of funding member states' job retention schemes, the SURE initiative has been labeled as one of the key pillars of the shift toward a return to Social Europe. Standing for "Support to Mitigate Unemployment Risks in an Emergency," SURE consisted of a share of financial assistance based on national income in the shape of loans from the EU to member states. The loans sustained the expenditure that member states had to incur to support markets and would have consequently saved, according to EU estimates, approximately 2.5 million firms and even more jobs. Within the EU, the adoption of SURE was considered a victory for Social Europe because it overcame the resistance of the most frugal member states to the benefit of Southern European countries, which could access a more favorable form of debt than is generally available to them.[8] While SURE might have helped to rebalance the long-standing skewed power dynamics between the core and the periphery of Europe, the effects on the people living in the periphery are less clear: SURE consisted simply of a loan to be returned and did not result in a redistribution of resources within the EU. It can be viewed, first and foremost, as an inexpensive and temporary macroeconomic tool to protect national markets from an ongoing crisis in order to avoid the risk of it spreading to the rest of Europe, targeted at the most unstable labor markets.

The other tool the EU used to address the social emergency of the pandemic was the NextGenerationEU (NGEU) package, which was launched in 2020 and put more money into the European market to avoid the risk of a spiraling crisis. NGEU was essentially a macroeconomic response, but, as discussed in chapter 3, the macroeconomic side of EU policies can have deep indirect effects on the social realm. NGEU was advertised as distinct from the austerity responses adopted in the Eurocrisis, but did it result in a substantial shift?[9] Despite being presented as a response to the economic and *social* damage caused by the crisis, the NGEU did not allocate resources per se to the social sphere.[10] Its main function was to release funding that member states could use to overcome the economic and social crisis triggered by Covid-19. The support offered by the EU during the Eurocrisis was conditional on reducing social programs, while the Recovery and Resilience Facility—the main mechanism of NGEU—was conditional on the final goal of achieving Europe's new growth strategy and the New Deal while still being attached to the overall prescriptions of the New Economic Governance established since 2008.[11]

Although no conditional rule for reducing social spending was set, no specific social targets were set either to support the socioeconomic damage triggered by Covid-19, as the focus was on economic growth. Its size and implications for member states have also been widely exaggerated, as the support received amounted to 1.8 percent of GDP and was always in the shape of returnable loans, for which member states are ultimately responsible.[12] Most important, the debate on whether NGEU was successful remains truly and uniquely a discussion on whether it served to relaunch the economy.[13] Despite its evident limitations for the socioeconomic sphere, a number of optimistic scholars of the EU and contributors to EU policymaking have authored enthusiastic pieces on the relaunch of Social Europe based on an analysis of changes in governance structures, or citing the lighter conditionality of the macroeconomic tools used in the Covid-19 crisis.[14] Looking at the macroeconomic side, the EU is seen as a tool for buffering and increasing the resilience of the European markets, while we move farther and farther away from assessing the impact of adopting these new macroeconomic mechanisms on the financial and work security of those who live in Europe.

The studies on EU governance that have considered the *longue durée* effect of the new governance structure adopted since 2008 for work and labor, which, as I discussed, was merely temporarily paused during Covid-19, have reached different conclusions from those that have focused on the macroeconomic outcomes. Roland Erne and his colleagues' systematic investigation of the qualitative impact of EU recommendations found that a "commodifying policy script" persisted in public services and in EU structural reforms more generally, which was not reversed during Covid-19. Even the more expansionary prescriptions that have been adopted in public services since 2016 were "not to address pressing social concerns but to rebalance the EU economy and to boost its growth and competitiveness."[15] Trapped in an economic-centered political script, EU institutions appear incredulous when an increasing number of citizens are drawn to the pledges of Euroskeptic populist parties, as occurred at the EU Parliament elections in 2024. Could the new politics of insecurity be used to reverse this trend?

Give Us Work, but Give Us Security Too

At the beginning of the twentieth century, suffragists and defenders of workers' rights started to use the political motto "Give us bread, but give us roses too," to refer to their dual political demand for material security and the emotional sense of fulfillment that the right to vote for women would bring. Since then, the political motto "bread and roses" has been used in multiple instances to refer to how the demands of workers aspire to more than fulfilling the basic necessities for survival. To this day, this aspiration is a fundamental drive of political support. Slightly editing its original formulation, a contemporary version of this motto would be asking politics not only to continue to create jobs, but also to provide the kind of socioeconomic security that, as demonstrated in previous chapters, is associated with antiestablishment politics.

Considering the changes in the world of work and in financial security that have taken place in the past decades, it is not difficult to understand why the electorate no longer believes that mainstream and established politics brings them bread and roses. What is less obvious is why insecurity has not led to a clear aggregation of political interest—e.g., to a new political class of insecure individuals who self-identify as members of the precariat. Standing's book theorized that precarity also had the function of aggregating political preferences into a new social class called "the precariat."[16] Standing's notion of the precariat was inspired by a relatively small but very active world of radical-left movements from Southern Europe, particularly no-global, autonomous, and activist groups, like the San Precario movement of workers in Italy. Some of these initiatives led to a cross-national aggregation of political demands by individuals facing extreme precarity under the umbrella of the precariat, for instance through the Middlesex declaration of the European precariat from the European social forum. It is evident that the social strata that compose these radical-left groups, and the substrata of those who live with insecurity and hold a populist outlook, whom I discussed in the previous chapter, represent extremely different constituencies, not just for the types of insecurity they endure, but also for the degree of self-identification with the precariat, and the political meaning they attach to their conditions of precarity.

Despite these individual and episodic attempts, insecurity is not leading to a coherent political aggregation around a new social class of individuals in shared conditions of insecurity. The existence of "the precariat" in itself presupposes a replacement of traditional class divisions with a new social class who are aware that they are part of the precariat by virtue of the similar work and living conditions they face. Sociological research on class and precarity has found a much more nuanced and articulated relationship between precarity and stratification and has problematized the idea that, despite the increasingly commonplace experiences of insecurity, individuals could aggregate and identify with a single precarious class. In the Great British Class Survey led by Mike Savage, precarity features not once but twice: first, as a self-contained class of individuals (defined as the precariat) with low income and low economic status who conduct manual jobs and live in old industrial cities; and, second, to describe the condition of younger workers in the service sector with high cultural capital and limited economic capital who face additional costs of living and struggle to enter the housing market due to their lack of savings.[17]

Hence, over and above its capacity to aggregate people into a self-contained group (the precariat) with specific political preferences, precarity seems useful to understand the political implications of the social reproduction of inequalities. On the one hand, precarity does not affect just a marginalized part of the population experiencing extreme forms of job insecurity; on the other, the assumption that everyone experiencing forms of work precariousness would automatically become part of a unified class is disproved by the unequal distribution of resources to navigate insecure events and uncertain lives among these groups.

The rise of the populist left in Europe vindicates, in some respects, the idea that precarity can be used to aggregate political support. After all, in continental Europe, Die Linke and La France Insoumise have referred to insecurity in one form or another in their agendas and political strategies, while in Southern Europe the rise of Podemos has been traced back to the anti-austerity movements that started with Occupy and have been led by young precarious workers (see chapter 4). Despite the—in the case of Die Linke, short-term—gains made by RPL parties, the possibility of aggregating the demands of the precarious through an agenda explicitly focused on opposing insecurity has not yet materialized in a continuous way. In contrast to Jonathan Hopkin's suggestion that left-wing antisystem politics would be more successful in debtor countries of the South with precarious highly educated younger populations,[18] Southern Europe has experienced one of the most dramatic spikes in RPR support. In general, the most popular form of populist support in the various parts of Europe remains RPR support. Why is it so difficult to translate shared experiences of insecurity into solidaristic forms of politics?

At a basic level, as mentioned earlier, RPR parties' appeal is based on their capacity to channel discontent through oppositional discourses that emphasize horizontal divisions in society based on race, ethnicity, and evaluations of worth in contemporary capitalism (e.g., deserving and undeserving, productive and nonproductive). A political offer that is based on a horizontal oppositional discourse resonates more with voters today as compared to the interwar period because productivism and meritocracy have become dominant cultural frames.

The aggregation of insecurity into solidaristic politics is also prevented by the absence of contemporary political aggregators. The political scientist Alex Mierke-Zatwarnicki has analyzed how socialist parties and interwar fascists across Germany, the Netherlands, and Great Britain have aggregated political support to identify the conditions that lead to various forms of political aggregation. The findings of her research suggest that insecurity cannot aggregate political preferences into an organized party because, unlike what occurred during the formation of the working-class movement, the precariat lacks a large, stratified organized group that is able to aggregate interests in a solidaristic way, as unions did in the twentieth century.[19] Hence, even if insecurity could potentially constitute the background societal state for politicizable in-group formation, the conditions to politicize insecure individuals into in-group politics are currently lacking. In the absence of a unified and organized group, those who feel as if they are outside of mainstream politics are more likely to be drawn into a political script, like those formulated by RPR parties, that draws on horizontal oppositional hierarchies.

We should not expect from insecurity what insecurity cannot provide. Insecurity is just a primal state individuals live in that does not necessarily lead to support for political responses that can actually address insecurity. Even if insecurity cannot be aggregated into a single social and political class (the precariat), the positive association between insecurity and populist sentiments, as well as the negative association between insecurity and mainstream support, indicates three ways in which insecurity is changing the political realm.

First, insecurity leads to a micro foundation of politics in opposition to the macro focus that dominates established political discourses. If the educated left is particularly receptive to progressive agendas that aim to address macro issues, like unemployment or inequality,[20] the new politics of insecurity does not require such a level of abstraction, and it connects with the two primary drivers for generating political support—financial concerns and working conditions, given that work is where many people spend most of their lives. RPR and RPL parties have already mobilized this side of the politics of insecurity, as analyzed in depth in chapter 4, and mainstream and established parties of the left and right are either centering their agendas on issues that are too remote for the average insecure voter to activate political support, such as macroeconomic interventions and economic stability, or borrowing microcentered agendas from the RPR and RPL and being surpassed by radical populist solutions from the right and left. The declining popularity of social democracy in Europe in particular can be understood as the unintended effect of having adopted horizontal oppositional frames centered on the deservingness of individuals in political discourses and policy reforms (see chapter 3). This resulted in Social Democratic parties being surpassed by newer or emerging parties that make even more stringent use of such horizontal divisional frames.

Second, just as it is evident that focusing on macroeconomic issues affects the capacity of parties to connect with voters' individual conditions, it is also clear that insecurity is framed by the RPL and RPR as an expander and aggregator of discontent. The broad conceptualization of insecurity used by RPL and RPR parties is in stark contrast with the idea—established by mainstream parties during the great insecurity shift described in chapter 3—that policies should fix a minority of precarious citizens and that the rest will be automatically protected from insecurity through job participation. Populist parties have been able to mobilize the new politics of insecurity through a social agenda that speaks to a larger set of social problems than extreme poverty and not being able to attain the bare minimum of survival; their agendas, as described in chapter 4, tap into recognition and into qualitative aspects of life, while mainstream and established parties are still anchored in a reductive framing of social disadvantage centered on out-of-work interventions and the reinclusion of a minority of socially excluded individuals. Adopting a politics of insecurity can also mean, however, using insecurity to reintegrate into politics a large portion of the population that has not been the target of a mainstream political agenda under the false assumption that their lives were secure.

Third, insecurity creates new coalitions across classes that transform the social bases behind parties' political support. With the decline of the traditional working-class support for the mainstream left and given the way insecurity contributes to the dynamic reconfiguration of class cleavages, parties cannot count on a singular class base to gain sufficient support. The political scene is a lot more fragmented nowadays than it was just a decade ago, with the vote being split across more parties, especially in proportional systems of political representation. This makes it necessary for parties to create cross-class coalitions to gain a sufficient number of votes to influence a coalition or insert themselves within mainstream politics; insecurity is a useful political tool to create such coalitions, as it is a condition that bonds the old working class, the new one, and the squeezed middle and hence has the potential to aggregate support across established social cleavages. Furthermore, insecurity can also potentially create alliances and coalitions between similar social groups across different countries.[21]

Restoring Security: Intervening in the Family, State, and Market Mix

Based on what I have just illustrated, restoring insecurity entails both a new discourse and a new policy strategy. Adopting oppositional discourses that emphasize horizontal divisions (e.g., based on race, ethnicity, productivity, or deservingness) over vertical divisions, as discussed in chapter 4, ends up increasing the future political demand for horizontal divisions. Given the political success of horizontal oppositional frames, political discourses tend to underplay the role of vertical hierarchies that are built on the opposition between the people and economic elites or the function of wealth redistribution. The support for parties that have discourses and policies revolving around horizontal oppositional frames in turn contributes to the diffusion of discourses and policies that reinforce these hierarchies, leading to a vicious circle. To stop this vicious circle, politicians would have to put policies in place that intervene in how the family, the state, and the market are used and balanced to provide security to individuals.

THE FAMILY

Despite the emphasis on individuals' independence embedded in contemporary welfare regimes, the family remains a fundamental source of stability to cushion and navigate insecurity through housing, via support in kind or through ad hoc financial support.[22] The issue, however, is that the family also represents one of the main drivers that reproduces inequalities: The more societies implicitly count on the family to navigate insecurity, the more we are creating societies in which buffering security is a privilege for the few. Instead of framing inequality and insecurity as two separate agendas,[23] a political response to the political relevance of insecurity would be to embrace the complex intricacies that exist between inequality and insecurity at the micro level, recognize the political implications of the exchanges that individuals have with their families, and address insecurity directly via policies to reduce family-generated inequalities.

Political parties that intend to tap into the declining capacity of the family to provide security to citizens would have to reframe their political discourses around how individuals are navigating their financial and work issues not by themselves but through the support of their families. The individualistic technocratic political scripts centered on competition among individuals and independence would have to be replaced by a collective political discourse to navigating insecurity that accounts for relations between family members. Referring to the role of the family in their political discourses and policy reforms is central to RPR political success, even if their understanding of familistic material relations is peppered with a framing of moralistic and cultural values based on anachronistic traditional gender and family roles. The alternative to that agenda is not individualism or independence, but an understanding of the contemporary material and cultural role that families play in sustaining people's insecure paths through life.

At the policy level, alongside the more macroeconomic solutions proposed by economists to eradicate inequalities (e.g., a progressive and global tax on wealth, initiatives to reduce tax dodging),[24] political actors can deepen the formulation of microlevel solutions that touch on the availability of family resources to navigate security. Some of the key policy proposals formulated to address inequalities also function as reducers of insecurity, such as the implementation of changes to progressive taxation that permit low- and lower-middle-income families to retain more resources to navigate insecurity, and the expansion or creation of a temporary universal basic income for children or young people to equalize the distribution of resources to navigate insecurity early on.[25]

THE STATE

Given the growing mismatch between lives and policies described in chapter 3, it is no surprise that the idea of a basic income strategy, with large variations on conditionality and universality, has gained popularity among parties and, depending on how issues are framed, also among voters.[26] A basic income policy that offers direct cash transfer and reduces conditionality or means-testing represents a diversion from the costly, and counterproductive in respect to security, spiral of our social protection systems toward means-testing. In Italy, the Five Star Movement, categorized as a center populist party, gained political support through its proposition of a citizen income, which offered relief to low-income families after the 2010 trend of austerity. Far from being universal, this form of basic income removed the conditionality of contributions present in other forms of unemployment benefits but was still welfare chauvinist in its emphasis on citizenship. The temporary emergency income adopted during the pandemic further removed some of the elements of conditionality because it was understood that means-testing had to be reduced to address the extraordinary rise in insecurity.

Basic income can take many different shapes, and there is nothing inherently progressive about basic income per se, as this tool has gained momentum even among venture-capitalist circles. Basic income could potentially decommodify people's lives by providing additional resources to navigate financial insecurity that are not based on preexisting inequalities, as family support is. Its effect, however, is based on its conditions and funding. In Europe, its implementation is assumed to rely almost entirely on the state, thereby excusing the market from having to pay the cost of decommodifying lives, and confusingly sending the bill to states and their taxpayers. A truly decommodifying basic income should be funded by the market while also being entirely deprived of market rules in its delivery, which seems a contradiction in terms.

Another major risk behind basic income is that it leaves virtually untouched one of the major drivers of insecurity: the world of work. The current state of work tends to attract two divergent opinions: the naive belief that having a job solves one's social issues, and the idea of fixing current issues by imagining an automated future without work. Those who believe in the role of work as an automatic social stabilizer in Europe have recently been looking at new European initiatives such as the proposal of a job guarantee: a resolution for a state-run program for long-term unemployed individuals, which was recently approved by the European Trade Union Confederation. Meanwhile, postcapitalist thinkers have pushed for antiwork solutions, imagining a future when we can remove ourselves from the world of paid work through automated technology.[27] Neither of these camps touches the core issues of current work-related insecurity nor can mobilize political support among people who are affected by existing insecurity. The policy solutions that are likely to ultimately reduce the insecurity of workers and potentially resonate with voters are those that intervene in the multidimensional aspects of work security illustrated in chapter 1. A number of policy strategies should be adopted to address the decline in the various aspects of work conditions. National policies and company-level initiatives to monitor and keep sustainable the staff/workload ratio should be introduced to address the rise of work pressure and the decline in work–life balance (even the now popular four-day-a-week initiative is unlikely to address work pressure and work–life balance unless it is accompanied by a public discussion of workloads during the working week); initiatives to embed lifelong learning in work would address career insecurity and recognition insecurity; policies that establish living wages and make work pay across sectors could address income insecurity; and employment regulations that discouraged the adoption of precarious contracts would tackle both job insecurity and employment insecurity. As discussed in chapter 3, autonomy and work pressure could be addressed indirectly by having more options to be out of work (in other words, by having more generous state interventions in passive social security), while the state could act as a mediator of tripartite negotiations, involving unions and employers, to restore workers' autonomy and reduce the spike in work pressure in the workplace.

THE MARKET

Any reversal of insecurity would need to bring the market in and ask employers to take back part of the insecurity generated by the markets, as well as sharing the inevitable higher costs of creating jobs that are secure in their tenure and conditions. What could be the state's negotiating power to push for such changes? The first major negotiating power comes from corporate welfare. While the use of conditionality in state interventions targeted at individuals and their families has become more mainstream, corporate welfare is, as discussed in chapter 3, based on unconditional state transfers to companies, and it could instead be used as a collective bargaining chip to collect corporate resources to fund collective mechanisms to buffer insecurity. Furthermore, many do not realize that in Europe, given the expansion of social investment, the cost of forming the labor force (i.e., the reproduction of the labor force to sustain capitalism in the knowledge economy) has been incurred mostly by the state in favor of the market. While some of these costs have also been transferred to the population, the reproduction of the labor force is directly controlled by state-owned services (i.e., health, education, and care), which also gives the state more negotiating leverage vis-à-vis the market than is generally discussed. To put it bluntly, it is much more expensive to run a business in a market in which the labor force is not as comprehensively assisted by the social investment state in health, education, and care as it is in Europe. A contemporary Bismarckian *Kassensystem* could be set up under the intermediation of the state by pooling the resources from employers, workers, and the market (e.g., via capital income taxation) to deliver funds for the mechanisms to navigate insecurity mentioned in the previous section.

As illustrated in chapter 3, with financial insecurity on the rise, and with a welfare discourse targeted at the very poor and leaving the rest to find individualized solutions to navigate insecurity, Europeans are increasingly turning to the use of private instruments to navigate insecurity, in the shape of customer debt. Learning from what has occurred in the United States, the employment of market-based credit mechanisms in Europe should be regulated using a typology that is more in tune with people's security rather than with the priorities of private lenders. In particular, public policy regulations should focus on transforming survival debt (a type of debt used for everyday expenses) into state-based support, while also forbidding the use of extractive debt (a type of debt that harms the borrower and benefits someone else), because the latter results in a societal exacerbation of financial insecurity.[28]

Summary

On April 23, 2024, the EU Parliament voted for a return to fiscal responsibility following its temporary suspension of the application of strict macroeconomic regulations during Covid-19. As I argued in the first part of the chapter, the pandemic has been a phase of experimentation but also a lost opportunity, during a period dedicated to addressing insecurity, given its static reliance on macroeconomic strategies and employment creation as the only mechanisms to address insecurity. The new politics of insecurity offers the opportunity to elaborate an alternative to the individualistic and technocratic approach used in established politics by providing a focus on the living conditions that form the social basis of political support. Insecurity has not resulted in a new political class that recognizes itself as the precariat, and, with the dominant cultural frames and in the absence of social aggregators of political support, it can be easily converted into horizontal oppositional political support. The new politics of insecurity is generating a change in the social basis of political support in several directions: by resituating the focus of politics on microlevel experiences rather than macroeconomic trends; by enlarging the public definition of what social disadvantage is; and by creating cross-party and cross-country coalitions around shared experiences of insecurity.

At this stage, it is not clear whether mainstream and populist parties intend to use the new politics of insecurity to gather political support. It is clear, however, that a political agenda that intends to tap into the new politics of insecurity and interrupt the toxic cycle of horizontal oppositional politics should adopt a double strategy in respect to political discourse and policy interventions. In respect to the discourse, the priority should be to move away from a discourse based on horizontal oppositional frames to one that emphasizes the existence of vertical hierarchies in society. The capacity of individuals to resonate with political discourses based on vertical hierarchies over horizontal oppositions can be facilitated by using political frames that connect with the difficulties that individuals and their families face in navigating insecurity as a result of the unequal concentration of resources. Furthermore, a policy agenda that responds to the political relevance of insecurity would need to emphasize the collective societal components of addressing insecurity over the individualistic and atomistic framings that are used in the current policy era. The state would need to reopen negotiations with employers to pool resources and fund cash-based mechanisms to navigate insecurity, and corporate initiatives would need to be established that can restore security in work conditions.

Epilogue

THE SOCIAL BASIS OF THE POPULISM MOMENTUM

MY AIM HAS been to investigate the social basis of the most recent populist momentum by focusing on microlevel insecurity—namely, the ordinary and everyday experiences of financial insecurity and insecurity in work conditions. By examining the political implications of the insecurity shifts that have occurred in European welfare states, and by empirically testing the role that experiences of insecurity play in the generation of support for populist views and populist voting, this book lays the ground for a political sociology of contemporary populism that integrates cultural and economic explanations of political support under the umbrella of insecurity.

If Lipset could visit Montesilvano and Hartlepool, he would find the current populist wave to be driven not by an authoritarian lower class but by a coalition of people with variegated positions in the societal class structure, bonded together by a perception that their life conditions have declined. The rise of populist voting has its roots in subtle and underground changes, which have affected the social matrix of European societies in respect to how security is provided and perceived. In the European context, "security" meant that the majority of the population did not struggle financially and had a job with relatively low pressure, high autonomy, and a good work–life balance. Part of the population was always going to be excluded from the social benefits of the European social model, but as long as the majority were benefiting from the project, the collective support for status quo politics was going to be maintained. As a large portion of individuals from the middle class who were previously secure began to experience declining fortunes alongside those classes who were already experiencing economic instability, insecurity reached a tipping point and became a commonplace feeling among voters. This passage occurred alongside a shift in the cultural script of welfare, which passed from providing security for insiders to enhancing the productive potential of individuals to compete in the labor market and find a job.

I utilized insecurity conceptually to overcome the popular two-dimensional division between the economic and cultural dimensions that oppose, respectively, conservativism and economic liberalism, and authoritarianism and cultural liberalism. Such a division, I argued, conceals the in-depth connections that exist between how economic and cultural attitudes are formed within populism. In line with the idealistic literature, I considered populism as a third dimension that is alternative to cultural authoritarianism and economic conservativism, which emerges from an agreement with two viewpoints: a belief in the centrality of the people, and a view of the political that is based on the opposition between the people and the elite. The new politics of insecurity combines both economic and cultural elements. Insecurity is the material condition that bonds people together in opposition to the secure elite. At the same time, the construction of the category of the people is a deeply cultural matter, because it is mediated by dominant cultural scripts that shape who is worthy of belonging to the construction of the people based on race, ethnicity, citizenship, or productivity.

How Europe's Path Toward Insecurity Opened the Way to Populism

Insecurity intervenes in people's socioeconomic lives and in the political offer that is presented to voters. Relatively speaking, each security regime (liberal, Southern, continental, Nordic, and Eastern), even though they presented different manifestations and levels of insecurity to start with, has been affected by a qualitative growth in the manifestations of financial and work insecurity. Furthermore, my quantitative analyses of work insecurity at the micro level in Europe show a prevalence of job dissatisfaction and bad career prospects, and widely diffused feelings among people that they are trapped in their job or are not paid fairly. The analysis of the trends in core aspects of security in the workplace that I offered also shows a decline in content and procedural autonomy and a steep increase in work pressure, with job quality being affected by restructuring and company-level changes that have had an impact on the workplace since the 1990s. Despite the differences across security regimes, I found that the lower-middle-income groups are extremely affected by experiences of financial insecurity—as much as, if not more than, the lowest income groups—making financial insecurity widely felt among the population.

Presented with a more open, global, and competitive economy, logics and assumptions on national welfare states in Europe have made welfare states more resilient and more investment-centered, but also less centered on providing—and less able to provide—security to individuals. The focus on activating and incentivizing individuals contributed to the generation of a job climate characterized by high work pressure for those in work as out-of-work options became less appealing. Welfare states have lost their compensatory role in respect to the market by accepting institutional exposure of individuals to cyclical market fluctuations. Families play a much greater role in buffering insecurity, but due to spiking income and wealth inequalities, the resources to intervene to navigate insecurity are concentrated among a smaller number of families. The desecuritization of European welfare states implies not only a reduction in the capacity of welfare states to address work and financial security, but also the use of new cultural narratives that frame states as actors that can externally assist individuals to manage and buffer insecurity, and cannot regulate its levels. The rise in financial and work insecurity among individuals can be interpreted as a casualty of the transition to a modern and transformed welfare state, which succeeded in keeping employment rates relatively high at the cost of people's security. At the micro level, individuals have experienced a squeeze in the material resources they can access to navigate insecurity (in particular, accessing resources from the state, the family, and the labor market), alongside an explicit and implicit demand by institutions to accept a more insecure life, in work and financially. My analysis contributes to the current critiques of welfare state transformations by adding to this literature an examination of how the transfer of responsibility and the privatization of risk at the institutional level affect the security of individuals and, in turn, influence their political attitudes and behaviors.[1]

The partial loss of welfare states' compensatory role has meant that the state and everyone who has been involved in state policies during such a political turn—that is, the establishment, particularly the biggest center-left and center-right parties in power—have been likely to be perceived as politically responsible for endorsing a shift that has come at a high social cost. The link between insecurity and politics is, however, not automatic, and insecurity is associated with a populist outlook and populist voting via the intermediation of cultural scripts. The cultural backlash that has been reported in the literature accounts for some of the major manifestations of the existing political discontent (i.e., through ethnonationalism) but covers up the more profound structural transformations behind it.[2] In contrast to the assumptions of cultural backlash theory, individuals do not appear to be postmaterialist or indifferent to the material insecurity they experience. The real cultural evolution manifested by populism concerns the resonance that the hegemonic cultural frame of worthiness has among insecure voters. Antimigration attitudes flourish in an economic climate of insecurity and competition, becoming an easy-to-mobilize horizontal oppositional frame within more general in-group/out-group dynamics based on cultural distinctions. Mainstream parties of the left and right made extensive use of oppositional framings way before the latest populist momentum. Politically, mainstream parties of the left and right have ceased to prioritize a political offer of socioeconomic security to gain support, aligning their agendas toward hegemonic cultural scripts of individual commodification and productive activation, and they have been surpassed by populist-right parties in their use of oppositional discourses.

The normalization of horizontal oppositional frames in European mainstream politics has left ample space for existing and new political actors to propose agendas that activate insecurity into political support through even more marked horizontal oppositional frames. In a cultural climate imbued with explicit and implicit out-group categorizations, populist parties gain political support mostly through an oppositional way of framing insecurity centered on ethnonationalism and economic-centered frames of worthiness, although political agendas that use a more solidaristic way to address insecurity are present through left populism. Furthermore, RPR parties have formulated new political plans to address insecurity through the combined use of state–family- and state–market-centered strategies, while RPL parties have proposed an agenda that restores faith in the state's role of providing security through decommodification.

The research I have undertaken and presented in this book offers strong empirical evidence that confirms the intuition of several political theorists, who had invoked socioeconomic insecurity to explain the rising popularity of populist voting in Europe.[3] Work insecurity and financial insecurity are consistently associated with populist views, particularly the two core ones (people-centrism and people versus the elites), in all the cases considered across different security regimes. Whether populist views are translated into populist voting depends on the offers of populist parties and on how parties draw from the hegemonic cultural scripts.

The Eastern European regime, where insecurity is also associated with populist views but not always with populist party voting, suggests that historical welfare politics within a regime influences the likelihood that insecurity will translate into populist support.

We are just at the beginning of disentangling the complex set of societal, cultural, and socioeconomic factors that interfere with the process that links insecurity to populism, but the empirical and theoretical analysis I have presented indicates that the effects of insecurity in politics are persistent and profound. The shifts between voting for populist parties and nonvoting in the presence of a rise in financial insecurity and insecurity in the workplace also suggest that populism is far from being a satisfactory solution for insecure individuals: It is as close to an exit option as voting could be, while still representing a way to voice opposition to the establishment through voting.

For a New Political Sociology of the Populist Momentum

The research presented has several implications for the way we investigate and understand our social realities and the political effects they generate. At the start, I asked readers to question how we select the social causes of political phenomena—whether only extreme poverty or the lack of a job represents a social problem that can have a political effect, or whether the insecurity and instability of people's lives are worth investigating for their social and political implications. Not just in the United States but in Europe too, it is worth asking what kind of societies our economies are serving and what kind of politics results from a work and financial model whereby unemployment rates are relatively low, but a large portion of the population reports dissatisfaction with their work and financial lives.[4] Fundamentally, this book represents another brick in the construction of a systematic field of insecurity studies centered on the analysis of insecurity and its political effects.

The cross-disciplinary interest in the populist moment that has emerged since 2016 gives us an opportunity to revise the fundaments and assumptions on populism within and beyond political sociology.[5] When the investigation of the politics of insecurity is limited to how populism responds to a mere physical notion of security (i.e., as a matter of national and personal defense),[6] or as macroeconomic risk, individually experienced socioeconomic insecurity is implicitly removed from the boundaries of research on populism. Instead, the emerging socioeconomic research on insecurity offers fertile ground to understand the changed socioeconomic conditions in our societies, which constitutes the first step for an investigation of populism that is grounded in contemporary socioeconomic conditions rather than frozen cleavages.

Building on the integrated approaches used in research on populism,[7] I offered an enlarged theoretical framework that does not separate the economic and cultural but integrates them in a continuous conversation with the world of politics. It is my hope that this framework will be useful for all social scientists who find the postmaterial conceptualization of the "cultural" in research on populism quite limiting and who, in addition to examining attitudes toward authoritarianism, migration, LGBTI+ rights, and gender equality, intend to analyze the political effects of the major cultural evolutions reported by sociological research. To this aim, my framework has greatly benefited by the use of research on symbolic boundaries that is pivotal to understand the cultural frames that individuals and groups employ to formulate a collective notion of the people in opposition to the elites. An important avenue that deserves to be explored in more depth is the political effect of the existence of cultural scripts that reflect the emphasis on productivism from social investment welfare economics and how it shapes parties' agendas, as well as how voters resonate with them through the internalized script of meritocracy.

In the first part of the book, I relied on new economic sociology and on sociological approaches to political economy to unravel the assumptions of dominant policy framings while also investigating the effects that institutional shifts have on individuals, in particular how they change both the forms of support individuals can rely on (the family, state, and market mix) and the outcomes in terms of how individuals experience work and financial security. My approach represented a move away from the focus on institutions that dominates qualitative political economic analysis, as well as from the emphasis on macroeconomic indicators that is predominant in quantitative political economic analysis, with the goal of untangling the impact of institutional changes on people's lives.

The results of my investigation reject the overly optimistic view of the transformed welfare state as an absorber of social shocks and an effective protector against populism.[8] The analysis of the microlevel effects of the transformed welfare state on individuals demonstrates that the welfare state might facilitate reinsertion in work but fulfills neither of these roles. As economics is rediscovering the use of empirical micro data over economic models,[9] my hope is that this approach inspires more attempts to connect institutional analyses of the welfare state with socioeconomic research on the societal effects of public interventions and on how individuals receive them. As demonstrated through my analysis, a key element in transitioning to a political economy grounded on people's lives is enlarging the set of microlevel variables used to understand people's lives beyond education and contract type, and embracing the use of overlooked subjective measures that explore people's lives beyond the individual-based notion of social status. After all, how can a people-centered phenomenon such as populism be properly studied without delving deeper into people's lives?

An important implication of this research for future analyses is the way cleavages, and in particular class cleavages, are used to discuss the populist momentum. Frozen cleavages can go stale, be redefined, and hold different cultural meanings across society. While class cleavage theory in political science has referred to macroeconomic insecurity as a factor behind the reconfiguration of cleavages,[10] I have shown that employing an individual-based notion of insecurity can advance the understanding of how insecurity is redefining old cleavages, as well as how insecurity can aggregate support across established social cleavages. I have also discussed how the existence of class cleavages is influenced by the presence of vertical and horizontal symbolic boundaries, referring to a field of research (that on symbolic boundaries) that remains detached from political analyses despite its major contribution to cleavage theory.[11] The notion of the working class that was heavily mobilized in the analysis of Brexit ended up reproducing national class boundaries while overlooking the transnational dynamics of inequalities that Brexit hinted at.[12] I considered the existence of structural inequalities in the distribution of security without assuming that the distribution of insecurity would be based on established cleavages, and hence I examined the phenomenon of insecurity independently from class divisions but entrenched with past and present inequalities.[13] My analysis of the new politics of insecurity suggests that different classes can face similar threats to what they had previously considered secure lives, but it also highlights how future research should clarify the paradox of insecurity: the idea that insecurity is felt by "everybody," as suggested by Astra Taylor's piece in *The New York Times*, or at least by a large and growing portion of the population, when there is clear evidence that insecurity and precarity are the products of an economy that is increasingly unequal.[14] Social status, and its connection with insecurity, is central to such an investigation, particularly when social status is investigated in relation to the structural conditions that influence it and not as a purely psychological measure of one's perceived position in the social ladder.[15] Status is increasingly evoked by political analyses in populism, though it is at times interpreted as a purely individualistic feeling of nostalgic discontent from the past that has no connection with changes to structural conditions that individuals experience in Europe.[16] Insecurity adds explanatory power to a process that social status flags in its outcome: Through insecurity we not only identify the presence of a widespread dissatisfaction with work and life, but we can also explore the conditions that lead people to feel like their status is under threat in the first place.

The analysis in this book is Eurocentric not because insecurity is present only in Europe (the emerging field of insecurity studies is indeed a global one), but because I did not want to extend my conclusions beyond my empirical focus. Pranab Bardhan suggests that the connection between insecurity and populism is also present in countries of the periphery and semiperiphery of global capitalism.[17] A global research agenda for the new politics of insecurity would require the development of international and comparative measures of insecurity, as well as consideration of the similarities and differences between the cultural and political scripts that exist in other parts of the world and those presented here. Research from Latin America, for instance, indicates the presence of comparable manifestations of financial insecurity to the ones presented here, while also highlighting the presence of specific cultural scripts that could explain the directions and forms that populism takes there.[18]

A recurrent theme in the book is the crisis that Europe and the EU project face. Berezin has already warned about the contributory role of the EU in the emerging polity of insecurity, and how this was feeding into Euroskepticism even before the Eurocrisis.[19] In my work, I examined the EU as an additional level to national security discourses, suggesting that EU organizations underestimate the political effects of reproducing welfare discourses based on an economic-centered vision of society, relying on a theory of welfare that conceptualizes people as a stock of human capital and that understands poverty as the only social problem to fix.[20] The stickiness of these notions derives from how social investment is not just a policy style but also an intellectual machine supported by academic policy entrepreneurs, with implicit assumptions about what to prioritize in social interventions (see chapter 3). In parallel to conducting an epistemic shift toward restoring socioeconomic security, EU and national politics could reverse the vicious circle of insecurity by using cultural frames that stress the existence of collective strategies to reduce the forms of insecurity that most people experience, while national and EU policies could implement policies that intervene to replenish the squeeze of resources that individuals get from the providers of material security (the state, the family, and the labor market).

What I am suggesting might seem so difficult as to sound impossible, but the different directions that populism has taken in Europe suggest that the new politics of insecurity is not necessarily a road to a more insecure and divided society. It can also be an opportunity to reconnect the social to the political to find political responses to growing insecurities shared by an increasing proportion of the population.

ACKNOWLEDGMENTS

I STARTED TO think about *Insecurity Politics* after the Brexit vote, but it was the pandemic period that, putting my love for academic research and writing to the ultimate test, gave me the push to write the book.

I am extremely grateful for the work of those who helped to produce the research illustrated in the book. I particularly appreciate the collaborations with Andrei Zhirnov, Roberta di Stefano, Jan Philipp Thomeczek, Carlo D'Ippoliti, Laszlo Horvath, Michele Scotto di Vettimo, and Martin Strobl, who have contributed to and coauthored the research presented in chapter 5 within and beyond the PRECEDE project. I am thankful for Strobl's assistance in the literature review and in producing the analyses presented in chapter 2, and for Thomeczek's work on the figures from the Manifesto Data in chapter 4. I want to express my gratitude to Zhirnov and Di Stefano for their willingness to implement my ideas and their statistical talent, which has informed the analyses presented in chapter 5. I am indebted to Thomeczek for having introduced me to the ideational definition of populism and for having been a great team player and project comanager. During my time at CES, I had the fortune to be assisted by two student assistants: Justin Hu, who has done fantastic work in improving figures that appear in this book, and Salvatore Valentino, who has helped with referencing. I am lucky to have had them as part of my team, and I remain inspired by their life journeys.

This book would have not been written without the generous support of the German Memorial Fellowship at the Minda de Gunzburg Center for European Studies (CES) at Harvard University, which allowed me to dedicate an entire academic year to thinking and writing about this topic. I am grateful for the support of the whole team at CES, especially Elaine Papoulias (executive director) and Elizabeth Johnson (director of operations). I also acknowledge the contribution of the Volkswagen Foundation through the project PRECEDE, funded by "Challenges for Europe" (96999), which provided research funding to guide Working Package 2 and work on this topic. I am thankful to the Department of Social Policy, Sociology, and Criminology of the University of Birmingham for granting me study leave, and to my colleagues for their support upon my return. I have also benefited from short periods in Paris both during the book proposal stage (Sciences Po, Centre d'études européennes, May–June 2022) and manuscript preparation (through a visiting position at the AxPo Center for Market Society Polarization and a research residence in Maison Suger, April–May 2025).

I have been very lucky to come across many supportive figures in academia who have encouraged me to write this book and shaped my way of navigating academia, but two of them warrant special mention. I am particularly grateful for the support I received from Danny Dorling, who remains a constant inspiration for how to navigate academia during and beyond our kayaking adventures. Danny's encouraging words have guided me through my low points of the writing journey, and his comments on the book have greatly improved the manuscript. I am indebted to Michèle Lamont for having opened my eyes to a new way to conceptualize culture in relation to politics, for welcoming me to the Weatherhead Cluster on Comparative Inequality and Social Inclusion at Harvard University, for connecting me with other scholars, and for her comments on the proposal and the manuscript, which have substantially improved the final work.

The proposal and manuscript have benefited from the comments I received at different stages, particularly by Bruno Palier and Pauliina Patana during my stays at Sciences Po (Paris); Peter Hall, Sirje Laurel Weldon, Stephen Hanson, Timur Ergen, Vivienne Schmidt, Georg Menz, Alex Mierke-Zatwarnicki, Elena Militello, Carmelo Ignaccolo, and all the other CES Visiting Scholars 2022/2023; Elena Ayala Hurtado (who has since become an excellent coauthor on writing and thinking on insecurity), Luca Carbone, Luuc Brans, Giovanni Matera, Poulomi Chakrabarti, Yael Cohen-Rimer, and the other members of the Cluster on Comparative Inequality and Social Inclusion.

My thinking on the topic has been shaped by intellectual exchanges with many political scientists, sociologists, economists, and other social researchers, particularly through the Cluster on Comparative Inequality and Social Inclusion (e.g., Jonathan Mijs, who has immensely influenced my understanding of how culture relates to politics), the Seminar on the State and Capitalism Since 1800 at CES (e.g., the provoking work of Sheri Berman), the Culture and Social Analysis Workshop (all at Harvard University), the Precarity Lab at Boston University, the EUSA conference in 2023 and my chats with the brilliant Aleksandra Sojka, and the special panel session co-organized by Paulus Wagner and Bruno Palier during the International Conference of Europeanists of the Council for European Studies in Lyon in 2024. I am particularly indebted to the participants of the insecurity miniconference at SASE (2024) for contributing to my thinking on the concept of insecurity (reflected in chapter 1): Elena Ayala-Hurtado, Albena Azmanova (who co-organized the session with me), David Joseph-Goteiner, Chrystin Ondersma, and Joaquín Prieto-Suarez. The part of the book that deals with EU policies has been enriched by the many exchanges I had with those who work in Brussels. I thank in particular Laura Caroli, Francesco Corti (with whom I coauthored a study cited in chapter 3), Bianca Luna Fabris, Silvia Righi, Slavina Spasova, Bart Vanhercke, and the researchers of the European Social Observatory and the European Trade Union Institute. I am thankful to László Andor and Ania Skrzypek for our exchanges on European politics and for the opportunities they created through the "Next Left" network of the Foundation of European Progressive Studies.

I am very grateful to Rebecca Brennan, my editor at Princeton University Press, and the entire PUP team for having been so receptive to my ideas and actively supporting me to produce the book I had in my mind. At PUP, I benefited from Anita O'Brien's precious assistance in editing the final manuscript, and Theresa Liu's meticulous help during the production stage. I am also extremely grateful for the work of the brilliant proofreader and editor Ben Corrigan, who has consistently improved my ability to express my thoughts for the past ten years.

This book would not have been written without the extended network of care, love, and friendship that I have been so lucky to access in the past years and that has deeply engaged with my academic work. In Cambridge, Massachusetts, I thank Farzan and Amir for being my home; our Boston crew, particularly Catherine for her wit; Laurel for her time and dedication—and for having come up with the right title for the book; Elena, Carmelo, and Costanza for being lovely humans; Peter and Rosemary for their eventful dinners; the Lamont-Dobbins family for its ability to connect academics; Luuc and Luca for their immense support and friendship; and Daria and Giovanni for reminding me I am (also) Italian. In Paris, I thank Hiba and Paulien. In Birmingham, I thank Anna, Pablo, Phil, and Luke for our interesting conversations and always being there for me; Foka Wolf for our exchanges on politics; and a wonderful network of supporting academic women around the world: Aleksandra, Bianca Luna, Laura, Maricia, and Raphaëlle. Special thanks to Chrys for showing me how to live deliciously within and outside academia. And, finally, I thank my old network of friends in Milan and across the world (Sibilla, Gaia, Marcella, and their families, and Alessandro and Giulia) and in Montesilvano (my childhood friends who keep me grounded, particularly Michaela and Francesca, and their kids).

Last but not least, I am thankful for the support of my family, especially my mum, our cat Wine, Elio, Ermes, and their partners. I don't think I would have been able to finish the book without the swimming and writing routine I had—I am very grateful for my mum for making that possible. This book is entirely for her.

METHODOLOGICAL APPENDIX

Overview

The book offers three types of data-based analyses: (1) empirical analyses to monitor the evolution of work and financial insecurity using, respectively, EWCS, ESS, and EU-SILC data (chapter 2)—hence using work and financial insecurity as dependent variables; (2) an empirical analysis of parties' manifestos using the Manifesto Data (chapter 4); and (3) empirical analyses of ad hoc online surveys and probability sampling datasets that use work and financial insecurity as explanatory variables and where the dependent variable is populist vote or populist outlook (chapter 5).

The book contains qualitative and quantitative comparative analyses conducted within Europe. The large-N cross-national design aims to identify generalizable patterns in the evolution of insecurity and in the impact of insecurity on voting, while the in-depth discussion of cases is used to limit the drawbacks of large-N comparisons by offering a conceptual analysis over a selected number of cases.[1] The qualitative discussion of security regimes (chapter 2) and populist supply (chapter 4) focuses on nine European case studies: the United Kingdom, the Netherlands, Italy, Germany, Spain, France, Sweden, Hungary, and Poland. These case studies were selected as they presented different varieties of welfare capitalism (which translated into different security regimes), as well as different types of populist party representation (left/right; in government/in opposition).[2] Depending on the type of study, the quantitative analyses conducted in chapters 2 and 5 included the highest number of available countries to maximize the potential for generalizing the results.

Methodology in Chapter 2

THE SYSTEMATIC REVIEW

The presentation of security regimes contains the results of a systematic review that included over two hundred publications on work and financial insecurity across the welfare regimes considered in this study before and after the European crisis that started between 2008 and 2010. Outputs were found using the search engines Web of Science and Google Scholar, reading and consulting about 210 academic outputs published between the 1990s and 2024. To be included in the scoping review, the abstracts or titles had to cover work and financial security in Europe and/or across the case studies, while academic outputs that use a different notion of insecurity than the one used in this study were excluded.

ANALYSIS OF WORK CONDITIONS

This section contains descriptive analyses of the European Working Conditions Survey (EWCS), the largest survey monitoring workers' conditions in Europe, run by Eurofound since 1990.[3] Figure 2.1 contains the descriptive analysis of the latest available round of EWCS, which took place in 2015 (the survey with the full variables is ongoing due to Covid-19 delays). Figures 2.2, 2.3, and 2.4 present the results of analyses of content autonomy, procedural autonomy, and work pressure that replicate the methodology used by Lopes and colleagues on a longer time span: between 1995 and 2015.[4] The full details of how the analysis has been conducted (e.g., use of variables and results of the full analyses) are contained in section 4.1 of a published article in *Social Policy & Administration*.[5] Table A.1 contains the variables used to define content autonomy,

Table A.1. Measures of Content Autonomy, Procedural Autonomy, and Work Pressure

Content autonomy	Q53b: Does your main paid job involve assessing yourself the quality of your own work? Q53c: Does your main paid job involve solving unforeseen problems on your own? Q53f: Does your main paid job involve learning new things?
Procedural autonomy	Q50e: Is your pace of work dependent on the direct control of your boss? Q54a: Are you able to choose or change your order of tasks? Q54b: Are you able to choose or change your methods of work? Q54c: Are you able to choose or change your speed or rate of work?
Work pressure	Q49a: Does your job involve working at very high speed? Q49b: Does your job involve working to tight deadlines? Q50a: Is your pace of work dependent on the work done by colleagues? Q50c: Is your pace of work dependent on numerical production targets or performance targets? Q61g: You have enough time to get the job done. Q61g_lt: You have enough time to get the job done.

procedural autonomy, and work pressure. To simplify the reading, the descriptive figures present an average for all countries available and twelve case studies from the different security regimes.

ANALYSIS OF FINANCIAL INSECURITY (ESS AND EU-SILC)

Figure 2.5 presents a descriptive analysis of a variable of financial insecurity using ten waves of the European Social Survey (ESS), from round 1 (2002) to round 10 (2020), in twenty-six countries.[6] The figure refers to the variable "hincfel" in ESS, a question that asks respondents to rate how they are feeling in respect to the household's income nowadays, giving them four options: "living comfortably," "coping," "finding it difficult," or "finding it very difficult" on present income.

Figures 2.6 and 2.7 present the analysis of the longitudinal dataset of the EU statistics on income and living conditions (EU-SILC), a cross-sectional and longitudinal sample survey in EU member states, coordinated by Eurostat.[7] The focus of the analysis is to identify households that have experienced financial strain in past survey waves and determine whether they have recovered or continue to face difficulties. The first step was to identify households that reported difficulties making ends meet in at least one of the previous three waves (hence over a four-year span). This was determined using a variable that measures the ability to make ends meet (HS120), which contains six response categories. Households were flagged as being in financial strain if they selected "with great difficulty," "with difficulty," or "with some difficulty" (excluding fairly easily, easily, and very easily). If households reported being able to make ends meet "easily" or "very easily" in a certain wave, they were considered to have recovered from financial strain and were unflagged. Households that reported "fairly easily" were still considered at risk and remained flagged because this response is close to the difficulty threshold, implying only a slight improvement and not a robust sign of recovery. The analysis computes the proportion of households that remain in financial difficulty, tracking them over time to determine whether they consistently face challenges or if they recover in certain periods. The analysis includes households that are present in the wave considered and have participated in at least one wave in the previous three years. The results are shown by calculating the share of households that remain flagged as facing financial insecurity, for each country and by different income classes, and with averages computed over country averages. To simplify the reading, the figures present an average of countries considered and twelve case studies from the various security regimes. The income categories are calculated as follows: bottom refers to households with income below 60 percent of the median income; lower refers to households with income between 60 and 75 percent of the median income; lower middle refers to households with income between 75 and 125 percent of the median income; upper middle refers to income between 125 and 166 percent of the median; and upper refers to households with income above 166 percent of the median income.[8]

Methodology in Chapter 4

The classification of parties as populist or not (table A.2) is mostly based on the PopuList classification proposed by Rooduijn and colleagues.[9] As this classification examines parties that are in parliament or have won at least 2 percent of the votes in an election since 1989, the other small populist parties were identified by consulting the ParlGov database and other experts-based continuous measures of populism, particularly POPPA, V-Dem, and the Timbro Authoritarian Populism Index (TAP).[10] The left and right party

Table A.2. Populist Parties Mapping Across Case Studies Since 1990

Country	Populist radical right	Populist radical left	Centrist populist
United Kingdom	UKIP; **Reform UK**	R; **SF**	
Sweden	**SD;** NyD; Centre Democrats, CD; Sjöbopartiet		
Spain	**Vox**	**ECP**; EM|GCE; **Podemos**	
Netherlands	CD; **FvD; PVV**	**SP**	LN; LPF
Italy	**FdI**; **LN/L**; LAM	PaP	LV; **M5S**; **FI/PdL** (*NB:* the status of FI/PdL as populist or mainstream varies across years)
Hungary	**FIDESZ; Jobbik**; MIÉP; MH		
Germany	**AfD**	**Linke**	
France	**DLR|DLF; FN/RN**	**FI**	
Poland	**Kukiz; PiS**		

Note: Parties that held seats are indicated in bold.

classification was conducted using the same databases, as well as the Chapel Hill Expert Survey (CHES).[11]

Figures 4.2–4.4 presents the scores of how parties are positioned using an analysis of the Manifesto Data.[12] The Manifesto Data project coded election programs in fifty-six countries between 1920 and 2021, including all parties that have won at least two seats in Europe, though the analysis presented in this book examined only the 2000–2021 period. The project provides saliency scores, namely, how many times terms and concepts have been mentioned in a party manifesto with a positive or negative

Table A.3. Dimensions and Coding in the Manifesto Data

Dimension	Item in the codebook	Item definition
Security agenda	Welfare state expansion (per504)	Favorable mentions of need to introduce, maintain, or expand any public social service or social security scheme, such as care and social housing.
	Labour groups: positive (per701)	Favorable references to all labor groups, the working class, and unemployed workers in general. Support for trade unions and calls for the good treatment of all employees, including good working conditions, fair wages.
	Equality: positive (per503)	Concept of social justice and the need for fair treatment of all people, including removal of class barriers and need for redistribution of resources.
Commodification	Incentives: positive (per402)	Favorable mentions of supply-side- oriented economic policies (assistance to businesses rather than consumers), including financial and other incentives such as subsidies and tax breaks; wage and tax policies to induce enterprise.
	Welfare state limitation (per505)	Limiting state expenditures on social services or social security. Favorable mentions of the social subsidiary principle (i.e., private care before state care).

connotation, depending on what the coding indicates. After preselecting relevant items pertaining to the provision of security, two variables were extracted through exploratory factor analysis that have been labeled as security agenda and commodification (see table A.3). More information on the coding of variables can be found in the Manifesto Data codebook.[13] Figures for the Liberal security regime (UK) and for the Eastern European regime (Hungary/Poland) were not included due to, respectively, the lack of populist parties in the Manifesto codebook to track (in the UK) and the frequent changes to the classification of populist parties in Eastern Europe over time.

Methodology in Chapter 5

This section presents a number of published or forthcoming empirical analyses that use socioeconomic indicators to explain populist vote or populist outlook. Some of the studies presented in this chapter use VAA-generated surveys conducted between 2016 and 2022 by Kieskompas. VAA-recruited data may be nonrepresentative of the general population as such data are affected by a twofold self-selection bias: the probability to opt into VAA usage and then into follow-up studies. Several techniques have been used to reduce such biases in the studies I present, such as raking weights for the analysis of vote choices. Studies that have investigated the relationships between variables using opt-in online panels show that, with weight adjustments, such data produce estimates that are sufficiently close to those obtained with probability samples, particularly when it comes to testing relationships between variables.[14] A recent study that examines the validity of VAA-generated surveys indicates that VAA is particularly reliable in the investigation of correlations between variables of interest, particularly with respect to socioeconomic variables.[15]

POPULISM AND THE INSECURE MIDDLE CLASS

The first part of the section (including fig. 5.1) presents the results of an analysis of the Brexit vote based on three data sources: an online opt-in panel that ran after the referendum (28 June–10 July 2016); the British Election Study Internet Panel referendum campaign wave; and a VAA-generated survey that was collected in June 2016 with 2,809 observations. Poststratification weights were applied to each respondent of the panel to make reasonable population-level inference. I presented the results of five mixed-effects logistic regressions with probability to vote Leave as the dependent variable and a number of individual-level variables, including education, perceptions on personal socioeconomic conditions, psychosocial variables, class, and income, controlling for age, gender, and political support. The full analyses and regression tables of these models are available in *Competition & Change*.[16]

ASSOCIATIONS BETWEEN INSECURITY AND POPULIST SUPPORT

The first part of the chapter refers to empirical research on insecurity and populism in the Netherlands and France (table 5.1; figs. 5.2 and 5.3). This analysis uses a VAA-generated survey conducted before and/or during the legislative elections: February 2017 in the Netherlands for the May elections, and May 2017 in France for the June elections. The VAA-generated survey consisted of 31,800 observations in the Netherlands and 6,992 in France. Poststratification weights were computed so that the joint distribution of gender, age, and education is matched exactly to the proportions in the census. Logistic regressions were run using insecurity of tenure and insecurity of work conditions as explanatory of the probability of voting for mainstream or radical/populist parties, while controlling for gender, age, and education.

It should be noted that the article "What's Work Got to Do with It?" which I coauthored with colleagues in 2023, uses a slightly more expansive operationalization of nonestablished left than what I used in the book. In line with a part of the literature, instead of referring to the populist left, it refers to the radical left, which includes populist left parties (e.g., FI) and a number of small, nonestablished radical left parties that operate in the French political context, as indicated in table A.4 (however, it is also evident that the RL results are driven by the main populist left party, namely, FI).[17] Readers can consult the published article in *Sociological Research Online* for the analysis of how the postweight survey compares to the census in the dataset and to see the full regression tables.

The second part of the chapter (table 5.2 and fig. 5.4) refers to the analysis of the VAA-generated survey conducted during the 2019 elections: the European Voter Election Survey (EVES), which included over 75,000 responses in total and over 60,000 complete responses in the ten countries considered (this study included Romania but not the UK, given that the British FPTP system does not allow a smooth comparison between the UK and other countries).[18] To address the overrepresentation of certain categories within EVES, the study used raking weights based on

Table A.4. Selection of Parties in the Study, France and the Netherlands

	Radical populist right (RPR) parties	Radical left (RL) parties	Mainstream parties
France	Front National (FN)	La France Insoumise (FI) Europe Écologie Les Verts (EELV) Front de gauche (FG) Parti communiste français (PCF) Parti communiste réunionnais (PCR) Parti de gauche (PG) Parti radical de gauche (PGR) Lutte Ouvrière (LO)	Les Républicains (LR) Parti socialiste (PS)
Netherlands	Partij voor de Vrijheid (PVV) Pim Fortuyn List (PFL) Forum voor Democratie (FvD)	Socialistische Partij (SP) Partij voor de Dieren (Pvd Dieren)	Christen-Democratisch Appèl (CDA) Partij van de Arbeid (PvdA)

the respondents' age group, education, sex, and region and the distributions of these variables among the adult population of the countries under investigation. Recalled vote choice was also used as an additional criterion for generating raking weights for the analysis of vote choices. At the end, the aggregates produced using the weights were significantly closer to the benchmark proportions (see the published article for the full analysis of the postweight dataset and benchmarks). The indicators of populism and the variables of insecurity (financial precarity; precarity of tenure; precarity at work) were extracted through confirmatory factor analyses.

The relationship between voters' insecurity and their populist attitudes was investigated through a linear model that controlled for age, gender, education, home ownership, income distribution, and work status for the model testing the effect of financial insecurity. The relationship between insecurity and voting was measured through multinomial logistic regressions based on the respondents' vote intentions, using the same control variables. The full discussion of the models, the regression tables, and the descriptives are included in the published article in the *European Sociological Review*.[19]

THE GENDERED EFFECT OF INSECURITY ON POPULISM

This section refers to the findings of research that used advanced statistical data matching with computational techniques to create a synthetic dataset of EWCS and ESS in twenty-three European countries based on demographics, region, industry sector, and educational attainment of respondents. The ESS provides information on voting and financial insecurity (through the variable presented in chapter 2, "hincfel"), while the EWCS allows a multidimensional analysis of work conditions. Statistical matching is preferred to group average-based imputation technique because the latter generates a distribution where the values are concentrated across the means, while a synthetic dataset derived from statistical data matching reproduces the density of the distribution of variables in the original dataset.

Through a nonlinear model, the probit, the study tested the association between populism and insecurity. All specifications controlled for all variables used in the matching—education level, contract, age, NACE, ISCO, health feeling, and country fixed effects. To avoid estimating too many parameters, health levels are aggregated through a binary variable and ISCO levels in three categories (high-skilled, semi-skilled, and low-skilled). To avoid omitted variable bias, a set of controls is added: income deciles grouped in five groups, trade union membership, and a binary variable that identifies those who find it difficult or very difficult to live on present income. The model also controls for variables of political attitudes in the ESS: cultural openness and system fairness, extracted through exploratory factor analysis. Information on the models, on the application of statistical matching, and the full regression tables are available in the working paper.[20]

INSECURITY AND THE EXCHANGES BETWEEN VOTING AND NONVOTING

To detect a relationship between precarity and voters' decisions, a follow-up longitudinal panel from the European Voter Electoral Study survey was conducted on a sample of 12,021 participants both in 2018 (before Covid) and in 2022 (after Covid) in six countries: France, Germany, Italy, Netherlands, Spain, and Sweden. Only the respondents who answered the question on vote preference and declared either no intention to vote or a preference for a populist or mainstream party were included. Individuals

Table A.5. Selection of Parties in the Study

Country	Populist right	Populist left	Populist center	Mainstream
Netherlands	Forum for Democracy, PVV, JA21	Socialist Party (SP)		PvdA, ChristenUnie, GroenLinks, CDA, VVD, D66
Germany	Alternative for Germany (AfD)	Linke		CDU/CSU, SPD, FDP, Die Grünen
Sweden	Sverigedemokraterna (SD)			Socialdemokraterna, Centerpartiet, Liberalerna, Moderaterna, Kristdemokraterna, Miljöpartiet
Italy	Lega, Fratelli d'Italia, Italia agli Italiani FN-FT, CasaPound Italia	Potere al Popolo!	Movimento 5 Stelle, Forza Italia	Noi con l'Italia UDC, +Europa, Partito Democratico, Liberi e Uguali, Insieme–Italia Europa, Civica Popolare, Art.1 / Sinistra Italiana Azione
France	FN (Front National), Debout la France, UPR, Reconquete	FI (La France Insoumise)		La République en marche!, Mouvement démocrate, Union des démocrates et indépendants, Europe Écologie Les Verts, Générations, Parti socialiste, Les Républicains
Spain	VOX	Podemos, Más País, Compromís, En Marea		Nueva Canarias, Foro de Ciudadanos/Foro Asturias, Partido Nacionalista Vasco, Partido Socialista Obrero Español, Esquerra Republicana de Catalunya, EH Bildu, Partido Popular, Ciudadanos, Partit Demòcrata Europeu Català, Compromís, Unión del Pueblo Navarro, Coalición Canaria

who are ineligible to vote, did not answer the vote preference question, or decided to vote for parties that are neither mainstream nor populist have been excluded. The categorization of parties as populist/mainstream was conducted according to the information in table A.5; the category of populist grouped together populist right, left, and center parties. The categorization is marginally more expansive than the one presented in A.2, as in this case the goal was to keep as many participants as possible in the longitudinal panel in order to have a sufficient panel size despite the attrition that affects longitudinal panels.

Work insecurity and financial insecurity were extracted through confirmatory factor analysis. The analysis was conducted through multinomial log-linear models, with intention to vote as the dependent variable divided into three categories (voting for mainstream parties, voting for populist parties, or not voting) and controls used for country fixed effects, gender, education, income, and job loss. The full discussion of the longitudinal panel, the implementation of the survey in the two waves, and the full regression tables are available in the working paper.[21]

GLOSSARY OF KEY TERMS

Demand (political). The analysis of what people entitled to vote want, ask for from politics, and vote for. Studies that investigate the demand side explore the range of factors and drivers that foster voters to opt for one political offer or another.

Desecuritization of the welfare state. The altered institutional language, values, goals, and targets of the state function in relation to the social sphere that affect individuals' sense of socioeconomic security. The desecuritization of European welfare states implies a reduction in the capacity of welfare states of addressing work and financial security, as well as the use of new cultural narratives that place the state as an actor that cannot regulate the levels of insecurity but only externally assist individuals to manage and buffer insecurity.

Family–market–state nexus. The interaction and balance between the main sources of welfare (the family, the state, and the market) to navigate insecurity. Changes to the nexus can affect the microlevel availability of resources, namely, the individual "welfare mix." The book refers, at times, to the specific market–state nexus and market–family nexus.

Insecurity. Microlevel socioeconomic instability that emerges from the lack of security in two areas of people's lives: work and finances. Work security entails having a stable job and secure work conditions, with respect to work pressure, autonomy, work–life balance, and recognition. Financial security refers to the ability to pay for necessary expenses, pay bills, cover unexpected expenses, and live without financial anxiety.

New politics of insecurity. The role of socioeconomic insecurity in contemporary politics. The book shows that insecurity enters in politics via the intersection of different security shifts: the spread of socioeconomic insecurity at the micro level, through the diffusion of new cultural scripts to manage security and due to changes to the political offer of socioeconomic security.

Oppositional frames. Cultural frames that reveal and reproduce the existence of distinctions between members of a society based on existing symbolic boundaries. **Horizontal oppositional frames** exclude others, from the construction of the people through existing cultural hierarchies of worth and value based on race, ethnicity, nativism, or productivity. **Vertical oppositional frames** emphasize the opposition between the people and those who have a higher position in the social hierarchy, such as the economic or cultural elites.

Populist outlook (*ideational definition*). Believing in the centrality of the people in politics (people-centrism) and in the fact that politics is characterized by an opposition between the people and the economic, intellectual, and political elites (people versus the elites). A third, albeit derivative, element of populism is holding a dualistic view of Good and Evil (Manichean outlook).

Scripts. How institutions or groups of people view the world. I refer both to **cultural scripts**, which refer to dominant views of the world in a certain society, and to **political scripts**, which pertain to parties' or institutions' views of the world.

Security regimes: Clusters of countries that are bonded together by a similar way in which welfare influences people's socioeconomic security at the micro level. Countries in the same security regime share strategies for upholding or increasing work and financial security and present similar sources of work and financial insecurity.

Security shifts. Changes to work and financial security that affect people's lives and are due to economic or institutional shifts (e.g., the desecuritization of the welfare state).

Social status. An assessment of one's position in the social hierarchy in relation to others. The **decline of social status** is the perceived loss of one's position in the social hierarchy compared to the past, while **social status threat** refers to the potential future risk that one could lose one's position in the social hierarchy.

Supply (political). The area of politics that is concerned with proposing political solutions to people entitled to vote. Political supply often refers to the types and number of parties that are available to voters before, during, and after electoral rounds, and to their main characteristics (e.g., their left/right positioning or whether they are categorized as populist or not).

Transformed welfare state(s). An umbrella term that summarizes the changes to welfare state interventions, visible particularly from the 1990s onward, in comparison to the Golden Age of welfare state development. The transformed welfare state has also been defined as the Schumpeterian workfare state, the enabling welfare state, the postindustrial welfare-state transition, the postcapitalist welfare state, and the social investment welfare state.

Welfare mixes. The welfare sources from the family, market, and state (i.e., providing resources in cash or kind) that individuals have or can access to navigate insecurity.

NOTES

Introduction. The Widespread Insecurity Thesis

1. *L'Espresso*, "Lo strano caso della cittadina abruzzese in cui sono diventati tutti leghisti," May 2019, https://lespresso.it/c/politica/2019/5/16/lo-strano-caso-della-cittadina-abruzzese-in-cui-sono-diventati-tutti-leghisti/37692.

2. Stefano Marchetti and Luca Secondi, "The Economic Perspective of Food Poverty and (In)Security: An Analytical Approach to Measuring and Estimation in Italy," *Social Indicators Research* 162, no. 3 (2022): 995–1020.

3. The Tees Valley is home to an important strand of studies on precarity and poverty in the UK, such as Tracy Shildrick et al., *Poverty and Insecurity: Life in Low-Pay, No-Pay Britain* (Bristol University Press, 2012).

4. An article in the *Independent* reflected: "British society is mired in class-consciousness, apathy and under-achievement. The future looks bleak. This is how Tony Horwitz of 'The Wall Street Journal' presented us to the world this month. It is an outsider's view, with a message that cuts across party politics." *The Independent* (London), "Britain 1992: The View from Wall Street," 23 February 1992, 3.

5. *The New Yorker*, "A Visit to the Pro-Brexit Coastal Town of Hartlepool," September 2019, https://www.newyorker.com/news/letter-from-the-uk/a-visit-to-the-pro-brexit-coastal-town-of-hartlepool.

6. John Burn-Murdoch, "What the 'Year of Democracy' Taught Us, in 6 Charts," *Financial Times*, 30 December 2024, https://www.ft.com/content/350ba985-bb07-4aa3-aa5e-38eda7c525dd.

7. These are a few examples of special issues and contributions in edited collections on Brexit, respectively, from sociology: Nigel Dodd, Michèle Lamont, and Mike Savage, "Introduction to BJS Special Issue," *British Journal of Sociology* 68, no. S1 (2017): S3–10; from economics: Thiemo Fetzer, "Did Austerity Cause Brexit?" *American Economic Review* 109, no. 11 (2019): 3849–86; Sascha O. Becker, Thiemo Fetzer, and Dennis Novy, "Who Voted for Brexit? A Comprehensive District-Level Analysis," *Economic Policy* 32, no. 92 (1 October 2017): 601–50; from human geography: Camilla Lenzi and Giovanni Perucca, "People or Places That Don't Matter? Individual and Contextual Determinants of the Geography of Discontent," *Economic Geography* 97, no. 5 (20 October 2021): 415–45; Danny Dorling, "Brexit: The Decision of a Divided Country," *BMJ* 354 (6 July 2016); and from social policy studies: Peter Taylor-Gooby, "Re-Doubling the Crises of the Welfare State: The Impact of Brexit on UK Welfare Politics," *Journal of Social Policy* 46, no. 4 (October 2017): 815–35.

8. Arlie Russel Hochschild, *Strangers in Their Own Land: Anger and Mourning on the American Right* (New Press, 2016); James Aho, *Far-Right Fantasy: A Sociology of American Religion and Politics* (Routledge, 2015).

9. I illustrate this point in more depth in the following section and in chapter 1.

10. Allison J. Pugh, *The Tumbleweed Society: Working and Caring in an Age of Insecurity* (Oxford University Press, 2015); Costanzo Ranci et al., "New Measures of Economic Insecurity Reveal Its Expansion Into EU Middle Classes and Welfare States," *Social Indicators Research* 158, no. 2 (2021): 539–62; Tom Barnes and Sally A. Weller, "Becoming Precarious? Precarious Work and Life Trajectories After Retrenchment," *Critical Sociology* 46, no. 4–5 (July 2020): 527–41.

11. A general discussion on the effects of economic insecurity on populism is offered by Yotam Margalit, "Economic Insecurity and the Causes of Populism, Reconsidered," *Journal of Economic Perspectives* 33, no. 4 (2019): 152–70. On the effects of trade on populism, see David Autor et al., "Importing Political Polarization? The Electoral Consequences of Rising Trade Exposure," *American Economic Review* 110, no. 10 (2020): 3139–83; Italo Colantone and

Piero Stanig, "The Trade Origins of Economic Nationalism: Import Competition and Voting Behavior in Western Europe," *American Journal of Political Science* 62, no. 4 (2018): 936–53. On the effects of austerity on populist voting, see Fetzer, "Did Austerity Cause Brexit?"; Simone Cremaschi et al., "Geographies of Discontent: How Public Service Deprivation Increased Far-Right Support in Italy," preprint (Harvard Business School Paper, 21 November 2023). On the effects of the economic crisis on populism, see Yann Algan et al., "The European Trust Crisis and the Rise of Populism," *Brookings Papers on Economic Activity* 2017, no. 2 (2017): 309–400.

12. Sergei Guriev and Elias Papaioannou, "The Political Economy of Populism," *Journal of Economic Literature* 60, no. 3 (2022): 753–832.

13. Benjamin Arditi, "Three Provocations Concerning the Uses of Populism," *Populism* 7, no. 1 (2 February 2024): 1–20; Matteo C. M. Casiraghi, "'You're a Populist! No, You Are a Populist!': The Rhetorical Analysis of a Popular Insult in the United Kingdom, 1970–2018," *The British Journal of Politics and International Relations* 23, no. 4 (1 November 2021): 555–75; Aurelien Mondon, "Populism, Public Opinion, and the Mainstreaming of the Far Right: The 'Immigration Issue' and the Construction of a Reactionary 'People,'" *Politics*, 23 June 2022, 02633957221104726.

14. Kacper Szulecki et al., "To Vote or Not to Vote? Migrant Electoral (Dis)Engagement in an Enlarged Europe," *Migration Studies* 9, no. 3 (1 September 2021): 989–1010.

15. Pippa Norris and Ronald Inglehart, *Cultural Backlash: Trump, Brexit, and Authoritarian Populism* (Cambridge University Press, 2019).

16. Numerous studies have used this framing. I am reporting here a few examples of highly cited works published right after Brexit: Sara B. Hobolt, "The Brexit Vote: A Divided Nation, a Divided Continent," *Journal of European Public Policy* 23, no. 9 (2016): 1259–77; Matthew J. Goodwin and Oliver Heath, "Brexit Vote Explained: Poverty, Low Skills and Lack of Opportunities," JRF, 26 August 2016, https://www.jrf.org.uk/report/brexit-vote-explained-poverty-low-skills-and-lack-opportunities; David Cutts et al., "Brexit, the 2019 General Election and the Realignment of British Politics," *The Political Quarterly (London 1930)* 91, no. 1 (2020): 7–23.

17. Norris and Inglehart, *Cultural Backlash*; Matthijs Rooduijn, "What Unites the Voter Bases of Populist Parties? Comparing the Electorates of 15 Populist Parties," *European Political Science Review* 10, no. 3 (August 2018): 351–68.

18. Take Sipma, Marcel Lubbers, and Niels Spierings, "Working Class Economic Insecurity and Voting for Radical Right and Radical Left Parties," *Social Science Research* 109 (1 January 2023): 102778; Rooduijn, "What Unites the Voter Bases of Populist Parties?"; Noam Gidron and Jonathan J. B. Mijs, "Do Changes in Material Circumstances Drive Support for Populist Radical Parties? Panel Data Evidence from the Netherlands During the Great Recession, 2007–2015," *European Sociological Review* 35, no. 5 (1 October 2019): 637–50.

19. Sheri Berman, "The Causes of Populism in the West," *Annual Review of Political Science* 24, no. 1 (2021): 74–75.

20. Norris and Inglehart, *Cultural Backlash*.

21. Lorenza Antonucci et al., "'The Malaise of the Squeezed Middle': Challenging the Narrative of the 'Left Behind' Brexiter," *Competition & Change* 21, no. 3 (2017): 211–29; Thomas Kurer and Bruno Palier, "'Shrinking and Shouting': The Political Revolt of the Declining Middle in Times of Employment Polarization," *Research & Politics* 6, no. 1 (1 January 2019): 2053168019831164; Thomas Kurer, "The Declining Middle: Occupational Change, Social Status, and the Populist Right," *Comparative Political Studies* 53, no. 10–11 (2020): 1798–1835.

22. See the recent paper by Alexi Gugushvili, Daphne Halikiopoulou, and Tim Vlandas, "Downward Class Mobility and Far-Right Party Support in Western Europe," *Political Behavior* (2025), https://doi.org/10.1007/s11109-025-10033-7.

23. Albena Azmanova, *Capitalism on Edge: How Fighting Precarity Can Achieve Radical Change Without Crisis or Utopia* (Columbia University Press, 2020), 20.

24. Hanspeter Kriesi et al. introduced the use of globalization to articulate new social cleavages in "Globalization and the Transformation of the National Political Space: Six European Countries Compared," *European Journal of Political Research* 45, no. 6 (2006):

921–56. After Brexit, Dani Rodrik went back to his framing of globalization's winners versus globalization's losers to discuss the link with populism in "Why Does Globalization Fuel Populism? Economics, Culture, and the Rise of Right-Wing Populism," *Annual Review of Economics* 13 (2021): 133–70.

25. The balance between economic growth and social cohesion was, for example, at the center of the Sapir Report in 2004: André Sapir et al., *An Agenda for a Growing Europe: The Sapir Report* (Oxford University Press, 2004).

26. Seymour Martin Lipset, "Democracy and Working-Class Authoritarianism," *American Sociological Review* 24, no. 4 (1959): 482–501.

27. Rooduijn, "What Unites the Voter Bases of Populist Parties?"; Antonucci et al., "'The Malaise of the Squeezed Middle'"; Kurer and Palier, "'Shrinking and Shouting.'"

28. There have been several attempts to understand the changing social cleavages in Europe within political science. While I do not delve into cleavage analysis in this book, for the reasons explained in the text, it is important to note that studies on social cleavages often refer to economic insecurity that emerged after the Eurocrisis. See, for example, Robert Ford and Will Jennings, "The Changing Cleavage Politics of Western Europe," *Annual Review of Political Science* 23 (11 May 2020): 295–314; Liesbet Hooghe and Gary Marks, "Cleavage Theory Meets Europe's Crises: Lipset, Rokkan, and the Transnational Cleavage," *Journal of European Public Policy* 25, no. 1 (2 January 2018): 109–35.

29. Anders Hylmö and Michèle Lamont, "The World Is Not a Field—an Interview with Michèle Lamont," *Sociologisk Forskning* 56, no. 2 (2019): 177.

30. At the moment of writing, Norris and Inglehart's book *Cultural Backlash* counts over 4,800 citations on Google Scholar. A few examples of relevant works that reproduce a similar framing of the cultural sphere are Marta Kotwas and Jan Kubik, "Symbolic Thickening of Public Culture and the Rise of Right-Wing Populism in Poland," *East European Politics and Societies* 33, no. 2 (1 May 2019): 435–71; Cas Mudde and Cristóbal Rovira Kaltwasser, "Studying Populism in Comparative Perspective: Reflections on the Contemporary and Future Research Agenda," *Comparative Political Studies* 51, no. 13 (1 November 2018): 1667–93; and Hooghe and Marks, "Cleavage Theory Meets Europe's Crises." The application has been challenged by Armin Schaefer, "Cultural Backlash? How (Not) to Explain the Rise of Authoritarian Populism," *British Journal of Political Science* 52, no. 4 (2022): 1977–93.

31. Ronald F. Inglehart, *Cultural Evolution* (Cambridge University Press, 2018), 232.

32. Inglehart, *Cultural Evolution*; Norris and Inglehart, *Cultural Backlash*.

33. Bart Bonikowski, "Ethno-Nationalist Populism and the Mobilization of Collective Resentment: Ethno-Nationalist Populism," *British Journal of Sociology* 68 (2017): S181–213; Michèle Lamont, "Addressing Recognition Gaps: Destigmatization and the Reduction of Inequality," *American Sociological Review* 83, no. 3 (2018): 419–44.

34. Lorenza Antonucci and Simone Varriale, "Unequal Europe, Unequal Brexit: How Intra-European Inequalities Shape the Unfolding and Framing of Brexit," *Current Sociology* 68, no. 1 (2020): 41–59.

35. I will refer particularly to the following empirical cases: the UK for the Liberal security regime; the Netherlands, France, and Germany for the Continental security regime; Spain and Italy for the Southern European security regime; Sweden for the Nordic security regime; and Hungary and Poland for the Eastern European security regime.

Chapter 1. Defining Insecurity in Life and Politics

1. This is a reference to Ridgeway's contention that social status is everywhere: Cecilia L. Ridgeway, *Status: Why Is It Everywhere? Why Does It Matter?* (Russell Sage Foundation, 2019). The concepts of insecurity and social status are profoundly related as I conceptualize social status as partially resulting from the dynamic process of insecurity (see chapter 4 and the epilogue).

2. Astra Taylor, "Why Does Everyone Feel So Insecure All the Time?," *New York Times*, August, 18, 2023, https://www.nytimes.com/2023/08/18/opinion/inequality-insecurity-economic-wealth.html.

3. I am referring to the preexisting research on insecurity published in socioeconomic studies and to the work on insecurity produced by the community of socioeconomic researchers built around the miniconference "Navigating Insecurities" that I have cochaired since 2024 within the Annual Conference of the Society of Socioeconomic Advanced Studies (SASE). I am also referring to the contributions included in the special issue on insecurity and inequality that I am co-editing with Elena Ayala-Hurtado for the *British Journal of Sociology*.

4. Pierre Bourdieu, "A Reasoned Utopia and Economic Fatalism," *New Left Review*, no. 1/227 (1 February 1998): 127; Judith Butler, *Notes Toward a Performative Theory of Assembly* (Harvard University Press, 2015); Michael J. Graetz and Ian Shapiro, *The Wolf at the Door: The Menace of Economic Insecurity and How to Fight It* (Harvard University Press, 2020).

5. Anthony Giddens, "Risk and Responsibility," *Modern Law Review* 62, no. 1 (1999): 1–10; Ulrich Beck, "Risk Society: Towards a New Modernity," *Sage*, 1992; Ulrich Beck and Elisabeth Beck-Gernsheim, *The Normal Chaos of Love* (Wiley, 2018).

6. Zygmunt Bauman, *Community: Seeking Safety in an Insecure World* (Wiley, 2013), 144.

7. Peter Taylor-Gooby offers an attempt to empirically test the arguments of risk society scholars in relation to social structures in "Pervasive Uncertainty in Second Modernity: An Empirical Test," *Sociological Research Online* 10, no. 4 (1 December 2005): 26–34.

8. Lorenza Antonucci, "Not All Experiences of Precarious Work Lead to Precarity: The Case Study of Young People at University and Their Welfare Mixes," *Journal of Youth Studies* 21, no. 7 (9 August 2018): 888–904; Pugh, *The Tumbleweed Society*; Sarah Damaske, *The Tolls of Uncertainty: How Privilege and the Guilt Gap Shape Unemployment in America* (Princeton University Press, 2021); Alexandrea J. Ravenelle, Ken Cai Kowalski, and Erica Janko, "The Side Hustle Safety Net: Precarious Workers and Gig Work during COVID-19," *Sociological Perspectives* 64, no. 5 (October 2021): 898–919; Elizabeth C. Martin, "Regulating the Risk of Debt: Exemption Laws and Economic Insecurity Across U.S. States, 1986–2012," *American Journal of Sociology* 128, no. 3 (1 November 2022): 728–67.

9. Arne Kalleberg and Steven Vallas, eds., *Probing Precarious Work: Theory, Research, and Politics*, vol. 31, Research in the Sociology of Work (Emerald Publishing, 2017); Arne L. Kalleberg, *Precarious Lives: Job Insecurity and Well-Being in Rich Democracies* (Polity Press, 2018).

10. Guy Standing, "Understanding the Precariat Through Labour and Work," *Development and Change* 45, no. 5 (2014): 963–80.

11. Leah F. Vosko, *Precarious Employment: Understanding Labour Market Insecurity in Canada* (McGill-Queen's Press, 2006); Juliet B. Schor et al., "Dependence and Precarity in the Platform Economy," *Theory and Society* 49, no. 5 (1 October 2020): 833–61.

12. Martin, "Regulating the Risk of Debt"; Jacob S. Hacker, Philipp Rehm, and Mark Schlesinger, "The Insecure American: Economic Experiences, Financial Worries, and Policy Attitudes," *Perspectives on Politics* 11, no. 1 (March 2013): 23–49.

13. Claire Parfitt and Tom Barnes, "Rethinking Economic Security in a Precarious World," *Critical Sociology* 46, no. 4–5 (July 2020): 487–94.

14. Dennis Arnold and Joseph R. Bongiovi, "Precarious, Informalizing, and Flexible Work: Transforming Concepts and Understandings," *American Behavioral Scientist* 57, no. 3 (March 2013): 289–308; Ian Campbell and Robin Price, "Precarious Work and Precarious Workers: Towards an Improved Conceptualisation," *Economic and Labour Relations Review* 27, no. 3 (2016): 314–32; Kalleberg, *Precarious Lives*.

15. Elena Ayala-Hurtado, "Narrative Continuity/Rupture: Projected Professional Futures amid Pervasive Employment Precarity," *Work and Occupations* 49, no. 1 (1 February 2022): 45–78.

16. Bourdieu, "A Reasoned Utopia and Economic Fatalism," 127.

17. Loïc Wacquant, "Ordering Insecurity," *Radical Philosophy Review* 11, no. 1 (2008): 12.

18. Michael Savage, *Class Analysis and Social Transformation* (Open University, 2000); Will Atkinson, "Beck, Individualization and the Death of Class: A Critique," *British Journal of Sociology* 58, no. 3 (2007): 349–66.

19. This is precisely the topic of the forthcoming special issue I am coediting with Elena Ayala-Hurtado in the *British Journal of Sociology*, titled "The Precarity of Work and Life: How Insecurity Equalizes and Stratifies People's Experiences."

20. Lorenza Antonucci, *Student Lives in Crisis: Deepening Inequality in Times of Austerity* (Policy Press, 2017); Antonucci, "Not All Experiences of Precarious Work Lead to Precarity."

21. Gabriella Alberti et al., "In, Against and Beyond Precarity: Work in Insecure Times," *Work, Employment and Society* 32, no. 3 (1 June 2018): 451.

22. For example, in the Great British Class Survey, precarity features twice as the defining experience of "the precariat" and as an experience affecting young emerging service workers: Savage et al., "On Social Class, Anno 2014."

23. Michèle Lamont, *The Dignity of Working Men: Morality and the Boundaries of Race, Class, and Immigration* (Russell Sage Foundation, 2000).

24. Wacquant, "Ordering Insecurity," 15; Pugh, *The Tumbleweed Society*, 2015; Damaske, *The Tolls of Uncertainty*.

25. Joseph Choonara, "The Precarious Concept of Precarity," *Review of Radical Political Economics* 52, no. 3 (2020): 427–46.

26. Arnold and Bongiovi, "Precarious, Informalizing, and Flexible Work," 289.

27. Daniel Beland, "Right-Wing Populism and the Politics of Insecurity: How President Trump Frames Migrants as Collective Threats," *Political Studies Review* 18, no. 2 (2020): 162–77.

28. Wacquant, "Ordering Insecurity," 12.

29. Patrick Emmenegger, Paul Marx, and Dominik Schraff, "Labour Market Disadvantage, Political Orientations and Voting: How Adverse Labour Market Experiences Translate Into Electoral Behaviour," *Socio-Economic Review* 13, no. 2 (2015): 189–213; Hanna Schwander, "Labor Market Dualization and Insider–Outsider Divides: Why This New Conflict Matters," *Political Studies Review* 17, no. 1 (2019): 14–29; Allison E. Rovny and Jan Rovny, "Outsiders at the Ballot Box: Operationalizations and Political Consequences of the Insider–Outsider Dualism," *Socio-Economic Review*, 10 January 2017.

30. Duncan Gallie, "The Quality of Work in a Changing Labour Market," *Social Policy & Administration* 51, no. 2 (2017), 243.

31. Duncan Gallie et al., "The Hidden Face of Job Insecurity," *Work, Employment and Society* 31, no. 1 (2017): 36–53.

32. Helena Lopes, Sérgio Lagoa, and Teresa Calapez, "Work Autonomy, Work Pressure, and Job Satisfaction: An Analysis of European Union Countries," *Economic and Labour Relations Review* 25, no. 2 (June 2014): 306–26; Gallie, "The Quality of Work in a Changing Labour Market"; Gallie et al., "The Hidden Face of Job Insecurity."

33. These indicators have also been used, particularly in US academia, as measures of "dignity at work."

34. European Foundation for the Improvement of Living and Working Conditions, *Convergence and Divergence of Job Quality in Europe 1995–2010: A Report Based on the European Working Conditions Survey* (EU Publications Office, 2015), https://data.europa.eu/doi/10.2806/053563; Mark Smith et al., "Job Quality in Europe," *Industrial Relations Journal* 39, no. 6 (2008): 586.

35. Heejung Chung and Steffen Mau, "Subjective Insecurity and the Role of Institutions," *Journal of European Social Policy* 24, no. 4 (1 October 2014): 303–18.

36. Andrew Clark, "Measures of Job Satisfaction: What Makes a Good Job? Evidence from OECD Countries," OECD Labour Market and Social Policy Occasional Papers, vol. 34, 13 August 1998, https://doi.org/10.1787/670570634774; Chung and Mau, "Subjective Insecurity and the Role of Institutions."

37. Kalleberg, *Precarious Lives*; Guy Standing, *The Precariat: The New Dangerous Class* (Bloomsbury Academic, 2011), 82.

38. Gallie et al., "The Hidden Face of Job Insecurity"; Lopes, Lagoa, and Calapez, "Work Autonomy, Work Pressure, and Job Satisfaction."

39. Clark, "Measures of Job Satisfaction"; Standing, *The Precariat*, 32.

40. Clark, "Measures of Job Satisfaction."

41. Kalleberg, *Precarious Lives*; Standing, *The Precariat*, 10.

42. Lamont, *The Dignity of Working Men*.

43. Standing, *The Precariat*.

44. Edmund Heery and John Salmon, eds., *The Insecure Workforce* (Routledge, 2000), 12.

45. Clark, "Measures of Job Satisfaction."

46. In addition to Clark's work, the importance of job satisfaction and quality of work for Europeans is also demonstrated by the systematic research on the values of Europeans in Loek Halman, Ruud Luijkx, and Marga van Zundert, *Atlas of European Values* (Brill, 2005). One should note, however, that expectations on job quality might change in Europe over time as older workers report higher job quality than younger workers. See José M. Arranz, Carlos García-Serrano, and Virginia Hernanz, "Job Quality Differences Among Younger and Older Workers in Europe: The Role of Institutions," *Social Science Research* 84 (1 November 2019): 102345.

47. Pranab Bardhan, *A World of Insecurity: Democratic Disenchantment in Rich and Poor Countries* (Harvard University Press, 2022); Joaquín Prieto, "A Multidimensional Approach to Measuring Economic Insecurity: The Case of Chile," *Social Indicators Research* 163, no. 2 (1 September 2022): 823–55.

48. Andrew E. Clark, "Your Money or Your Life: Changing Job Quality in OECD Countries," *British Journal of Industrial Relations* 43, no. 3 (2005): 377–400.

49. Paul Marx and Georg Picot, "Three Approaches to Labor-Market Vulnerability and Political Preferences," *Political Science Research and Methods* 8, no. 2 (2020): 357.

50. Pugh, *The Tumbleweed Society*; Ranci et al., "New Measures of Economic Insecurity"; Barnes and Weller, "Becoming Precarious?"; Prieto, "A Multidimensional Approach to Measuring Economic Insecurity"; Bardhan, *A World of Insecurity*.

51. Standing, *The Precariat*.

52. Hacker, Rehm, and Schlesinger, "The Insecure American."

53. Peter Townsend, "Deprivation," *Journal of Social Policy* 16, no. 2 (1987): 125–46.

54. Anne-Catherine Guio et al., "Improving the Measurement of Material Deprivation at the European Union Level," *Journal of European Social Policy* 26, no. 3 (2016): 219–333.

55. Elaine Kempson and Sharon Collard, "Developing a Vision for Financial Inclusion" (University of Bristol, 2012); Ranci et al., "New Measures of Economic Insecurity."

56. Kristy L. Archuleta, Anita Dale, and Scott M. Spann, "College Students and Financial Distress: Exploring Debt, Financial Satisfaction, and Financial Anxiety," *Journal of Financial Counseling and Planning* 24, no. 2 (2013): 50–62.

57. Zhen Jie Im et al., "The 'Losers of Automation': A Reservoir of Votes for the Radical Right?," *Research & Politics* 6, no. 1 (January 2019): 205316801882239; Massimo Anelli, Italo Colantone, and Piero Stanig, "Individual Vulnerability to Industrial Robot Adoption Increases Support for the Radical Right," *Proceedings of the National Academy of Sciences–PNAS* 118, no. 47 (2021).

58. Heery and Salmon, *The Insecure Workforce*.

59. Bob Jessop, "Towards a Schumpeterian Workfare State? Preliminary Remarks on Post-Fordist Political Economy," *Studies in Political Economy* 40, no. 1 (1993): 13.

60. Without wanting to enter in the debate on the definition and utility of the concept of neoliberalism (which I use very sparsely in this book in favor of other specific concepts and manifestations), I recommend Jessop's nuanced contribution to the utility of neoliberalism in social sciences: Bob Jessop, "Putting Neoliberalism in Its Time and Place: A Response to the Debate," *Social Anthropology* 21, no. 1 (2013): 65–74. Jessop has also offered a useful typology of neoliberalism, particularly in investigating the state-market nexus through the notion of neoliberalism policies: Bob Jessop, "The Heartlands of Neoliberalism and the Rise of the Austerity State," in *Handbook of Neoliberalism* (Routledge, 2016).

61. Danny Dorling, *Peak Injustice: Solving Britain's Inequality Crisis* (Bristol University Press, 2024), 206.

62. Antonucci, *Student Lives in Crisis*.

63. Paul Pierson, "The New Politics of the Welfare State," *World Politics* 48, no. 2 (1996): 143–79.

64. Kees van Kersbergen, Barbara Vis, and Anton Hemerijck, "The Great Recession and Welfare State Reform: Is Retrenchment Really the Only Game Left in Town?," *Social Policy & Administration* 48, no. 7 (2014): 883–904.

65. Jon Kvist, "The Post-Crisis European Social Model: Developing or Dismantling Social Investments?," *Journal of International and Comparative Social Policy* 29, no. 1 (2013): 91–107.

66. Torben Iversen and David Soskice, *Democracy and Prosperity: Reinventing Capitalism Through a Turbulent Century* (Princeton University Press, 2019).

67. Jochen Kluve, "The Effectiveness of European Active Labor Market Programs," *Labour Economics* 17, no. 6 (1 December 2010): 904–18.

68. Bea Cantillon, "The Paradox of the Social Investment State: Growth, Employment and Poverty in the Lisbon Era," *Journal of European Social Policy* 21, no. 5 (2011): 432–49; Alain Noel, "Is Social Investment Inimical to the Poor?," *Socio-Economic Review* 18, no. 3 (2020): 857–80.

69. Mattias Bengtsson, Caroline de la Porte, and Kerstin Jacobsson, "Labour Market Policy Under Conditions of Permanent Austerity: Any Sign of Social Investment?," *Social Policy & Administration* 51, no. 2 (2017): 367–88.

70. Emanuele Ferragina, "Welfare State Change as a Double Movement: Four Decades of Retrenchment and Expansion in Compensatory and Employment-Oriented Policies Across 21 High-Income Countries," *Social Policy & Administration* 56, no. 5 (2022): 705–25.

71. Jacob S. Hacker, "Privatizing Risk Without Privatizing the Welfare State: The Hidden Politics of Social Policy Retrenchment in the United States," *American Political Science Review* 98, no. 2 (2004): 243–60.

72. Pugh, *The Tumbleweed Society*, 2015.

73. Antonucci, *Student Lives in Crisis*.

74. A. B. Atkinson, "After Piketty?," *British Journal of Sociology* 65, no. 4 (2014): 619–38.

75. Luigi Guiso et al., "The Financial Drivers of Populism in Europe," *SSRN Electronic Journal*, BAFFI CAREFIN Centre Research Paper no. 166, 2021. This point is also investigated and argued by J. Lawrence Broz, Jeffry Frieden, and Stephen Weymouth, "Populism in Place: The Economic Geography of the Globalization Backlash," *International Organization* 75, no. 2 (February 2021): 464–94, as well as by Chase Foster and Jeffry Frieden, "Compensation, Austerity, and Populism: Social Spending and Voting in 17 Western European Countries," working paper (December 2023).

76. Benjamin H. Snyder, *The Disrupted Workplace: Time and the Moral Order of Flexible Capitalism* (Oxford University Press, 2016); Pugh, *The Tumbleweed Society*; Ayala-Hurtado, "Narrative Continuity/Rupture."

77. Cecilia L. Ridgeway, "Why Status Matters for Inequality," *American Sociological Review* 79, no. 1 (1 February 2014): 1–16.

78. Tali Mendelberg, "Status, Symbols, and Politics: A Theory of Symbolic Status Politics," *RSF: The Russell Sage Foundation Journal of the Social Sciences* 8, no. 6 (1 November 2022): 51.

79. Bonikowski, "Ethno-Nationalist Populism and the Mobilization of Collective Resentment."

80. Lamont, "Addressing Recognition Gaps."

81. The concept of a Manichaean attitude is a borrowed term from the philosophy of Manichaeism, which is an old religion that breaks all judgment down into good or evil.

82. Mabel Berezin, *Illiberal Politics in Neoliberal Times: Culture, Security and Populism in the New Europe* (Cambridge University Press, 2009), 44.

83. Daniel Beland, "Ideas and Institutional Change in Social Security: Conversion, Layering, and Policy Drift," *Social Science Quarterly* 88, no. 1 (2007): 20–38; Beland, "Right-Wing Populism and the Politics of Insecurity."

84. Jenny Andersson, *Between Growth and Security: Swedish Social Democracy from a Strong Society to a Third Way* (Manchester University Press, 2006), 10.

85. Kees van Kersbergen, *Social Capitalism: A Study of Christian Democracy and the Welfare State* (Routledge, 1995).

86. Florence Faucher-King and Patrick Le Galès, *The New Labour Experiment: Change and Reform Under Blair and Brown* (Stanford University Press, 2010).

87. Azmanova, *Capitalism on Edge*, 73.

88. This nuance is evident in the work of critical social policy scholars, such as Fiona Williams, who recognizes the exclusionary elements embedded in European welfare states. See her essay "Race/Ethnicity, Gender, and Class in Welfare States: A Framework for Comparative Analysis," in *Rethinking European Welfare: Transformations of European Social Policy*, ed. Janet Finke, Gail Lewis, and John Clarke (Open University, 2001), 131–60. At the same time, she stresses that the move to an active welfare subject during New Labour resulted in a loss of a collective notion of socioeconomic security. See the discussion and conclusion in Fiona Williams, "Good-Enough Principles for Welfare," *Journal of Social Policy* 28, no. 4 (October 1999).

89. C. J. van Kersbergen and S. N. Kalyvas, "Christian Democracy," *Annual Review of Political Science* 13, no. 1 (2010): 183–209; Johannes Karreth, Jonathan T. Polk, and Christopher S. Allen, "Catchall or Catch and Release? The Electoral Consequences of Social Democratic Parties' March to the Middle in Western Europe," *Comparative Political Studies* 46, no. 7 (2013): 791–822; Hanspeter Kriesi, "The Political Consequences of the Financial and Economic Crisis in Europe: Electoral Punishment and Popular Protest," *Swiss Political Science Review* 18, no. 4 (2012): 518–22.

90. Sheri Berman and Maria Snegovaya, "Populism and the Decline of Social Democracy," *Journal of Democracy* 30, no. 3 (2019): 5–19.

91. Azmanova, *Capitalism on Edge*, 73.

92. Tim Bale et al., "If You Can't Beat Them, Join Them? Explaining Social Democratic Responses to the Challenge from the Populist Radical Right in Western Europe," *Political Studies* 58, no. 3 (2010): 410–26.

93. Paul Pierson, "Irresistible Forces, Immovable Objects: Post-Industrial Welfare States Confront Permanent Austerity," *Journal of European Public Policy* 5, no. 4 (1998): 539–60.

94. Vivien A. Schmidt, "Does Discourse Matter in the Politics of Welfare State Adjustment?," *Comparative Political Studies* 35, no. 2 (2002): 168–93.

95. Tony Cutler Waine, "Social Insecurity and the Retreat from Social Democracy: Occupational Welfare in the Long Boom and Financialization," *Review of International Political Economy* 8, no. 1 (2001): 96–118.

96. Schmidt, "Does Discourse Matter in the Politics of Welfare State Adjustment?"

97. Andersson, *Between Growth and Security*.

98. Certain authors refer explicitly to the leftist agenda of populist right parties: Gilles Ivaldi, "Towards the Median Economic Crisis Voter? The New Leftist Economic Agenda of the Front National in France," *French Politics* 13, no. 4 (2015): 346–69; Juliana Chueri, "An Emerging Populist Welfare Paradigm? How Populist Radical Right-Wing Parties Are Reshaping the Welfare State," *Scandinavian Political Studies* 45 (December 2022). Philip Rathgeb, instead, using data on the policies that are enacted by the populist right once in power, places more emphasis on the neoliberal and selective nature of populist right welfare state policies. See Philip Rathgeb, *How the Radical Right Has Changed Capitalism and Welfare in Europe and the USA* (Oxford University Press, 2024).

99. Williams, "Race/Ethnicity, Gender, and Class in Welfare States."

100. A recent book that systematized this argument is Peter Mair, *Ruling the Void: The Hollowing of Western Democracy* (Verso, 2013).

101. Guglielmo Meardi and Igor Guardiancich, "Back to the Familialist Future: The Rise of Social Policy for Ruling Populist Radical Right Parties in Italy and Poland," *West European Politics* 45, no. 1 (2022): 129–53.

102. See Luke March and Charlotte Rommerskirchen, "Out of Left Field? Explaining the Variable Electoral Success of European Radical Left Parties," *Party Politics* 21, no. 1 (2015): 40–53; Jonathan Hopkin, *Anti-System Politics: The Crisis of Market Liberalism in Rich Democracies* (Oxford University Press, 2020), particularly chapter 2.

103. Chantal Mouffe, *For a Left Populism* (Verso, 2018).

104. Íñigo Errejón, Chantal Mouffe, and Owen Jones, *Podemos: In the Name of the People* (Lawrence & Wishart, 2016), 67.

Chapter 2. The Fear of Keeping Your Job and of Having a Stagnant Life

1. Alan B. Krueger, "The Workplace: For Workers, Happiness Is Next to Productivity," *New York Times*, December 2005, https://www.nytimes.com/2005/12/13/business/worldbusiness/the-workplace-for-workers-happiness-is-next-to.html.

2. Etienne Mercier, "29 Percent of Europeans Say They Are in a Precarious Financial Situation," Ipsos, Second European Barometer on Poverty and Precariousness conducted for French Secours Populaire (September 2023), https://www.ipsos.com/en/29-europeans-say-they-are-currently-precarious-financial-situation.

3. A number of scholars have used a microlevel focus in welfare regime analysis, including Robert E. Goodin, ed., *The Real Worlds of Welfare Capitalism* (Cambridge University Press, 1999). A security-based focus in welfare regime analysis has also been used to understand the impact of welfare regimes across the world; see, for example, Geof Wood and Ian Gough, "A Comparative Welfare Regime Approach to Global Social Policy," *World Development* 34, no. 10 (2006): 1696–1712.

4. While the empirical analysis included Portugal, Czech Republic, and Romania, the presentation of the case-study analysis will focus on other countries from the same security regime in part due to space limitations, but also because covering these countries would not add much to the understanding of the regimes and to the empirical analysis of populist voting presented in the second part.

5. José M. Magone, Brigid Laffan, and Christian Schweiger, eds., *Core-Periphery Relations in the European Union: Power and Conflict in a Dualist Political Economy*, Routledge/UACES Contemporary European Studies 32 (Routledge, 2016).

6. Ipsos, Second European Barometer on Poverty and Precariousness.

7. Economic-based approaches tend to confute the presence of widespread insecurity, but they only examine job insecurity: Alan Manning and Graham Mazeine, "Subjective Job Insecurity and the Rise of the Precariat: Evidence from the United Kingdom, Germany, and the United States," *Review of Economics and Statistics* (2022), 1–45.

8. Faucher-King and Le Galés, *The New Labour Experiment*.

9. Duncan Gallie et al., "The Quality of Work in Britain Over the Economic Crisis,'" *International Review of Sociology* 24, no. 2 (2014): 207–24.

10. David N. F. Bell and David G. Blanchflower, "UK Unemployment in the Great Recession," *National Institute Economic Review* 214 214 (2010): 201; Annette Walling and Gareth Clancy, "Underemployment in the UK Labour Market," *Economic & Labour Market Review* 4, no. 2 (2010): 16–24.

11. Nikhil Datta, Giulia Giupponi, and Stephen Machin, "Zero-Hours Contracts and Labour Market Policy," *Economic Policy* 34, no. 99 (2019): 369–427; Cominetti Clark and Stephen Nye, "Setting the Record Straight: How Record Employment Has Changed the UK," Resolution Foundation, 14 January 2019, https://www.resolutionfoundation.org/publications/setting-the-record-straight-how-record-employment-has-changed-the-uk/.

12. Guy Standing, "Understanding the Precariat Through Labour and Work."

13. Gallie et al., "The Hidden Face of Job Insecurity."

14. Monica Costa Dias et al., "The Challenges for Labour Market Policy During the COVID-19 Pandemic," *Fiscal Studies* 41, no. 2 (2020): 371–82.

15. Sophia Parker, ed., *The Squeezed Middle: The Pressure on Ordinary Workers in America and Britain* (Bristol University Press, 2013); Paul Langley, "Financialization and the Consumer Credit Boom," *Competition & Change* 12, no. 2 (2008): 133–47.

16. Danny Dorling, *Shattered Nation: Inequality and the Geography of A Failing State* (Verso, 2023), 232.

17. OECD, *Under Pressure: The Squeezed Middle Class* (2019), https://doi.org/10.1787/689afed1-en; Matthew Whittaker, "Squeezed Britain 2013," Resolution Foundation, 13 February 2013, https://www.resolutionfoundation.org/publications/squeezed-britain-2013/.

18. Ranci et al., "New Measures of Economic Insecurity."

19. Zhiming Cheng et al., "Working Parents, Financial Insecurity, and Childcare: Mental Health in the Time of COVID-19 in the UK," *Review of Economics of the Household* 19, no. 1 (2021): 123–44; Heather Brown, Susanna Mills, and Viviana Albani, "Socioeconomic Risks of Food Insecurity During the Covid-19 Pandemic in the UK: Findings from the Understanding Society Covid Survey," *BMC Public Health* 22, no. 1 (2022): 590.

20. Francesca Marino and Luca Nunziata, "The Labor Market in Italy, 2000–2016," *IZA World of Labor*, 2017, https://doi.org/10.15185/izawol.407.

21. Anna Sanz-De-Galdeano and Anastasia Terskaya, "The Labor Market in Spain, 2002–2018," *IZA World of Labor*, 2020, https://doi.org/10.15185/izawol.403.v2.

22. Maribel Casas-Cortés and Sebastian Cobarrubias, "Precariedad Everywhere?! Rethinking Precarity and Emigration in Spain," in *Mapping Precariousness, Labour Insecurity and Uncertain Livelihoods*, vol. 1 (Routledge, 2017), 170–86; Isabel Tavoral and Paula Rodriguez-Modrono, "The Impact of the Crisis and Austerity on Low Educated Working Women: The Cases of Spain and Portugal," *Gender, Work, and Organization* 25, no. 6 (2018): 621–36.

23. Christine Erhel et al., "Trends in Job Quality During the Great Recession: A Comparative Approach for the EU," working papers halshs-00966898, HAL, 2014; Duncan Gallie and Zhou Ying, "Job Control, Work Intensity, and Work Stress," in *Economic Crisis, Quality of Work, and Social Integration*, ed. Duncan Gallie (Oxford University Press, 2013), 115–41.

24. Marino and Nunziata, "The Labor Market in Italy, 2000–2016"; Athina Avagianou et al., "Being NEET in Youthspaces of the EU South: A Post-Recession Regional Perspective," *Young* 30, no. 5 (2022): 425–54.

25. Valeria Cirillo, Marta Fana, and Dario Guarascio, "Labour Market Reforms in Italy: Evaluating the Effects of the Jobs Act," *Economia Politica* 34, no. 2 (2017): 211–32.

26. Matteo Jessoula, Paolo R. Graziano, and Ilaria Madama, "'Selective Flexicurity' in Segmented Labour Markets: The Case of Italian 'Mid-Siders,'" *Journal of Social Policy* 39, no. 4 (2010): 561–83.

27. Ranci et al., "New Measures of Economic Insecurity"; Maria Petmesidou, ed., *Economic Crisis and Austerity in Southern Europe: Threat or Opportunity for a Sustainable Welfare State*, South European Society and Politics (Taylor & Francis, 2015).

28. Pepper D. Culpepper, "The Political Economy of Unmediated Democracy: Italian Austerity Under Mario Monti," *West European Politics* 37, no. 6 (2 November 2014): 1264–81.

29. Tito Boeri, Andrea Brandolini, and Nicola Rossi, "The Age of Discontent: Italian Households at the Beginning of the Decade," *Giornale Degli Economisti e Annali Di Economia* 63 (Anno 117), no. 3/4 (2004): 449–90; Riccardo Massari, Maria Grazia Pittau, and Roberto Zelli, "A Dwindling Middle Class? Italian Evidence in the 2000s," *Journal of Economic Inequality* 7, no. 4 (2009): 333–50; Steven Pressman, "The Decline of the Middle Class: An International Perspective," *Journal of Economic Issues* 41, no. 1 (2007): 181–200.

30. Thomas Amossé et al., *Que sait-on du travail?* (Sciences Po; Le Monde, 2023).

31. Sotiria Theodoropoulou, *Labour Market Policies in the Era of Pervasive Austerity: A European Perspective* (Policy Press, 2018).

32. Philippe Askenazy, "The Changing of the French Labor Market, 2000–2017," *IZA World of Labor*, 2018; Philippe Askenazy and Bruno Palier, "France: Rising Precariousness Supported by the Welfare State," in *Inequality and Inclusive Growth in Rich Countries: Shared Challenges and Contrasting Fortunes*, ed. Brian Nolan (Oxford University Press, 2018).

33. Erhel et al., "Trends in Job Quality During the Great Recession"; Janine Leschke and Andrew Watt, "Challenges in Constructing a Multi-Dimensional European Job Quality Index," *Social Indicators Research* 118, no. 1 (2014): 1–31.

34. Ranci et al., "New Measures of Economic Insecurity."

35. Jake Bradley and Alice Kügler, "Labor Market Reforms: An Evaluation of the Hartz Policies in Germany," *European Economic Review* 113 (2019): 108–35.

36. Jens Alber and Jan Paul Heisig, "Do New Labour Activation Policies Work? A Descriptive Analysis of the German Hartz Reforms," Wissenschaftszentrum Berlin für Sozialforschung, WZB (2011).

37. Kalleberg, *Precarious Lives.*

38. Karl Brenke, Ulf Rinne, and Klaus F. Zimmermann, "Short-Time Work: The German Answer to the Great Recession," *International Labour Review* 152, no. 2 (2013): 287–305.

39. Erhel et al., "Trends in Job Quality During the Great Recession."

40. Boris Chafwehé, Mattia Ricci, and Daniel Stoehlker, "The Impact of the Cost-of-Living Crisis on European Households," JRC Working Papers on Taxation and Structural Reforms, 2024.

41. Miles Corak, Michael Fertig, and Marcus Tamm, "A Portrait of Child Poverty in Germany," *Review of Income and Wealth* 54, no. 4 (2008): 547–71; Marco Giesselmann, "Differences in the Patterns of In-Work Poverty in Germany and the UK," *European Societies* 17, no. 1 (2015): 27–46.

42. Nicole Rippin, "Multidimensional Poverty in Germany: A Capability Approach," *Forum for Social Economics* 45, no. 2–3 (2016): 230–55.

43. Sabine Pfeiffer, Tobias Ritter, and Andreas Hirseland, "Hunger and Nutritional Poverty in Germany: Quantitative and Qualitative Empirical Insights," *Critical Public Health* 21, no. 4 (1 December 2011): 425.

44. Sotiria Theodoropoulou, *Labour Market Policies in the Era of Pervasive Austerity: A European Perspective* (Policy Press, 2018).

45. Erhel et al., "Trends in Job Quality During the Great Recession"; Leschke and Watt, "Challenges in Constructing a Multi-Dimensional European Job Quality Index."

46. Leschke and Watt, "Challenges in Constructing a Multi-Dimensional European Job Quality Index."

47. Johanna Louisa Ypeij, *Single Motherhood and Poverty: The Case of the Netherlands* (Amsterdam: Aksant, 2009); Cäzilia Loibl et al., "Which Financial Stressors Are Linked to Food Insecurity Among Older Adults in the United Kingdom, Germany, and the Netherlands? An Exploratory Study," *Food Security* 14, no. 2 (2022): 533–56.

48. Josien Arts and Marguerite Van Den Berg, "Pedagogies of Optimism: Teaching to 'Look Forward' in Activating Welfare Programmes in the Netherlands," *Critical Social Policy* 39, no. 1 (1 February 2019): 66–86.

49. Tomas Berglund, Kristina Håkansson, and Tommy Isidorsson, "Occupational Change on the Dualised Swedish Labour Market," *Economic and Industrial Democracy* 43, no. 2 (2022): 918–42; Jørgen Svalund and Tomas Berglund, "Fixed-Term Employment in Norway and Sweden: A Pathway to Labour Market Marginalization?," *European Journal of Industrial Relations* 24, no. 3 (2018): 261–77; Tomas Berglund et al., "Temporary Contracts, Employment Trajectories and Dualisation: A Comparison of Norway and Sweden," *Work, Employment and Society* 37, no. 2 (2023): 505–24.

50. Hulya Ulku and Silvia Muzi, "Labor Market Regulations and Outcomes in Sweden: A Comparative Analysis of Recent Trends," Policy Research Working Paper, 7229 (2015), http://hdl.handle.net/10986/21843.

51. Tomas Berglund et al., "Temporary Employment and the Future Labor Market Status," *Nordic Journal of Working Life Studies* 7, no. 2 (2017); Lisa Laun and Mårten Palme, "The Recent Rise of Labor Force Participation of Older Workers in Sweden," NBER Working Paper Series, 2018.

52. Erhel et al., "Trends in Job Quality During the Great Recession."

53. B. Halleröd, "Making Ends Meet: Perceptions of Poverty in Sweden," *Scandinavian Journal of Social Welfare* 4, no. 3 (1995): 174–89. Regarding insecurity among migrants, see Kræn Blume et al., "At the Lower End of the Table: Determinants of Poverty Among Immigrants to Denmark and Sweden," *Journal of Ethnic and Migration Studies* 33, no. 3 (2007): 373–96; Christel Kesler, "Welfare States and Immigrant Poverty: Germany, Sweden, and the United Kingdom in Comparative Perspective," *Acta Sociologica* 58, no. 1 (2015): 39–61; Ognjen Obucina, "Paths into and out of Poverty Among Immigrants in Sweden," *Acta Sociologica* 57, no. 1 (2014): 5–23. Regarding insecurity among young people, see Timo M. Kauppinen et al., "Social Background and Life-Course Risks as Determinants of Social Assistance Receipt Among Young Adults in Sweden, Norway and Finland," *Journal of European Social Policy* 24, no. 3 (2014): 273–88.

54. Ranci et al., "New Measures of Economic Insecurity."

55. Anneli Marttila et al., "Controlled and Dependent: Experiences of Living on Social Assistance in Sweden," *International Journal of Social Welfare* 19, no. 2 (2010): 142–51.

56. Duncan Gallie, ed., *Economic Crisis, Quality of Work, and Social Integration: The European Experience* (Oxford University Press, 2013); Bob Deacon, "Eastern European Welfare States: The Impact of the Politics of Globalization," *Journal of European Social Policy* 10, no. 2 (2000): 146–61; Dorothee Bohle and Béla Greskovits, "Neoliberalism, Embedded Neoliberalism and Neocorporatism: Towards Transnational Capitalism in Central-Eastern Europe," *West European Politics* 30, no. 3 (2007): 443–66; Alfio Cerami and Pieter Vanhuysse, eds., *Post-Communist Welfare Pathways: Theorizing Social Policy Transformations in Central and Eastern Europe* (Palgrave Macmillan, 2009); Zsuzsa Ferge, "Welfare and 'Ill-Fare' Systems in Central-Eastern Europe," in *Globalization and European Welfare States* (Macmillan Education UK, 2001), 127–52.

57. Deacon, "Eastern European Welfare States."

58. Zsuzsa Ferge and Katalin Tausz, "Social Security in Hungary: A Balance Sheet After Twelve Years," *Social Policy & Administration* 36, no. 2 (2002): 176–99; Zsuzsa Ferge, Katalin Tausz, and Ágnes Darvas, *A Case Study of Hungary*, vol. 1 (International Labour Office, Central and Eastern European Team, 2002).

59. Ferge and Tausz, "Social Security in Hungary."

60. Sara Hungler, "Labor Law Reforms After the Populist Turn in Hungary," *Review of Central and East European Law* 47, no. 1 (2022): 84–114; Levente Alpek and Robert Tésits, "Measuring Regional Differences in Labour Market Sensitivity in Hungary," *Applied Spatial Analysis and Policy* 12, no. 1 (2019): 127–46.

61. Zoltán Lakner and Katalin Tausz, "From a Welfare to a Workfare State: Hungary," in *Challenges to European Welfare Systems*, ed. Klaus Schubert, Paloma de Villota, and Johanna Kuhlmann (Springer International, 2016), 325–50.

62. Piotr Lewandowski, Góra Marek, and Lis Maciej, "Temporary Employment Boom in Poland: A Job Quality vs. Quantity Trade-Off?," IZA Discussion Papers, no. 11012, Institute of Labor Economics, Bonn, 2017.

63. Leschke and Watt, "Challenges in Constructing a Multi-Dimensional European Job Quality Index."

64. Lewandowski, Marek and Maciej, "Temporary Employment Boom in Poland."

65. Meardi and Guardiancich, "Back to the Familialist Future."

66. Renata Siemienska and Anna Domaradzka, "Politics of Welfare: The Polish Welfare System in the First Decades of the 21st Century," in *Routledge Handbook of European Welfare Systems*, 2nd ed. (Routledge, 2019).

67. Werner Eichhorst and Paul Marx. "How Stable Is Labour Market Dualism? Reforms of Employment Protection in Nine European Countries," *European Journal of Industrial Relations* 27, no. 1 (2021): 93–110.

68. Naoki Akaeda and Nadine M. Schöneck, "Socio-Economic Insecurity Perceptions and Their Societal Determinants: Europe in the Aftermath of the Great Recession," *European Societies* 24, no. 3 (2022): 310–32.

69. Sławomir Kalinowski, Aleksandra Łuczak, and Adam Koziolek, "The Social Dimension of Security: The Dichotomy of Respondents' Perceptions During the COVID-19 Pandemic," *Sustainability* 14, no. 3 (2022): 1363.

70. B. ter Weel, "The Rise of Temporary Work in Europe," *De Economist (Netherlands)* 166, no. 4 (2018): 397–401.

71. Gallie, "The Quality of Work in a Changing Labour Market."

72. Kevin Doogan, "Insecurity and Long-Term Employment," *Work, Employment and Society* 15, no. 3 (2001): 419–41.

73. Clark, "Your Money or Your Life."

74. Lopes, Lagoa, and Calapez, "Work Autonomy, Work Pressure, and Job Satisfaction"; European Foundation for the Improvement of Living and Working Conditions, *Convergence and Divergence of Job Quality in Europe 1995–2010: A Report Based on the European Working Conditions Survey* (EU Publications Office, 2015), https://data.europa.eu/doi/10.2806/053563.

75. Agnieszka Piasna, "Bad Jobs Recovery? European Job Quality Index 2005–2015," *ETUI Research Paper*, working paper (January 2018).

76. Lopes, Lagoa, and Calapez, "Work Autonomy, Work Pressure, and Job Satisfaction."

77. Parker, *The Squeezed Middle.*

78. OECD, *Under Pressure.*

79. Branko Milanović, *Global Inequality: A New Approach for the Age of Globalization* (Belknap Press of Harvard University Press, 2018).

80. Daniel Vaughan-Whitehead, ed., *Europe's Disappearing Middle Class? Evidence from the World of Work* (Edward Elgar, 2016).

81. Christopher T. Whelan, Brian Nolan, and Bertrand Maitre, "Polarization or 'Squeezed Middle' in the Great Recession? A Comparative European Analysis of the Distribution of Economic Stress," *Social Indicators Research* 133, no. 1 (2017): 163–84.

82. Ranci et al., "New Measures of Economic Insecurity."

83. Some scholars who examine deprivation look only at who reports finding it difficult or very difficult to live on current income, while here I include also those who are coping (namely, who report to be able to live on current income despite the difficulties) because, in alignment with other studies on insecurity, my aim is to include the entire portion of the population that is not secure, namely, those who do not live comfortably on present income.

84. Whelan, Nolan, and Maitre, "Polarization or 'Squeezed Middle' in the Great Recession?"

85. Marius R. Busemeyer and Julian L. Garritzmann, "Compensation or Social Investment? Revisiting the Link Between Globalisation and Popular Demand for the Welfare State," *Journal of Social Policy* 48, no. 3 (2019): 427–48; Jochen Clasen, "Motives, Means and Opportunities: Reforming Unemployment Compensation in the 1990s," *West European Politics* 23, no. 2 (2000): 89–112.

Chapter 3. The Transformed Welfare States and the Effects on Insecurity

1. Rudi Dornbusch, "Euro Fantasies," *Foreign Affairs* 75, no. 5 (1996): 110–25, quote on 120.

2. J. Magnus Ryner, *Capitalist Restructuring, Globalization and the Third Way: Lessons from the Swedish Model* (London: Routledge, 2002), 35.

3. Rolf Heinze and Wolfgang Streeck, "An Arbeit fehlt es nicht," *Der Spiegel* 19 (May 10, 1999), 38.

4. The intellectual work by Streeck and his colleagues also constitutes the intellectual basis of the Hartz reforms that followed, according to Jürgen Klute and Sandra Kotlenga, eds., *Sozial- und Arbeitsmarktpolitik nach Hartz: fünf Jahre Hartzreformen; Bestandsaufnahme, Analysen, Perspektiven* (Univ.-Verl. Göttingen, 2008).

5. Wolfgang Streeck, "The Return of the Repressed," *New Left Review*, no. 104 (1 April 2017): 5. Note that Streeck refers to neoliberalism in particular, but, as discussed earlier, neoliberalism is different from what happened in Europe, and the reforms he is criticizing are the result of specific political and institutional choices.

6. van Kersbergen, Vis, and Hemerijck, "The Great Recession and Welfare State Reform; Kvist, "The Post-Crisis European Social Model."

7. Yascha Mounk, *The Age of Responsibility: Luck, Choice, and the Welfare State* (Harvard University Press, 2017); Jacob S. Hacker, *The Great Risk Shift: The New Economic Insecurity and the Decline of the American Dream*, second ed. (Oxford University Press, 2019).

8. Gurminder K. Bhambra and John and Holmwood, "Colonialism, Postcolonialism and the Liberal Welfare State," *New Political Economy* 23, no. 5 (3 September 2018): 574–87; Fiona Williams, "Extraction, Exploitation, Expropriation and Expulsion in the Domestic Colonial Relations of the British Welfare State in the Twentieth and Twenty-First Centuries," *British Journal of Sociology* 73, no. 1 (2022): 23–34.

9. Fernand Braudel, *Civilization and Capitalism, 15th–18th Century*, vol. 1: *The Structure of Everyday Life*, trans. Siân Reynold (1992); Immanuel Maurice Wallerstein, *The Modern World System. 1: Capitalist Agriculture and the Origins of the European World-Economy in*

the Sixteenth Century: With a New Prologue Studies in Social Discontinuity (University of California Press, 2011).

10. Standing, *The Precariat.*

11. Milanović, *Global Inequality.*

12. Nihel Chabrak, Russell Craig, and Nabyla Daidj, "Financialization and the Employee Suicide Crisis at France Telecom," *Journal of Business Ethics* 139, no. 3 (1 December 2016): 501–15.

13. Milanović, *Global Inequality.*

14. Jessop, "Towards a Schumpeterian Workfare State?"

15. Kevin Farnsworth, *Social Versus Corporate Welfare: Competing Needs and Interests Within the Welfare State* (Springer, 2012).

16. Fabio Bulfone, Timur Ergen, and Manolis Kalaitzake, "No Strings Attached: Corporate Welfare, State Intervention, and the Issue of Conditionality," *Competition & Change* 27, no. 2 (2023): 253–76.

17. Bulfone, Ergen, and Kalaitzake, 70.

18. Manuel B. Aalbers, "The Variegated Financialization of Housing," *International Journal of Urban and Regional Research* 41, no. 4 (2017): 542–54.

19. Bernhard Ebbinghaus, "The Privatization and Marketization of Pensions in Europe: A Double Transformation Facing the Crisis," *European Policy Analysis* 1, no. 1 (2015): 56–73; Adam D. Dixon, "Financialization and the Welfare State," in *The New Geography of Capitalism: Firms, Finance, and Society*, ed. Adam D. Dixon (Oxford University Press, 2014).

20. Jessop, "Towards a Schumpeterian Workfare State?"

21. Neil Gilbert, *Transformation of the Welfare State: The Silent Surrender of Public Responsibility* (Oxford University Press, 2002); Standing, *The Precariat*; Wolfgang Streeck, "How Will Capitalism End?," *New Left Review* (2014): 35–64; Iversen and Soskice, *Democracy and Prosperity.*

22. Iversen and Soskice, *Democracy and Prosperity.*

23. Francesco Laruffa, "Social Investment: Diffusing Ideas for Redesigning Citizenship After Neo-Liberalism?," *Critical Social Policy* 38, no. 4 (1 November 2018): 688–706.

24. Jean-Claude Barbier and Matthias Knuth, "Of Similarities and Divergences: Why There Is No Continental Ideal-Type of 'Activation Reforms,'" *Documents de Travail Du Centre d'Economie de La Sorbonne*, October 2010; Bengtsson, de la Porte, and Jacobsson, "Labour Market Policy Under Conditions of Permanent Austerity."

25. Jon Kvist, "A Framework for Social Investment Strategies: Integrating Generational, Life Course and Gender Perspectives in the EU Social Investment Strategy," *Comparative European Politics* 13, no. 1 (2015): 131–49.

26. Julian L. Garritzmann et al., eds., *The World Politics of Social Investment*, vol. 1: *Welfare States in the Knowledge Economy*, International Policy Exchange (Oxford University Press, 2022), 60.

27. Jane Jenson, "Redesigning Citizenship Regimes After Neoliberalism: Moving Towards Social Investment," in *Towards a Social Investment Welfare State?* (Policy Press, 2011), 69.

28. Bruno Palier, Julian L. Garritzmann, and Silja Häusermann, "Toward a Worldwide View on the Politics of Social Investment," in *The World Politics of Social Investment*, vol. 1: *Welfare States in the Knowledge Economy*, ed. Julian L. Garritzmann, Silja Häusermann, and Bruno Palier (Oxford University Press, 2022).

29. Silja Häusermann, Julian L. Garritzmann, and Bruno Palier, "The Politics of Social Investment: A Global Theoretical Framework," in Garritzmann, Häusermann, and Palier, *The World Politics of Social Investment*, vol. 1, 60.

30. Anton Hemerijck, Stefano Ronchi, and Ilze Plavgo, "Social Investment as a Conceptual Framework for Analysing Well-Being Returns and Reforms in 21st Century Welfare States," *Socio-Economic Review* 21, no. 1 (1 January 2023): 479–500.

31. Häusermann, Garritzmann, and Palier, "The Politics of Social Investment," 66–67.

32. Hartley Dean, "Critiquing Capabilities: The Distractions of a Beguiling Concept," *Critical Social Policy* 29, no. 2 (2009): 261–78.

33. Neil Gilbert, *Never Enough: Capitalism and the Progressive Spirit* (Oxford University Press, 2016).

34. Len Doyal and Ian Gough, "A Theory of Human Needs," *Critical Social Policy* 4, no. 10 (1984): 6–38; Gøsta Esping-Andersen, *The Three Worlds of Welfare Capitalism* (Polity, 1990).

35. Karl Polanyi, *The Great Transformation* (Beacon Press, 2001), 185.

36. Josien Arts and Marguerite Van Den Berg, "Pedagogies of Optimism: Teaching to 'Look Forward' in Activating Welfare Programmes in the Netherlands," *Critical Social Policy* 39, no. 1 (2019): 66–86; Anneli Marttila et al., "Controlled and Dependent: Experiences of Living on Social Assistance in Sweden," *International Journal of Social Welfare* 19, no. 2 (2010): 142–51.

37. Cantillon, "The Paradox of the Social Investment State."

38. Walter Korpi and Joakim Palme, "The Paradox of Redistribution and Strategies of Equality: Welfare State Institutions, Inequality, and Poverty in the Western Countries," *American Sociological Review* 63, no. 5 (1998): 661–87; Dimitri Gugushvili and Tijs Laenen, "Two Decades After Korpi and Palme's 'Paradox of Redistribution': What Have We Learned So Far and Where Do We Take It from Here?," *Journal of International and Comparative Social Policy* 37, no. 2 (2021): 112–27.

39. Werner Eichhorst et al., "Quantity Over Quality? A European Comparison of the Changing Nature of Transitions Between Non-Employment and Employment," in *Regulating the Risk of Unemployment: National Adaptations to Post-Industrial Labour Markets in Europe*, ed. Jochen Clasen and Daniel Clegg (Oxford University Press, 2011), 281.

40. Bengtsson, de la Porte, and Jacobsson, "Labour Market Policy Under Conditions of Permanent Austerity."

41. Chung and Mau, "Subjective Insecurity and the Role of Institutions"; Christopher J. Anderson and Jonas Pontusson, "Workers, Worries and Welfare States: Social Protection and Job Insecurity in 15 OECD Countries," *European Journal of Political Research* 46, no. 2 (2007): 211–35.

42. Giuliano Bonoli, "The Political Economy of Active Labor-Market Policy," *Politics & Society* 38, no. 4 (2010): 435–57.

43. Lorenza Antonucci, Hyojin Seo, and Martin Strobl, "Quantity Over Quality? How Economic Factors and Welfare State Interventions Affected Job Insecurity and Job Quality Before, During and After the Economic Crises," *Social Policy & Administration* 58, no. 2 (2024): 277–98.

44. Heejung Chung and Wim van Oorschot, "Institutions Versus Market Forces: Explaining the Employment Insecurity of European Individuals During (the Beginning of) the Financial Crisis," *Journal of European Social Policy* 21, no. 4 (2011): 287–301.

45. Iversen and Soskice, *Democracy and Prosperity*.

46. Cantillon, "The Paradox of the Social Investment State."

47. Olaf Van Vliet and Chen Wang, "Social Investment and Poverty Reduction: A Comparative Analysis Across Fifteen European Countries," *Journal of Social Policy* 44, no. 3 (2015): 611–38.

48. Sarah Marchal, Ive Marx, and Natascha Van Mechelen, "The Great Wake-Up Call? Social Citizenship and Minimum Income Provisions in Europe in Times of Crisis," *Journal of Social Policy* 43, no. 2 (April 2014): 247–67.

49. Olivier Pintelon et al., "The Social Stratification of Social Risks: The Relevance of Class for Social Investment Strategies," *Journal of European Social Policy* 23, no. 1 (2013): 52–67; Bea Cantillon and Wim Van Lancker, "Three Shortcomings of the Social Investment Perspective," *Social Policy and Society* 12, no. 4 (2013): 553–64.

50. Cantillon, "The Paradox of the Social Investment State."

51. Ferragina, "Welfare State Change as a Double Movement."

52. Lyle A. Scruggs and Gabriela Ramalho Tafoya, "Fifty Years of Welfare State Generosity," *Social Policy & Administration* 56, no. 5 (2022): 791–807.

53. Marchal, Marx, and Mechelen, "The Great Wake-Up Call?"

54. Kersbergen, Vis, and Hemerijck, "The Great Recession and Welfare State Reform"; Kvist, "The Post-Crisis European Social Model."

55. See the discussion of the rise of credit use in Europe in Akos Rona-Tas and Alya Guseva, "Consumer Credit in Comparative Perspective," *Annual Review of Sociology* 44 (2018): 55–75.

56. Silvia Magri et al., "The Expansion of Consumer Credit in Italy and the Main Euro Area Countries," *European Review* 30, no. 3 (2022): 322–52.

57. Stephen P. Jenkins, ed., *The Great Recession and the Distribution of Household Income*, Reports for the Fondazione Rodolfo Debenedetti (Oxford University Press, 2013).

58. Both the authors who are critical of EU's role (see the following references) and those who are more positive about the postausterity shift recognize that 2010 was a period of austerity for EU policies. See, for example, Jonathan Zeitlin and Bart Vanhercke, "Socializing the European Semester: EU Social and Economic Policy Co-Ordination in Crisis and Beyond," *Journal of European Public Policy* 25, no. 2 (2018): 149–74.

59. A. Crespy and G. Menz, "Conclusion: Social Europe Is Dead. What's Next?," in *Social Policy and the Euro Crisis. Palgrave Studies in European Union Politics* (Palgrave Macmillan, 2015), 199–200.

60. P. Copeland and M. Daly, "The European Semester and EU Social Policy," *Journal of Common Market Studies* 56, no. 5 (2018): 1001–18.

61. Vivien A. Schmidt, "Speaking to the Markets or to the People? A Discursive Institutionalist Analysis of the EU's Sovereign Debt Crisis," *British Journal of Politics & International Relations* 16, no. 1 (2013): 188–209.

62. Joan Miró, "In the Name of Competitiveness: A Discursive Institutionalist Analysis of the EU's Approach to Labour Market Structural Reform, 2007–2016," *Socio-Economic Review* 19, no. 2 (2021): 711–33.

63. Philip Rathgeb and Arianna Tassinari, "How the Eurozone Disempowers Trade Unions: The Political Economy of Competitive Internal Devaluation," *Socio-Economic Review* 20, no. 1 (2022): 323–50.

64. Valerie J. D'Erman et al., "The European Semester in the North and in the South: Domestic Politics and the Salience of EU-Induced Wage Reform in Different Growth Models," *JCMS: Journal of Common Market Studies* 60, no. 1 (2022): 21–39.

65. Sotiria Theodoropoulou, "National Social and Labour Market Policy Reforms in the Shadow of EU Bailout Conditionality: The Cases of Greece and Portugal," in *The Sovereign Debt Crisis, the EU and Welfare State Reform*, ed. Caroline De La Porte and Elke Heins, Work and Welfare in Europe (Palgrave Macmillan UK, 2016), 95–130.

66. Sotiria Theodoropoulou, *Labour Market Policies in the Era of Pervasive Austerity: A European Perspective* (Policy Press, 2018); Sotiria Theodoropoulou and Andrew Watt, "Withdrawal Symptoms: An Assessment of the Austerity Packages in Europe," SSRN Scholarly Paper, 4 May 2011.

67. On austerity in the UK, see Kevin Farnsworth, "Retrenched, Reconfigured and Broken: The British Welfare State After a Decade of Austerity," *Social Policy and Society* 20, no. 1 (2021): 77–96; on German austerity, see Berndt Keller, "The Continuation of Early Austerity Measures: The Special Case of Germany," *Transfer: European Review of Labour and Research* 20, no. 3 (2014): 387–402.

68. Jonathan Zeitlin and Bart Vanhercke, "Socializing the European Semester: EU Social and Economic Policy Co-Ordination in Crisis and Beyond," *Journal of European Public Policy* 25, no. 2 (2018): 149–74.

69. Amandine Crespy and Vivien A. Schmidt, "The EU's Economic Governance in 2016: Beyond Austerity?," in *Social Policy in the European Union: State of Play 2017* (European Social Observatory, 2017), 107–23.

70. Lorenza Antonucci and Francesco Corti, "Inequalities in the European Semester," FEPS, 2020.

71. Rakesh Kochhar, "Middle Class Fortunes in Western Europe," *Policy File* (Pew Research Center, 2017); Vaughan-Whitehead, *Europe's Disappearing Middle Class?*

72. This point is made by Caroline de La Porte and Bruno Palier, "The Politics of European Union's Social Investment Initiatives," in *The World Politics of Social Investment*, vol. 1: *Welfare States in the Knowledge Economy*, ed. Julian Garritzmann, Bruno Palier, and

Silja Hausermann (Oxford University Press, 2022), 132. An example of a paper written to push for the adoption of social investment policies at the EU level is Frank Vandenbroucke, Anton Hemerijck, and Bruno Palier, "The EU Needs a Social Investment Pact," SSRN Scholarly Paper (Rochester, NY, 1 May 2011).

73. Patrick Emmenegger, ed., *The Age of Dualization: The Changing Face of Inequality in Deindustrializing Societies*, International Policy Exchange Series (Oxford University Press, 2012).

74. De La Porte and Palier, "The Politics of European Union's Social Investment Initiatives."

75. European Central Bank, "Interview with the Wall Street Journal," 24 February 2012, https://www.ecb.europa.eu/press/key/date/2012/html/sp120224.en.html.

76. I briefly referred to this debate in chapter 1. See the contribution by Jessop, "Putting Neoliberalism in Its Time and Place."

77. Alberto Alesina and Francesci Giavazzi, *The Future of Europe, Reform or Decline* (Cambridge University Press, 2006), cited in Berezin, *Illiberal Politics in Neoliberal Times*, 5.

Chapter 4. Demand and Supply in the New Politics of Insecurity

1. Paris Aslanidis, "Is Populism an Ideology? A Refutation and a New Perspective," *Political Studies* 64, no. 1_suppl (1 April 2016): 88–104, stresses how populism is at times used in a derogatory way in the public and academic debate.

2. Cas Mudde, "The Far Right and the 2024 European Elections," *Intereconomics* 59, no. 2 (2024): 61–65.

3. Aurelien Mondon and Aaron Winter, *Reactionary Democracy: How Racism and the Populist Far Right Became Mainstream* (Verso, 2020).

4. The approach I use is different from the categorization employed by Cas Mudde, who includes the populist right and nonpopulist extreme right under the umbrella of the far right in *The Far Right Today* (Wiley, 2019). Readers should note, however, that in current politics the two categories very frequently overlap, and that Mudde himself has been involved in the categorization of populist parties via the PopuList. Populist left parties are categorized, by some nonideational scholars, as radical left parties. See Luke March, *Radical Left Parties in Europe*, Routledge Studies in Extremism and Democracy (Routledge, 2011).

5. Kirk Andrew Hawkins et al., eds., *The Ideational Approach to Populism: Concept, Theory, and Analysis*, Routledge Studies in Extremism and Democracy (Routledge, 2019).

6. Ian Shapiro, "Problems, Methods, and Theories in the Study of Politics, or What's Wrong with Political Science and What to Do About It," *Political Theory* 30, no. 4 (2002): 596–619.

7. Even if we did consider political choice as working like markets do, the field of economic sociology has long moved beyond rational, e.g., through the classic work of Polanyi and Poulantzas and, most recently, through New Economic Sociology.

8. Berezin, *Illiberal Politics in Neoliberal Times*.

9. Bonikowski, "Ethno-Nationalist Populism and the Mobilization of Collective Resentment."

10. Tim Bale et al., "If You Can't Beat Them, Join Them? Explaining Social Democratic Responses to the Challenge from the Populist Radical Right in Western Europe," *Political Studies* 58, no. 3 (2010): 410–26; D. Adascalitei and F. Vegetti, "Deregulation, Job Security and Employability During the Great Recession," in *Job Quality in an Era of Flexibility*, ed. Tommy Isidorsson and Julia Kubisa (Routledge, 2018).

11. Johannes Karreth, Jonathan T. Polk, and Christopher S. Allen, "Catchall or Catch and Release? The Electoral Consequences of Social Democratic Parties' March to the Middle in Western Europe," *Comparative Political Studies* 46, no. 7 (2013): 791–822.

12. Berezin, *Illiberal Politics in Neoliberal Times*.

13. Noam Gidron and Peter A. Hall, "The Politics of Social Status: Economic and Cultural Roots of the Populist Right," *British Journal of Sociology* 68, no. S1 (2017).

14. Cecilia L. Ridgeway and Hazel Rose Markus, "The Significance of Status: What It Is and How It Shapes Inequality," *RSF: The Russell Sage Foundation Journal of the Social Sciences* 8, no. 7 (1 November 2022): 1–25.

15. Michèle Lamont and Virág Molnár, "The Study of Boundaries in the Social Sciences," *Annual Review of Sociology* 28 (1 August 2002): 167–95.

16. Juliana Chueri, "An Emerging Populist Welfare Paradigm? How Populist Radical Right-Wing Parties Are Reshaping the Welfare State," *Scandinavian Political Studies* 45 (2022).

17. Leonce Röth, Alexandre Afonso, and Dennis C. Spies, "The Impact of Populist Radical Right Parties on Socio-Economic Policies," *European Political Science Review* 10, no. 3 (2018): 325–50; Andrej Zaslove, "The Populist Radical Right: Ideology, Party Families and Core Principles," *Political Studies Review* 7, no. 3 (2009): 309–18.

18. I made this point earlier, referring to the argument in Wacquant, "Ordering Insecurity," 1–19; Beland, "Right-Wing Populism and the Politics of Insecurity."

19. Gilles Ivaldi and Oscar Mazzoleni, "Producerist Populist Attitudes and Electoral Support for Populism in the USA and Western Europe," *Socio-Economic Review*, 17 June 2024.

20. Lamont, *The Dignity of Working Men*.

21. Bonikowski, "Ethno-Nationalist Populism and the Mobilization of Collective Resentment," 202.

22. Hawkins et al., *The Ideational Approach to Populism*, 238.

23. Cédric M. Koch, Carlos Meléndez, and Cristóbal Rovira Kaltwasser, "Mainstream Voters, Non-Voters and Populist Voters: What Sets Them Apart?," *Political Studies* 71, no. 3 (2023): 893–913.

24. Rathgeb, *How the Radical Right Has Changed Capitalism and Welfare in Europe and the USA*.

25. My use of "resonance" relies on the work of political communication scholars, in particular by Gamson, that underlines how certain frames resonate with people as they appear as natural and familiar to them: Willam A. Gamson, "Mass Media," in *Concise Encyclopedia of Comparative Sociology* (Brill, 2014), 246. The idea here is that insecurity would resonate with individuals as it becomes common and widespread within the population and across social strata.

26. Meardi and Guardiancich, "Back to the Familialist Future"; Matteo Jessoula, Marcello Natili, and Emmanuele Pavolini, "'Exclusionary Welfarism': A New Programmatic Agenda for Populist Right-Wing Parties?," *Contemporary Politics* 28, no. 4 (2022): 447–68.

27. Michèle Lamont, *Seeing Others: How Recognition Works—and How It Can Heal a Divided World* (Simon and Schuster, 2025); Lamont, "Addressing Recognition Gaps."

28. March, *Radical Left Parties in Europe*; Ivaldi, "'Towards the Median Economic Crisis Voter?"

29. Luke March and Charlotte Rommerskirchen, "Out of Left Field? Explaining the Variable Electoral Success of European Radical Left Parties," *Party Politics* 21, no. 1 (2015): 40–53.

30. Laura Chazel and Vincent Dain, "Left-Wing Populism and Nationalism: A Comparative Analysis of the Patriotic Narratives of Podemos and France Insoumise," *Journal for the Study of Radicalism* 15, no. 2 (2021): 73–94; Donatella Bonansinga, "'A Threat to Us': The Interplay of Insecurity and Enmity Narratives in Left-Wing Populism," *British Journal of Politics and International Relations* 24, no. 3 (2022): 511–25.

31. Anthony Kevins and Naomi Lightman, "Immigrant Sentiment and Labour Market Vulnerability: Economic Perceptions of Immigration in Dualized Labour Markets," *Comparative European Politics* 18, no. 3 (2020): 460–84.

32. Lincoln Quillian, "Prejudice as a Response to Perceived Group Threat: Population Composition and Anti-Immigrant and Racial Prejudice in Europe," *American Sociological Review* 60, no. 4 (1995): 586–611.

33. Michael Wallace and Rodrigo Figueroa, "Determinants of Perceived Immigrant Job Threat in the American States," *Sociological Perspectives* 55, no. 4 (2012): 583–612.

34. Wallace and Figueroa, 603.

35. Joakim Ruist, "How the Macroeconomic Context Impacts on Attitudes to Immigration: Evidence from Within-Country Variation," *Social Science Research* 60 (2016): 125–34.

36. Joonghyun Kwak and Michael Wallace, "The Impact of the Great Recession on Perceived Immigrant Threat: A Cross-National Study of 22 Countries," *Societies* 8, no. 3 (2018): 52.

37. Anabel Kuntz, Eldad Davidov, and Moshe Semyonov, "The Dynamic Relations Between Economic Conditions and Anti-Immigrant Sentiment: A Natural Experiment in Times of the European Economic Crisis," *International Journal of Comparative Sociology* 58, no. 5 (2017): 392–415.

38. Javier G. Polavieja, "Labour-Market Competition, Recession and Anti-Immigrant Sentiments in Europe: Occupational and Environmental Drivers of Competitive Threat," *Socio-Economic Review* 14, no. 3 (2016): 395–417.

39. Tim Reeskens and Wim van Oorschot, "Disentangling the 'New Liberal Dilemma': On the Relation Between General Welfare Redistribution Preferences and Welfare Chauvinism," *International Journal of Comparative Sociology* 53, no. 2 (2012): 132.

40. Jonathan J. B. Mijs, "The Paradox of Inequality: Income Inequality and Belief in Meritocracy Go Hand in Hand," *Socio-Economic Review* 19, no. 1 (2021): 7–35.

41. Ruth Levitas, *The Inclusive Society? Social Exclusion and New Labour* (Springer, 2005).

42. Erwin Gielens, Femke Roosma, and Peter Achterberg, "Deservingness in the Eye of the Beholder: A Vignette Study on the Moderating Role of Cultural Profiles in Supporting Activation Policies," *International Journal of Social Welfare* 28, no. 4 (2019): 442–53.

43. The classification used to categorize parties in this book mostly relies on the PopuList (see the methodological appendix for the full rationale of the classification): Matthijs Rooduijn et al., "The PopuList: A Database of Populist, Far-Left, and Far-Right Parties Using Expert-Informed Qualitative Comparative Classification (EiQCC)," *British Journal of Political Science* 54, no. 3 (2024): 969–78.

44. Lorenza Antonucci and Jan Philipp Thomeczek, "Commodification and Security Agendas of Parties in Europe Using the Manifesto Data Project," working paper, OSF, September 19, 2024, https://doi:10.17605/OSF.IO/JVXW4.

45. Paolo Segatti and Francesco Capuzzi, "Five Stars Movement, Syriza and Podemos: A Mediterranean Model?" in *Beyond Trump: Populism on the Rise*, ed. Alberto Martinelli (ISPI, 2016), 47–72.

46. Hopkin, *Anti-System Politics*.

47. Samuele Mazzolini and Arthur Borriello, "The Normalization of Left Populism? The Paradigmatic Case of Podemos," *European Politics and Society* 23, no. 3 (2022): 285–300.

48. Alejandro Pizzi and Verònica Gisbert-Gracia, "Vox of Whom? An Assessment of Vox through Discourse Analysis and Study of the Profile of Its Social Base," in *Populism and Postcolonialism* (Routledge, 2019); Stuart J. Turnbull-Dugarte, "Explaining the End of Spanish Exceptionalism and Electoral Support for Vox," *Research & Politics* 6, no. 2 (1 April 2019): 2053168019851680.

49. Loris Zanatta, "Il Populismo. Sul Nucleo Forte Di Un'ideologia Debole," *Polis*, no. 2/2002 (2002): 286.

50. Berezin, *Illiberal Politics in Neoliberal Times*.

51. Lorenzo Mosca and Filippo Tronconi, "Beyond Left and Right: The Eclectic Populism of the Five Star Movement," in *Varieties of Populism in Europe in Times of Crises* (Routledge, 2021).

52. Meardi and Guardiancich, "Back to the Familialist Future."

53. Gianfranco Baldini, Filippo Tronconi, and Davide Angelucci, "Yet Another Populist Party? Understanding the Rise of Brothers of Italy," *South European Society and Politics* 27, no. 3 (2022): 387.

54. Jens Rydgren, "Radical Right-Wing Populism in Denmark and Sweden: Explaining Party System Change and Stability," *SAIS Review of International Affairs* 30, no. 1 (2010): 57–71.

55. Ov Cristian Norocel, "Populist Radical Right Protectors of the Folkhem: Welfare Chauvinism in Sweden," *Critical Social Policy* 36, no. 3 (2016): 371–90; Isabel Airas and Carl Truedsson, "Contesting and Envisioning 'Trygghet': The Sweden Democrats, Social Democrats, and the 2018 Swedish General Election," *Area* 55, no. 1 (2023): 26–37.

56. Jens Rydgren, "Radical Right Populism in Sweden: Still a Failure, but for How Long?," *Scandinavian Political Studies* 25, no. 1 (2002): 27–56.

57. SD Sverigedemokraternas principprogram 2011 [SD's principle programme 2011], 34, as translated in Ov Cristian Norocel, "Populist Radical Right Protectors of the Folkhem: Welfare Chauvinism in Sweden," *Critical Social Policy* 36, no. 3 (2016): 379.

58. Andersson, *Between Growth and Security.*

59. Pierre Blavier, *Gilets jaunes, la révolte des budgets contraints: La révolte des budgets contraints* (Humensis, 2021).

60. Ivaldi, "Towards the Median Economic Crisis Voter?"

61. Daniel Béland and Randall Hansen, "Reforming the French Welfare State: Solidarity, Social Exclusion and the Three Crises of Citizenship," *West European Politics* 23, no. 1 (2000): 47–64.

62. Matteo Jessoula, Marcello Natili, and Emmanuele Pavolini, "'Exclusionary Welfarism': A New Programmatic Agenda for Populist Right-Wing Parties?," *Contemporary Politics* 28, no. 4 (2022): 447–68.

63. Jessoula, Natili, and Pavolini.

64. See William Rispin, *The French Centre Right and the Challenges of a Party System in Transition* (Springer International, 2021), chapter 4.

65. A translation of Mélenchon's discourses in 2016 by Paolo Chiocchetti, "'Make Way for the People!' Left-Wing Populism in the Rhetoric of Jean-Luc Mélenchon's 2012 and 2017 Presidential Campaigns," in *Left Radicalism and Populism in Europe* (Routledge, 2019), 117.

66. Bonansinga, "'A Threat to Us.'"

67. Manès Weisskircher, "The Strength of Far-Right AfD in Eastern Germany: The East-West Divide and the Multiple Causes Behind 'Populism,'" *Political Quarterly* 91, no. 3 (2020): 614–22.

68. Martin Seeleib-Kaiser, "Social Democratic Reforms of the Welfare State: Germany and the UK Compared," in *Modernising the Welfare State: The Blair Legacy*, ed. Martin Powell (Policy Press, 2008), 235–54.

69. Jörg Michael Dostal, "The Crisis of German Social Democracy Revisited," *Political Quarterly* 88, no. 2 (2017): 230–40.

70. Ralf Havertz, "Strategy of Ambivalence: AfD Between Neoliberalism and Social Populism 1," in *Radical Right Populism in Germany* (Routledge, 2021).

71. Achim Goerres, Dennis C. Spies, and Staffan Kumlin, "The Electoral Supporter Base of the Alternative for Germany," *Swiss Political Science Review* 24, no. 3 (2018): 259.

72. Benjamin T. Bowyer and Mark I. Vail, "Economic Insecurity, the Social Market Economy, and Support for the German Left," *West European Politics* 34, no. 4 (2011): 683–705.

73. Stathis N. Kalyvas and Kees van Kersbergen, "Christian Democracy," *Annual Review of Political Science* 13 (2010): 183–209.

74. David Smith, David Deacon, and John Downey, "Inside out: The UK Press, Brexit and Strategic Populist Ventriloquism," *European Journal of Communication* 36, no. 1 (2021): 21–37.

75. Geoffrey Evans, Roosmarijn de Geus, and Jane Green, "Boris Johnson to the Rescue? How the Conservatives Won the Radical-Right Vote in the 2019 General Election," *Political Studies* 71, no. 4 (2023): 984–1005.

76. Karine Tournier-Sol, "From UKIP to Brexit: The Right-Wing Populist Surge in the UK," in *The Faces of Contemporary Populism in Western Europe and the US*, ed. Karine Tournier-Sol and Marie Gayte (Springer International, 2021), 1–22.

77. Jake Watts and Tim Bale, "Populism as an Intra-Party Phenomenon: The British Labour Party Under Jeremy Corbyn," *British Journal of Politics and International Relations* 21, no. 1 (2019): 99–115.

78. Peter Dorey, "Jeremy Corbyn Confounds His Critics: Explaining the Labour Party's Remarkable Resurgence in the 2017 Election," *British Politics* 12, no. 3 (2017): 308–34.

79. Eunice Goes, "The Labour Party Under Keir Starmer: 'Thanks, but No "Isms" Please!,'" *Political Quarterly* 92, no. 2 (2021): 176–83.

80. Stijn van Kessel, "Populist Parties in Poland," in *Populist Parties in Europe: Agents of Discontent?*, ed. Stijn van Kessel (Palgrave Macmillan UK, 2015), 121–43.

81. Attila Melegh et al., "Positional Insecurity and the Hegemony of Radical Nationalism: Migration and Justice in the Hungarian Media," *International Spectator* 54, no. 3 (2019): 54–71.

82. Katharina Bluhm and Mihai Varga, "Introduction: Toward a New Illiberal Conservatism in Russia and East Central Europe," in *New Conservatives in Russia and East Central Europe* (Routledge, 2018).

83. Jochen Roose and Ireneusz Pawel Karolewski, "The National Conservative Parties in Poland and Hungary and Their Core Supporters Compared: Values and Socio-Structural Background," in *New Conservatives in Russia and East Central Europe* (Routledge, 2018).

84. Meardi and Guardiancich, "Back to the Familialist Future."

85. Stanley Bill, "How PiS Lost Power in Its Heartland," *Notes from Poland* (blog), 30 October 2023, https://notesfrompoland.com/2023/10/30/how-pis-lost-power-in-its-heartland/.

Chapter 5. From Insecure People to Populist Voters

1. Rodrik, "Why Does Globalization Fuel Populism?"; Thomas Piketty, *Capital and Ideology* (Harvard University Press, 2021).

2. Tito Boeri et al., "A Dialogue Between a Populist and an Economist," *AEA Papers and Proceedings* 108 (2018): 191–95, quote on 194.

3. See notes 5, 6, and 9 for a list of sources from political science that use the approach described here.

4. The model considers whether individuals state that they have an insufficient income or find it difficult to live on their present income (i.e., extreme forms of insecurity). The discussion on the socioeconomic triggers of populism focuses on the level of unemployment in the country.

5. There is a large strand of research that uses the insider/outsider division in relation to voting. A few influential studies are Patrick Emmenegger, Paul Marx, and Dominik Schraff, "Labour Market Disadvantage, Political Orientations and Voting"; Schwander, "Labor Market Dualization and Insider–Outsider Divides"; Rovny and Rovny, "Outsiders at the Ballot Box."

6. The analyses of the most recent populist surge operationalize socioeconomic disadvantage and insecurity as the risk/presence of unemployment. In their highly influential paper, "Trump, Brexit, and the Rise of Populism: Economic Have-Nots and Cultural Backlash" (Harvard Kennedy School Working Paper, 2016), https://doi.org/10.2139/ssrn.2818659), Ronald Inglehart and Pippa Norris operationalized material factors through unemployment and receipt of welfare. Other examples are Sipma, Lubbers, and Spierings, "Working Class Economic Insecurity and Voting for Radical Right and Radical Left Parties"; and Rooduijn, "What Unites the Voter Bases of Populist Parties?"

7. I am referring to the limited number of items that investigate insecurity in the European Social Survey (the dataset used in Boeri et al., "A Dialogue Between a Populist and an Economist," 2018; Ronald F. Inglehart and Pippa Norris, "Trump, Brexit, and the Rise of Populism: Economic Have-Nots and Cultural Backlash," July 29, 2016, HKS Working Paper No. RWP16-026, http://dx.doi.org/10.2139/ssrn.2818659; and numerous other studies on populism). This dataset contains only one general question asking individuals to assess how they navigate their financial commitments with their household income ("hincfel," the variable I use in chapter 2).

8. Goodwin and Heath, "Brexit Vote Explained."

9. Several influential studies use this approach in political science: Matthew J. Goodwin and Oliver Heath, "The 2016 Referendum, Brexit and the Left Behind: An Aggregate-Level Analysis of the Result," *Political Quarterly* 87, no. 3 (2016): 323–32; Hobolt, "The Brexit Vote"; and, in sociology, Lisa Mckenzie, "The Class Politics of Prejudice: Brexit and the Land of No-Hope and Glory," *British Journal of Sociology* 68, no. S1 (2017): S265–80.

10. Antonucci et al., "'The Malaise of the Squeezed Middle.'"

11. Becker, Fetzer, and Novy, "Who Voted for Brexit?"; Dorling, "Brexit: The Decision of a Divided Country"; Fetzer, "Did Austerity Cause Brexit?"

12. This was not entirely a new finding, although scholars have previously overlooked these intermediate segments by referring to the negative correlation between education and the Leave vote. See Goodwin and Heath, "Brexit Vote Explained."

13. Sonja Avlijaš, "From Brexit to Trump: Why Mobilising Anger in a Constructive Way Is Now One of the Key Challenges in Modern Politics," *EUROPP* (blog), 30 June 2016, https://blogs.lse.ac.uk/europpblog/2016/06/30/brexit-trump-mobilising-anger/.

14. Kurer and Palier, "'Shrinking and Shouting.'"

15. Lorenza Antonucci et al., "What's Work Got to Do with It? How Precarity Influences Radical Party Support in France and the Netherlands," *Sociological Research Online* 28, no. 1 (2023): 110–31.

16. Marx and Picot, "Three Approaches to Labor-Market Vulnerability and Political Preferences," 357.

17. See the studies on labor market outsiders cited in note 4. For an application of this framework to the realm of populist voting post-2016, see, for example, Sipma, Lubbers, and Spierings, "Working Class Economic Insecurity and Voting for Radical Right and Radical Left Parties"; Rooduijn, "What Unites the Voter Bases of Populist Parties?"

18. Gidron and Hall, "The Politics of Social Status."

19. Andrei Zhirnov, Lorenza Antonucci et al., "Precarity and Populism: Explaining Populist Outlook and Populist Voting in Europe Through Subjective Financial and Work-Related Insecurity," *European Sociological Review*, 40, no. 4 (2024): 704–20.

20. Here, I am referring to all the previous research that focuses on work-related insecurity: the studies that conceptualize insecurity as the risk of losing one's job (see notes 4 and 5), as well as our previous research investigating insecurity of job tenure and work conditions.

21. The measures of subjective job insecurity related to the tenure of work/work conditions only permit an investigation of insecurity among those who are in paid and formal employment, as they exclude those who are not—that is, retired people and those in unpaid work or care work. This is not an insignificant proportion: In our surveys, those who state that they are not in work constitute about 50 percent of the sample. For example, the sample for all ten countries in Zhirnov et al. (2024) goes from 60,043 respondents to 29,660 respondents once we consider only those who state that they are in paid work.

22. For an introduction to the ideational approach to populism, see Hawkins et al., *The Ideational Approach to Populism*.

23. This is in contrast to the focus on unemployment/risk of unemployment that is present in several influential studies cited earlier, such as Rooduijn, "What Unites the Voter Bases of Populist Parties?"; Sipma, Lubbers, and Spierings, "Working Class Economic Insecurity and Voting for Radical Right and Radical Left Parties"; and Inglehart and Norris, "Trump, Brexit, and the Rise of Populism."

24. Lorenza, Antonucci, Roberta Di Stefano et al., "Gender, Insecurity and Populism in Europe: Expanding the Investigation of Insecurity and Populist Voting Through Statistical Matching," Harvard CES Open Forum Series, No. 53, January 2025, https://ces.fas.harvard.edu/uploads/files/Open-Forum-Paper-Antonucci-January-2025.pdf.

25. Niels Spierings and Andrej Zaslove, "Gender, Populist Attitudes, and Voting: Explaining the Gender Gap in Voting for Populist Radical Right and Populist Radical Left Parties," *West European Politics* 40, no. 4 (2017): 821–47.

26. Gidron and Hall, "The Politics of Social Status."

27. Lamont, *The Dignity of Working Men*.

28. Gabriele Dietze and Julia Roth, "Right-Wing Populism and Gender: A Preliminary Cartography of an Emergent Field of Research," in *Right-Wing Populism and Gender: European Perspectives and Beyond*, ed. Gabriele Dietze and Julia Roth (transcript Verlag, 2020), 7–22.

29. Niels Spierings et al., "Gender and Populist Radical-Right Politics: An Introduction," *Patterns of Prejudice* 49, no. 1–2 (15 March 2015): 3–15; Spierings and Zaslove, "Gender, Populist Attitudes, and Voting."

30. Gidron and Hall, "The Politics of Social Status."

31. Pugh, *The Tumbleweed Society.*

32. Marta Fana et al., "The COVID Confinement Measures and EU Labour Markets," JRC, 29 April 2020, https://doi.org/10.2760/079230.

33. Marta Fana et al., "Telework, Work Organisation and Job Quality During the COVID-19 Crisis: A Qualitative Study," JRC Working Papers Series on Labour, Education and Technology, 2020, https://www.econstor.eu/handle/10419/231343.

34. T. Murat Yildirim and Hande Eslen-Ziya, "The Differential Impact of COVID-19 on the Work Conditions of Women and Men Academics During the Lockdown," *Gender, Work & Organization* 28, no. S1 (2021): 243–49; Gundula Zoch, Ann-Christin Bächmann, and Basha Vicari, "Who Cares When Care Closes? Care-Arrangements and Parental Working Conditions During the COVID-19 Pandemic in Germany," *European Societies* 23, no. sup1 (2021): S576–88.

35. Andrew E. Clark, Conchita D'Ambrosio, and Anthony Lepinteur, "The Fall in Income Inequality During COVID-19 in Four European Countries," *Journal of Economic Inequality* 19, no. 3 (2021): 489–507; Amelia Fiske et al., "The Second Pandemic: Examining Structural Inequality Through Reverberations of COVID-19 in Europe," *Social Science & Medicine* 292 (2022): 114634.

36. Liad Bareket-Bojmel, Golan Shahar, and Malka Margalit, "COVID-19-Related Economic Anxiety Is as High as Health Anxiety: Findings from the USA, the UK, and Israel," *International Journal of Cognitive Therapy* 14, no. 3 (2021): 566–74.

37. Antonucci, Di Stefano et al., "Gender, Insecurity and Populism in Europe."

Chapter 6. The Future of the Politics of Insecurity

1. Mudde and Kaltwasser, "Studying Populism in Comparative Perspective."

2. Ernesto Laclau, *On Populist Reason* (Verso, 2005); Chantal Mouffe, *On the Political* (Routledge, 2011).

3. Isabel Baptista et al., "Social Protection and Inclusion Policy Responses to the COVID-19 Crisis," *An Analysis of Policies in 35 Countries*, ESPN (European Commission, 2021).

4. Baptista et al.

5. Jan Drahokoupil and Torsten Müller, "Job Retention Schemes in Europe: A Lifeline During the Covid-19 Pandemic," *ETUI Research Paper-Working Paper*, 2021, https://papers.ssrn.com/sol3/papers.cfm?abstract_id=3931230.

6. Bernhard Ebbinghaus and Lukas Lehner, "Cui Bono—Business or Labour? Job Retention Policies During the COVID-19 Pandemic in Europe," *Transfer: European Review of Labour and Research* 28, no. 1 (2022): 47–64.

7. Drahokoupil and Müller, "Job Retention Schemes in Europe."

8. Joan Miró et al., "Buffering National Welfare States in Hard Times: The Politics of EU Capacity-Building in the Social Policy Domain," *Social Policy & Administration* 58, no. 2 (2024): 215–27.

9. Stella Ladi and Dimitris Tsarouhas, "EU Economic Governance and Covid-19: Policy Learning and Windows of Opportunity," *Journal of European Integration* 42, no. 8 (2020): 1041–56.

10. European Council, Conclusions of the European Council meeting, 17–21 July, Brussels, https://www.consilium.europa.eu/media/45109/210720-euco-final-conclusions-en.pdf.

11. Klaus Armingeon et al., "Voices from the Past: Economic and Political Vulnerabilities in the Making of next Generation EU," *Comparative European Politics* 20, no. 2 (2022): 144–65.

12. Armingeon et al.

13. David Howarth and Lucia Quaglia, "Failing Forward in Economic and Monetary Union: Explaining Weak Eurozone Financial Support Mechanisms," *Journal of European Public Policy* 28, no. 10 (3 October 2021): 1555–72.

14. Maarten Keune and Philippe Pochet, "The Revival of Social Europe: Is This Time Different?," *Transfer: European Review of Labour and Research* 29, no. 2 (1 May 2023): 173–83.

15. Roland Erne et al., *Politicising Commodification: European Governance and Labour Politics from the Financial Crisis to the Covid Emergency* (Cambridge University Press, 2024), 249.

16. Standing, *The Precariat.*

17. Mike Savage et al., "On Social Class, Anno 2014," *Sociology* 49, no. 6 (2015): 1011–30.

18. Hopkin, *Anti-System Politics.*

19. Alex Mierke-Zatwarnicki, "Identity Politics, Old and New: Party-Building in the Long Twentieth Century," PhD dissertation, Harvard University Graduate School of Arts and Sciences, November 21, 2023, https://dash.harvard.edu/handle/1/37378031.

20. Piketty, *Capital and Ideology.*

21. A transnational movement of the populist left, the Democracy in Europe Movement 2025 (DiEM25), has attempted to aggregate political support around a common agenda that includes ending precarity, although it has failed to elect representatives in the European Parliament so far. Possible reasons for the low appeal of DiEM25 include its transnational nature and the use of a highly politicized notion of precarity.

22. Antonucci, *Student Lives in Crisis*; Pugh, *The Tumbleweed Society.*

23. Graetz and Shapiro, *The Wolf at the Door.*

24. Piketty, *Capital and Ideology.*

25. Anthony B. Atkinson, *Inequality: What Can Be Done?* (Harvard University Press, 2015); Lorenza Antonucci, "Towards EU Youth Policies? The Limits of Current Welfare States and the Potential for a 'Youth Truzansition Fund' (YTF)," *Progressive Structural Reforms*, 2015, 59.

26. Tijs Laenen, *The Popularity of Basic Income: Evidence from the Polls* (Springer Nature, 2023).

27. Nick Srnicek and Alex Williams, *Inventing the Future: Postcapitalism and a World Without Work* (Verso, 2015).

28. Chrystin Ondersma, *Dignity Not Debt: An Abolitionist Approach to Economic Justice* (University of California Press, 2024).

Epilogue. The Social Basis of the Populism Momentum

1. Existing research on welfare transformations in relation to responsibility and risk includes, respectively, Mounk, *The Age of Responsibility*, and Hacker, *The Great Risk Shift*, to which I add a deeper empirical focus and a more specific analysis of the micro effects of institutional transformations on people, societies, and politics.

2. Norris and Inglehart, *Cultural Backlash*; Inglehart, *Cultural Evolution.*

3. Azmanova, *Capitalism on Edge*; Berman and Snegovaya, "Populism and the Decline of Social Democracy."

4. At the end of *The Tumbleweed Society*, her book on US insecurity, Pugh asks what kind of societies our economies are serving.

5. Dodd, Lamont, and Savage, "Introduction to BJS Special Issue."

6. Beland, "Right-Wing Populism and the Politics of Insecurity."

7. Gidron and Hall, "The Politics of Social Status"; Ivaldi and Mazzoleni, "Producerist Populist Attitudes and Electoral Support for Populism in the USA and Western Europe"; Gugushvili, Halikiopoulou, and Vlandas, "Downward Class Mobility and Far-Right Party Support in Western Europe."

8. Iversen and Soskice, *Democracy and Prosperity.*

9. Thomas Piketty, *Capital in the Twenty-First Century* (Belknap Press, 2014).

10. Hooghe and Marks, "Cleavage Theory Meets Europe's Crises"; Kriesi et al., "Globalization and the Transformation of the National Political Space."

11. Lamont and Molnár, "The Study of Boundaries in the Social Sciences."

12. Antonucci and Varriale, "Unequal Europe, Unequal Brexit."

13. Mike Savage, *The Return of Inequality: Social Change and the Weight of the Past* (Harvard University Press, 2021).

14. Taylor, "Why Does Everyone Feel So Insecure All the Time?"

15. The importance of social status is stressed by classic qualitative sociological research: Lamont, *The Dignity of Working Men.* Most recently, Ridgeway presented a psycho-social

investigation of status; see the special issue Ridgeway and Markus, "The Significance of Status." A helpful synthesis of the uses of social status in politics is offered by one of the contributions of the special issue: Mendelberg, "Status, Symbols, and Politics."

16. An example of this status protection is framed in Philip Rathgeb, *How the Radical Right Has Changed Capitalism and Welfare in Europe and the USA*. In contrast, social status protection is discussed in relation to structural socioeconomic transformations in Brian Nolan and David Weisstanner, "Rising Income Inequality and the Relative Decline in Subjective Social Status of the Working Class," *West European Politics* 45, no. 6 (19 September 2022): 1206–30.

17. Bardhan, *A World of Insecurity*, 16.

18. Prieto, "A Multidimensional Approach to Measuring Economic Insecurity." In fact the ideational approach to populism is based on the empirical investigation of populism across the world, particularly in Europe and Latin America: Hawkins et al., *The Ideational Approach to Populism.*

19. Berezin, *Illiberal Politics in Neoliberal Times.*

20. Hemerijck, Ronchi, and Plavgo, "Social Investment as a Conceptual Framework for Analysing Well-Being Returns and Reforms in 21st Century Welfare States."

Methodological Appendix

1. This allows an in-depth exploration of cases. See B. Ebbinghaus, "When Less Is More: Selection Problems in Large-N and Small-N Cross-National Comparisons, in *Soziale Ungleichheit, kulturelle Unterschiede: Verhandlungen des*, ed. K. Rehberg (Kongresses der Deutschen Gesellschaft für Soziologie in München), 4013–21 (2006).

2. Peter Hall and David Soskice *Varieties of Capitalism: The Institutional Foundations of Comparative Advantage* (Oxford University Press, 2001).

3. More information about the EWCS dataset is available at https://www.eurofound.europa.eu/en/surveys/european-working-conditions-surveys-ewcs.

4. Lopes, Lagoa, and Calapez, "Work Autonomy, Work Pressure, and Job Satisfaction."

5. Antonucci, Seo, and Strobl, "Quantity Over Quality?"

6. For more information about the dataset, see https://www.europeansocialsurvey.org/.

7. More information about the dataset is available at https://ec.europa.eu/eurostat/web/microdata/european-union-statistics-on-income-and-living-conditions.

8. These are the categories used to investigate income groups in Parker, *The Squeezed Middle.*

9. Rooduijn et al., "The PopuList." See also https://www.popu-list.org.

10. Holger Döring and Philip Manow, "ParlGov" (Parliaments and Governments Database), 2021; Maurits J. Meijers and Andrej Zaslove, "Populism and Political Parties Expert Survey 2018 (POPPA). Harvard Dataverse, V2," 2020; Michael Coppedge et al., "V-Dem: Dataset V11. 1," 2020, https://ueaeprints.uea.ac.uk/id/eprint/92180/.

11. Ryan Bakker et al., "Chapel Hill Expert Survey," version 1.2, 2019.

12. Antonucci and Thomeczek, "Commodification and Security Agendas of Parties in Europe Using the Manifesto Data Project."

13. Manifesto Data Project codebook, https://manifesto-project.wzb.eu/.

14. Dimiter Toshkov and Jeroen Romeijn, "How to Estimate the Policy Preferences of Party Supporters: Disaggregating Data from Voting Advice Applications Versus Modeling Survey Responses," *Electoral Studies* 74 (2021): 102403; Evelyn Bytzek and Ina E. Bieber, "Does Survey Mode Matter for Studying Electoral Behaviour? Evidence from the 2009 German Longitudinal Election Study," *Electoral Studies* 43 (September 2016): 41–51; Ruth Dassonneville et al., "The Effects of Survey Mode and Sampling in Belgian Election Studies: A Comparison of a National Probability Face-to-Face Survey and a Nonprobability Internet Survey," *Acta Politica* 55, no. 2 (1 April 2020): 175–98.

15. Michele Scotto di Vettimo et al., "Research Contexts Conducive to the Bias in the Estimates with VAA-Generated Data," PRECEDE WP3 paper, forthcoming.

16. Antonucci et al., "'The Malaise of the Squeezed Middle.'"

17. March, *Radical Left Parties in Europe.*

18. Andre Krouwel, Yordan Kutiyski, and Jan Philipp Thomeczek, *EVES: European Voter Election Studies Survey Data* (Kieskompas, 2019).

19. Zhirnov et al., "Precarity and Populism."

20. Antonucci, Di Stefano et al, "Gender, Insecurity and Populism in Europe."

21. Lorenza Antonucci, Roberta Di Stefano et al, "The Political Effects of Widespread Insecurity: How Work and Financial Insecurity Changed Support for Populist, Mainstream and Non-voting During Covid-19," WP2 Working Paper and SASE conference paper, 2024.

INDEX

Page numbers in *italics* refer to figures and tables.

Abruzzo, Italy, 2
active labor market policies (ALMPs), 70–73, *74*
Alesina, Alberto, 84
Alleanza Nazionale (AN), 100
Alternative für Deutschland (AfD), 106–7
anti-elitism, 6, 29–30, 136
artificial intelligence (AI), 25
austerity, 26, 77–84, 92, 141, 143, 148; in Germany, 80; in Italy, 42, 99, 148; regressiveness of, 79–80; in the UK, 80, 115
Austria, 123, 139
automation, 25, 149
autonomy, 19, *20*, 48, 123–24; content, 50, 51, 71; procedural, 50, 51, *52*, 71
Azmanova, Albena, 7, 31

Beck, Ulrich, 15
Bardhan, Pranab, 159
basic income, 148
Bauman, Zygmunt, 15
Berezin, Mabel, 30, 88, 159
Berlusconi, Silvio, 100
Berman, Sheri, 6–7
Boeri, Tito, 113
Bonikowski, Bart, 29, 91
Bourdieu, Pierre, 15, 16
Brexit, 2, 4, 8, 80, 92, 98, 109, 114, 115–17, 158
Brothers of Italy, 1, 101
Butler, Judith, 15

Cantillon, Bea, 73
canvassing, 137
career security, 19, *20*
cash transfers, 27, 42, 47, 59, 73, 76, 139, 148
centrism, 31
China, 63
Christian Democrats, 1, 30–32, 87–88
collective bargaining, 43, 150
colonialism, 17, 63
commodification, 69, 88, 99, 102, 103, 106, *107*, 155
compensation theory, 28, 44, 58–60
content autonomy, 50, 51, 71
continental security regime, 42–44, 55, 58, 104–8, 118
Corbyn, Jeremy, 92, 109
corporate welfare, 64–65, 140, 149–50
cost-of-living crisis, 2, 10, 36, 44, 55, 68, 132, 138
country-specific recommendations (CSRs), 81–82, 142
Covid-19 pandemic, 13, 36, 48–49, 55, 77, 150; cash transfers during, 76, 148; insecurity heightened by, 40–41, 114, 115, 132, 138–39; job retention schemes during, 139–40; as missed opportunity, 138–42, 150; nonvoting during, 134; in Poland, 47; populist support linked to, 134, *135*; remote work during, 132
cultural backlash, 6–7, 9–11
cultural sociology, 10
Czech Republic, 46

de la Porte, Caroline, 82
debt, *23*, 75, 76; extractive, 150; survival, 150
Democracy and Prosperity (Iversen and Soskice), 27
Democratic Christian Party, 1
Denmark, 45
deprivation, 22, *23*
deservingness, 11, 84, 90–91, 95–96, 101, 108, 112, 145–46
disengagement, 6, 132–35
division of labor, 63
Dorling, Danny, 40
Dornbusch, Rudi, 61, 83
Draghi, Mario, 83
dualism, 29, 86, 124, 126

Eastern European security regime, 46–47, 57, 58, 110–11, 129, 156
elites, people vs., 24, 35, 89, 91, 112, 124, 126, 155, 157
Errejón, Íñigo, 34
ethnonationalism, 5, 24, 155
European Monetary Union, 61
European Semester, 80, 82
European Social Survey (ESS), 37, 115, 129–30

European Union (EU), 77–83, 88, 159
European Voter Election Study (EVES), 123
European Working Conditions Survey (EWCS), 37, 49, 50, 115, 129
Euroskepticism, 30, 88, 142, 159
EU-SILC (EU Statistics on Income and Living Conditions), 37, 56
exchange rates, 64
extractive debt, 150

family policy, 11, 92, 101, 105, 111, 147–48
Fidesz Party, 46, 110
financial insecurity, 4, 12, *23*, *56*, 123–24, 126, 156; in comparative perspective, *55*, *57*, *59*; defined, 54; in Germany, 44; growth of, 37; indicators of, 13, *38*, 39, 124–25; in Italy, 42; policy reforms linked to, 16, 27–28, 40, 43; populist voting linked to, 126, *127*, 131, *134*, 135, 136; in Spain, 42; among "squeezed middle," 7, 13, 53–54, 58, 114, 115, 117; in Sweden, 45; uneven effects of, 9, 17, 28, 69; among women, 131; work insecurity linked to, 21–22. *See also* work insecurity
first-past-the-post electoral system, 98, 108
Five Star Movement, 1, 98, 101, 148
flexible work arrangements, 43–48, 63, 114, 119
folkhem, 102
food insecurity, 2, 44
Forza Italia (FT), 100
France, 38, 97, 139; consumer debt in, 76; declining job quality in, 42, 43, 58, 123; insecurity in, 37, 39, 42, 119; populism in, 85, 104–6, 118, *121*, *122*; progressive taxation in, 80; temporary employment in, 48
France Insoumise, La (FI), 97, 104, 105, 120, 143
France Télécom, 64

gender: equality of, 6, 7, 156; populist support and, 129–31, 136, 173
Germany, 38, 61, 76, 78, 84, 97, 123; austerity in, 80; financial and work insecurity in, 43–44, 106; populism in, 106–8, 112, 144; productivist model of, 82
Giavazzi, Francesco, 84
Gidron, Noam, 130
Gilbert, Neil, 68
globalization, 7–8, 18, 58, 63–65
glossary, 177–78
Graetz, Michael, 15
Great Recession, 39, 41, 43, 47, 54
Greece, 48, 79, 139

Hacker, Jacob, 22, 28
Hall, Peter, 130
Hartlepool, England, 2
Hartz, Peter, 43
Hawkins, Kirk Andrew, 91
Heckscher-Ohlin model, 113–14
Hemerijck, Anton, 67
higher education, 28
Hopkin, Jonathan, 99, 144
horizontal opposition, 30, 35, *88*, 93, 111, 145, 151, 177; defined, 29; effectiveness of, 94–96, 98, 108, 112; to migration, 95, 101, 106, 109–10, 155; populist parties linked to, 33, 34, 89–90, 98, 99, 100, 104, 105, 107, 121, 138, 144; race and ethnicity linked to, 89–90, 144, 146
housing, 14, 40, 65, 109, 137, 143, 147
Hungary, 38, 46–47, 97, 110, 123, 126

income security, 19, *20*
India, 63
individualization, 15, *24*, 104
Inglehart, Ronald F., 6, 10
insecurity: cultural links to, 24, 28–30; defined, 3–4; food-related, 2, 44; inequality linked to, 9, 14, 17; objective vs. subjective measures of, 4–5, 21; politics of, 24, 30, 35, 145–46, 153; populism linked to, 3, 4, 6–15, 86–93, 125–26, *127*, 136, 153; precarity distinguished from, 3–4, 17–18; socioeconomic, 12, 15–23, 25–28, 35; of tenure, 119; as unifier and divider, 11. *See also* financial insecurity; tenure insecurity; work insecurity
Ireland, 79
Italy, 38, 48, 76, 97, 108, 123, 139, 142; austerity in, 42, 99, 148; populism in, 1–2, 100; work insecurity in, 41–42
Iversen, Torben, 27

Jessop, Bob, 25–26
Johnson, Boris, 109
Juncker Commission, 80, 82

Keynesian welfare state (KWS), 25, 65, 72–73
knowledge economy, 25, 67, 70, 150
Krueger, Alan, 36

labor market outsiders, 114; in welfare states, 18, 34, 39–42, *59*
labor market policy, 25, 27, 70–72, 88, 92
Laclau, Ernesto, 137–38
Lamont, Michèle, 9, 29, 130
Law and Justice (PiS) Party, 47, 128

Lega (Italian political party), 1, 98, 100, 101
LGBTQ+ rights, 6, 7, 28, 87, 111, 156
liberal security regime, 39–41, 108–10
Linke, Die (German political party), 97, 108, 143–44
Lipset, Seymour Martin, 9, 152
Luxembourg, 80

Macron, Emmanuel, 42, 106, 120
manifestos, 98, 102, 105, 109, 111
Matthew effect, 70
means-testing, 46, 139, 148
Mélenchon, Jean-Luc, 85, 105
Meloni, Giorgia, 101
Memorandums of Understanding (MoUs), 79
Mendelberg, Tali, 29
meritocracy, 91, 93, 95–96, 101, 104, 107–9, 112, 144, 157
migration, 6, 10–11, 63, 156; hostility toward, 30, 35, 87, 93–96, 100, 101, 105, 109–10, 155
Mijs, Jonathan, 95–96
Montesilvano, Italy, 1–2
Monti, Mario, 41
Mouffe, Chantal, 109, 137–38
Mudde, Cas, 137
multiculturalism, 6, 7

National Rally (National Front, France), 85, 92, 104–5, 112, 120–21
nativism, 29, 34, 93, 96
neoliberalism, 15, 26, 66, 67, 83
Netherlands, 38, 48, 69, 84, 96, 97, 112, 118, 123; populist voting in, *121*, *122*, 144; productivism in, 44, 108; work insecurity in, 44, 119–20
New Popular Front (NPF, France), 85
NextGenerationEU (NGEU), 141
nonvoting, 132–35, 136, 156, 173–75
Nordic security regime, 45, 55, 57–58, 66, 101–4
Norris, Pippa, 6, 10

Orbán, Viktor, 46
ordoliberalism, 106, 108
otrygghet, 31, 103

Palier, Bruno, 82
passive labor market policies (PLMPs), 71–72, 75
pensions, 65, 81
people vs. elites, 24, 35, 89, 90, 112, 124, 126, 155, 157
people-centrism, 6, 29, 124, 126, 136, 155, 158
performance-based compensation, 25
Pfeiffer, Sabine, 44
Pierson, Paul, 26
Piketty, Thomas, 113
Podemos (Spanish political party), 99–100, 109, 112, 143
Poland, 38, 46, 47, 48, 97, 110–11, 123, 126, 128
Polanyi, Karl, 68–69
political demand, 142, 146, 177
political supply, 96–111, 178
Poor Laws, 4, 96
populism: cultural backlash theory of, 6–7, 9–11; defined, 85–86; dualism linked to, 29, 86, 124, 126; as dynamic process, 5–6; in Germany, 43–44; insecurity linked to, 3, 4, 6–15, 86–93, 125–26, *127*, 136, 153; in Italy, 1–2, 100; media coverage of, 2, 5; in the United Kingdom, 108–9, 112, 115, 144. *See also* radical populist left (RPL) parties; radical populist right (RPR) parties
Portugal, 48, 79
precarity, 9, 13, 16–17, 22, 48, 78, 119–30, 142–45; insecurity distinguished from, 3–4, 17–18; measures of, 36–37, 118; in Sweden, 45; in the UK, 39–40; among youth, 109. *See also* financial insecurity; tenure insecurity; work insecurity
privatization, 64, 65, 81
procedural autonomy, 50, 51, *52*, 71
producerism, 90, 91
productivism, 90–91, 93, 106, 111, 112, 138, 144, 157; in Germany, 82; insecurity linked to, 69; in the Netherlands, 44, 108; in Poland, 47; in the UK, 96; welfare state imperiled by, 32
proportional representation, 97–98
Pugh, Allison, 28

radical populist left (RPL) parties, 13, *24*, 35, 87, *88*, 122–26; economic elites linked to, 95; exclusionary elements of, 89, 92–93; in France, 104, 112, 118, 119–20; in Germany, 105–6, 108; leftward shift of, 92; in the Netherlands, 118, 119–20; in Spain, 34, 99, 112; in the UK, 98, 109
radical populist right (RPR) parties, 13, *24*, 34, 35, 47, 87–92, 95, 125; in Eastern Europe, 110–11, 129; family discourse of, 147; in France, 104–6, 120; in Germany, 106–8, 112; men's support for, 130; in Poland, 110–11; in Southern Europe, 144; in the UK, 98, 108–10, 112

Ranci, Costanzo, 54
rational choice theory, 86
recognition, 10
Reeskens, Tim, 95
Renzi, Matteo, 41
risk, 3, 17, 18, 58, 67; housing insecurity linked to, 65; insecurity distinguished from, 15, 34; social, 15, 28, 32, 39; technological, 25, 27
Rodrik, Dani, 113
Roma people, 47
Romania, 46, 123
Rovira Kaltwasser, Cristóbal, 137
Rydgren, Jens, 102

Savage, Mike, 143
savings, *23*, 124
Schmidt, Vivien, 80
Schumpeterian welfare state (SWS), 25, 52, 64, 65, 73, 77
scripts 33, 104; cultural, 14, 24, 29, 153, 155, 157, 159; economic-centered, 96; political, 8, 69, 147, 159
security regimes, 37; types of, 38–39, 123, 133, 154, 155
Shapiro, Ian, 15
short-termism, 65
Social Democrats, 30–32, 87–88, 145
social investment, 25, 65, 82–83, 150, 157; assumptions of, 66–70; criticisms of, 69–71, 73; defined, 66–67; after economic crisis (2010), 26, 75; financial insecurity linked to, 27–28; neoliberalism linked to, 66, 67; in Nordic countries, 66; as poverty reduction, 68, 70, 73; support for, 27, 62, 71; types of, 66, 71; in the UK, 66
social status, 10, 29, 88–89, 158–59, 177; threats to, 8, 89, 130, 159
Soskice, David, 27
Southern European security regime, 41–42, 57, 58, 99–101
Spain, 34, 38, 48, 76, 97, 123; financial insecurity in, 42; populism in, 99–100; unemployment in, 41
"squeezed middle," 7, 13, 53–54, 58, 114, 115, 117
Standing, Guy, 16, 19, 142
Starmer, Keir, 109–10
status threat, 8, 89, 130, 159
Streeck, Wolfgang, 62
SURE (Support to mitigate Unemployment Risk in an Emergency), 140
survival debt, 150
Sweden, 31, 38, 45, 69, 84, 97, *103*, 123; radical left in, 104; right-wing populism in, 99, 101–3, 112
symbolic boundaries, 10, 67, 68, 87, 89, 95, 157, 158

taxation, 64, 80, 147
Taylor, Astra, 14, 158
Tees Valley, 2
temporary employment, 45, 47, 48, 114, 119
tenure insecurity, 20, 44, 49, 63, 123, 126, 128, 129; during Covid-19 pandemic, 132, 139; in France, 43, 104, 118, 119; limited range of, 18–19; measures of, *125*; populist support linked to, 120–21, *122*, *127*
Theodoropoulou, Sotiria, 79–80
Titmuss, Richard, 64
Townsend, Peter, 22
trade shocks, 4, 7–8
trade unions, 32, 144
Trump, Donald, 2, 115
trygghet, 31, 102, 103

unemployment, 6, 27–28, 34, 40; Brexit vote and, 2, 4, 8, 80, 92, 98, 109, 114, 115–17, 158; in France, 42; in Germany, 43; in Hungary, 46; insecurity linked to, 68; insurance for, 59, 71, 74–75, *76*, 139; in Poland, 47; populism linked to, 114; in Spain, 41; in the UK, 39
unexpected expenses, 4, 22, *23*, 124, *125*, *133*
United Kingdom, 31, 37, 38, 97; anti-immigrant sentiment in, 109; austerity in, 80, 115; insecurity normalized in, 39, 40; Poor Laws in, 4, 96; populism in, 108–9, 112, 115, 144; productivism in, 96; social investment in, 66; unemployment in, 39

van Oorschot, Wim, 95
vertical opposition, 29, 34, 35, *88*, 93, 101, 108, 138, 146, 177
Vox (Spanish political party), 99–101

Wacquant, Loïc, 16–17, 18
wage bargaining, 79
Watt, Andrew, 79–80
welfare chauvinism, 47, 90, 101, 102, 105, 106, 108, 126, 148
welfare mixes, 17, 23
welfare states: desecuritization of, 83, 177; in Europe, 12, 23, 26–28, 62, 66;

financialization of, 65; Keynesian (KWS), 25, 65, 72–73; labor market outsiders in, 18, 34, 39–42, *59*; populism linked to reductions in, 27, 28, 62; RPR parties' support for, 90; Schumpeterian (SWS), 25, 52, 64, 65, 73, 77; social investment form of, 65–76
work insecurity, 10, 12, 16, 18–21, 29, *59*, 126; in European periphery, 38; financial insecurity linked to, 21–22; in Italy, 41–42; of labor market outsiders, 43; measures of, *130*, *133*; in the Netherlands, 44, 119–20; in Poland, 47; policy reforms linked to, 41; RPR voting linked to, *121*; in Sweden, 45; in the United Kingdom, 117–18
workfare, 25, 28, 34, 65
working conditions, 36, 37, 40, 54, *59*, 118; gender and, 130–31, 132; precarity of tenure distinguished from, 120; quantity of work counterpoised to, 70–71; work pressures and, 4, 19, 20, 34, 47–52, *53*, 129, 136; work-life balance in, 19, *20*, 43, 44, 48, 81, 119–20, 123–24, 132, 149
world-systems theory, 63

Yellow Vests movement, 104

A NOTE ON THE TYPE

THIS BOOK has been composed in Miller, a Scotch Roman typeface designed by Matthew Carter and first released by Font Bureau in 1997. It resembles Monticello, the typeface developed for The Papers of Thomas Jefferson in the 1940s by C. H. Griffith and P. J. Conkwright and reinterpreted in digital form by Carter in 2003.

Pleasant Jefferson ("P. J.") Conkwright (1905–1986) was Typographer at Princeton University Press from 1939 to 1970. He was an acclaimed book designer and AIGA Medalist.